THE
R. CRUMB
HANDBOOK

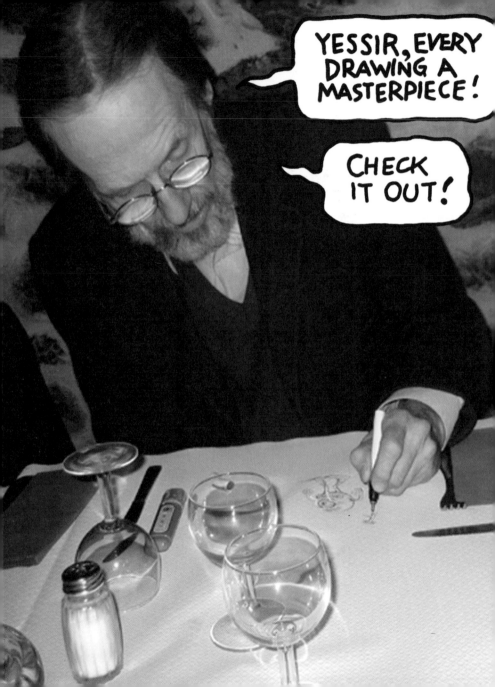

THE R. CRUMB HANDBOOK

R. CRUMB
and
PETER POPLASKI

MQP

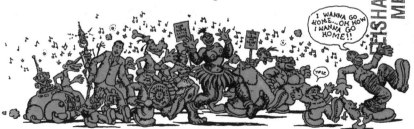

I WANNA GO HOME...OH HOW I WANNA GO HOME!!

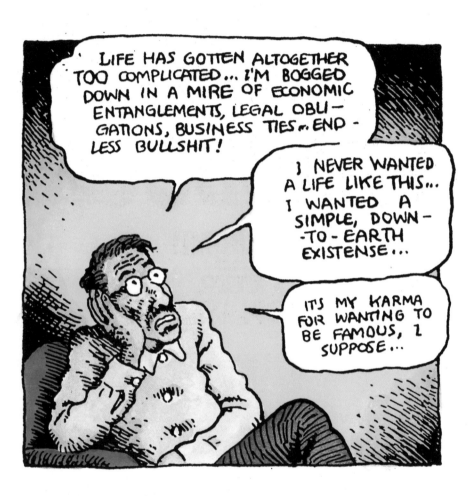

CONTENTS

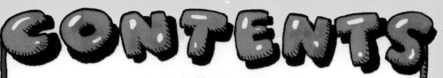

FOREWORD:
A Well Plowed Field

FEAR

CLARITY

POWER

OLD AGE

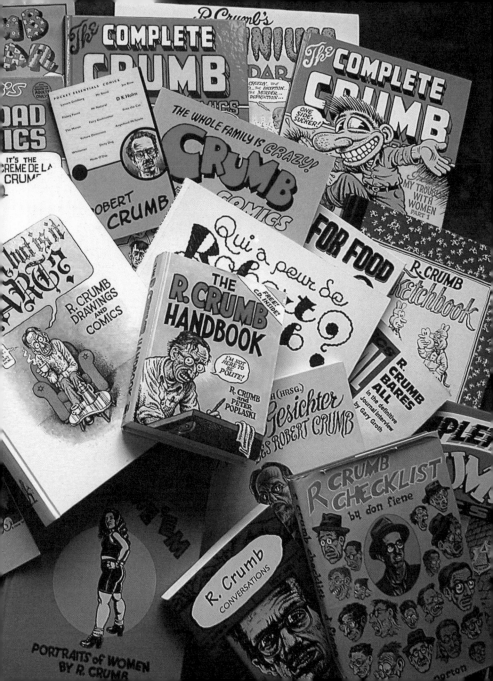

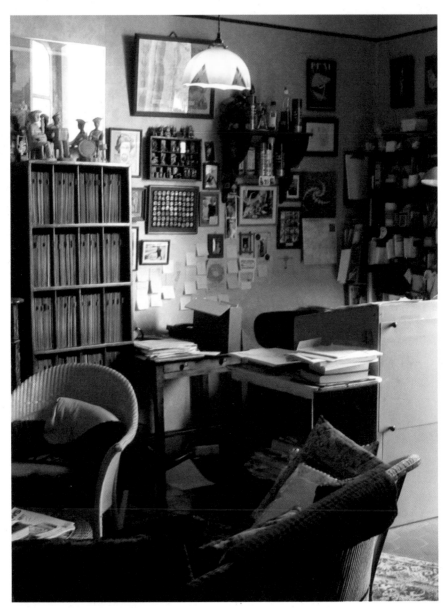

R. Crumb's studio, south of France

Foreword

A Well Plowed Field

"I spend more time on business than I do on drawing, as the Crumb empire expands beyond my control," complained Robert Crumb, the bad boy cartoonist of the 1960s hippie culture whose work has recently been appropriated by the fine art establishment and placed in the "blue chip" category.

It was *apéritif* time in the beautiful south of France, 6:30 in the evening, and the great man stood over two neat piles of correspondence on the writing desk in the far corner of his studio. Next to the desk was a slanted glass top printer's light table with an unfinished drawing casually set aside. Crumb squinted at it momentarily before gesturing that I pour myself a glass from a bottle of *Domaine de Baubiac* and help myself to the potato chips in a blue ceramic bowl. The wine is intended for guests, for Crumb himself drinks only soda water mixed with ginger syrup.

Crumb's studio is a cozy, womb-like room which, like the entire house he shares with his wife and fellow artist Aline, is a universe of wacky knicknacks from past decades. It functions like a decompression chamber to keep the outside forces of the present at bay. The only two modern conveniences are the photocopier on the right by the door, and the telephone which, in the manner of telephones, suddenly rang. It was someone calling about Japanese toy designs of Crumb's cartoon characters.

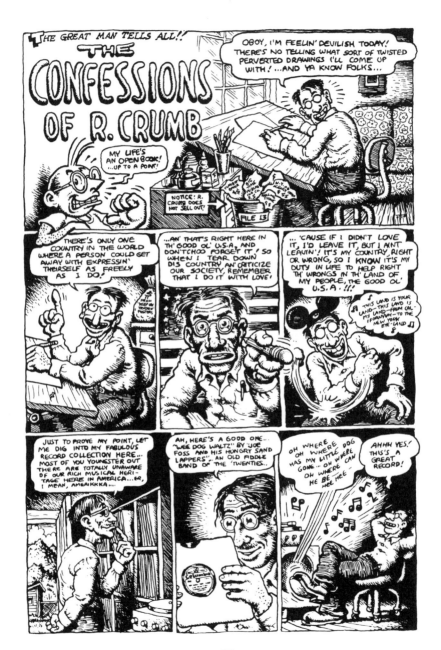

"*Jeeziz,*" he muttered, as he hung up and launched into a self-mocking sales pitch. "*We have the R. Crumb empire going ovah here! I am a money maker on all levels. First, you have your entry level, which is the schlock: the stickers the kids can put on their notebooks, the bumper stickers, the patches and the badges, the cigarette lighters, the Mr. Natural incense ... We have all that happening big time, BIG TIME! All that shit. Up above that, we have the publishing empire! You got all the books, the comics, the commentaries, all coming out, like this Handbook, for instance. On the highest level, the museums are showing the original art, and the galleries are selling the original art for all the cake eaters! We have lots of action on that level ... a lot of shows. I got museum shows. I got auctions. Like that ... a lot happening for all levels of the culture.*"

He ended his tirade with outstretched arms, palms open, head bowed low. Was he putting me on? Or did he really feel he was being crucified? Probably a bit of both.

The purpose of my summons to Crumb's inner sanctum was to discuss the approach this volume should take. There were so many books about Robert Crumb out there already, the big question was, did the world really need another one? Was there really anything that the world at large didn't know about Crumb's life and loves? Was there any artwork out there that hadn't seen print in some collection? How could anyone get a fresh perspective on Crumb's life and work?

I'd gone through this process with Robert eight years before, and *The R. Crumb Coffee Table Art Book* was the result. My first reaction to this new challenge was "*Oh no, not again!*" But eight years can bring major changes in anyone's life, perhaps even more in an artist's. So we stood on our heads and meditated on the coming ordeal. "*Terence McKenna says, you must always create media, never consume it,*" Robert said.

Personally, I thought too much blood was getting to his head. Anyway, we agreed that the influence of the media in people's lives might be an interesting point to stress. Viewing Crumb's life as a transformation from a "L.S." (Loser Schmuck) into a "C.I." (Cultural Icon) could even give readers a new way of assessing their own growth potential. And then, the use of the paradigm of the Toltec Indians' four enemies of man—fear, clarity, power and old age—would structure the book into four concise segments, giving the so-called "Dean of Underground Cartoonists" ample room to express his ideas and opinions, past and present.

When Crumb professed to be *"not a Star,"* but *"... half a Star,"* I had to remind Robert that most human beings forget 97% of what they learn, so the sordid details of some of his more outrageous adventures, which the general public is already familiar with, will seem new. Finally, the inclusion of a music CD of Robert's favorite tunes, played with various musicians over his thirty-year musical career, is the gilding that makes the whole damned package an irresistible monument.

"I want to give you a piece of advice about fame," the master said as we were about to begin the interviews. *"You should get down on your knees and thank the baby Jesus every day that you are on your side of the microphone and not on mine. Think about it!"*

My tape recorder took down this initial statement for the benefit of the purchasers of this book, and the game was afoot. Still, I knew my old friend would rather be alone, playing one of the amazing 78 rpm records from his vast collection of 1920s dance band music. It is only his sense of duty to the hundreds of thousands of Crumb fans that drives him on. R. Crumb will never let his people down.

Peter Poplaski, 23 April 2004

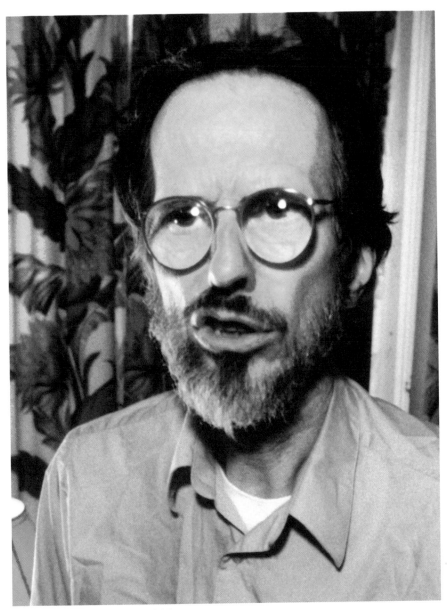

R. Crumb, San Francisco, 1996

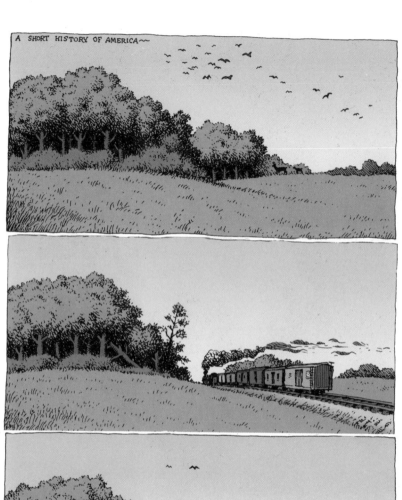

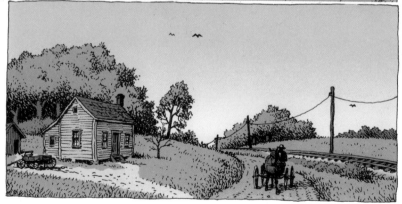

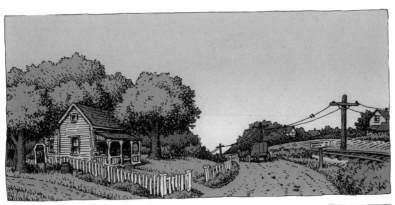

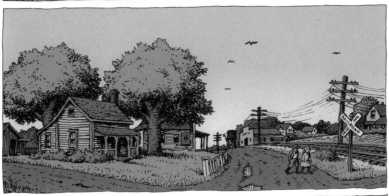

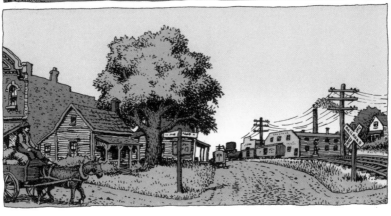

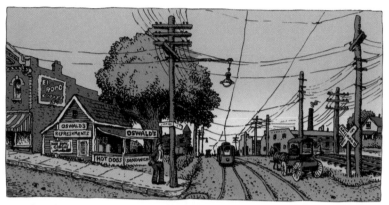

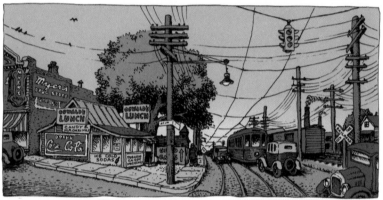

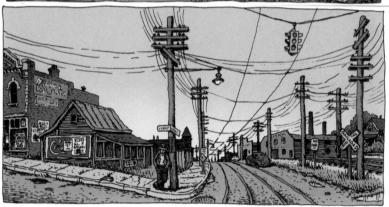

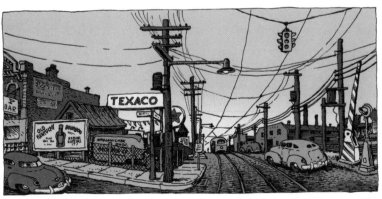

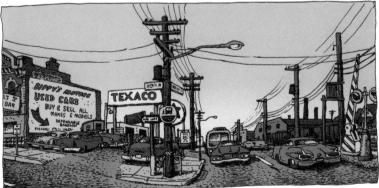

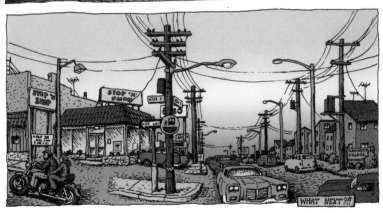

WHAT NEXT?!!

JAMES HOWARD KUNSTLER
WRITER AND COMMENTATOR

The spread of slums, the hypergrowth and congestion of manufacturing cities, the noise and stench of the industrial process, debased urban life all over the western world and led to a great yearning for escape ... in America, with its superabundance of cheap land, simple property laws, social mobility, mania for profit, zest for practical invention, and bible drunk sense of history, the yearning to escape industrialism expressed itself as a renewed search for Eden. America reinvented that paradise, described so briefly and vaguely in the book of Genesis, called it suburbia, and put it up for sale.

from *The Geography Of Nowhere,* 1993

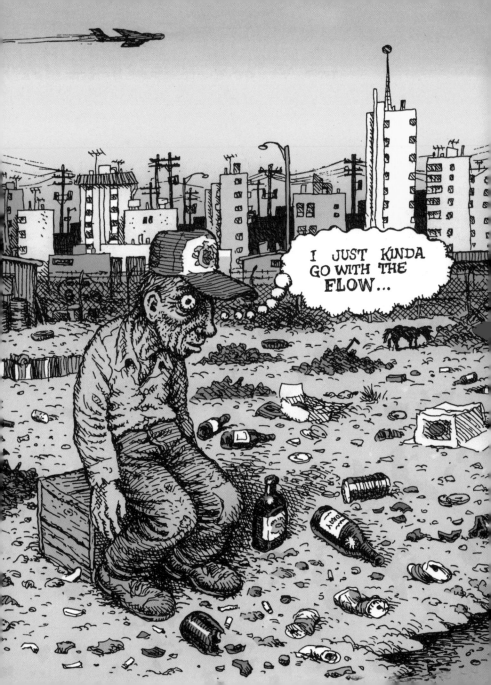

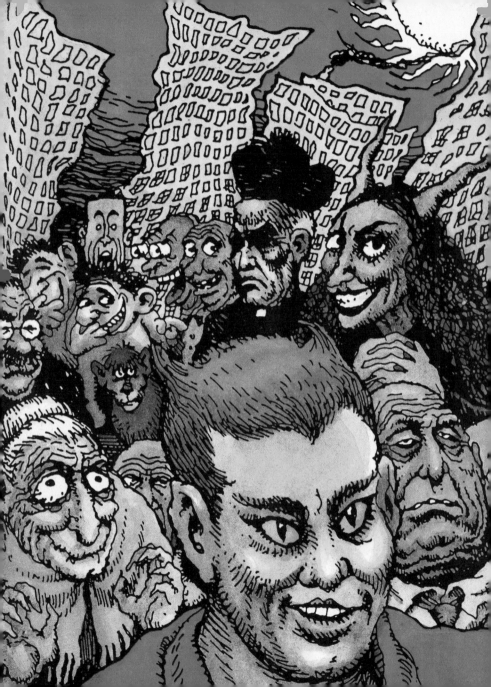

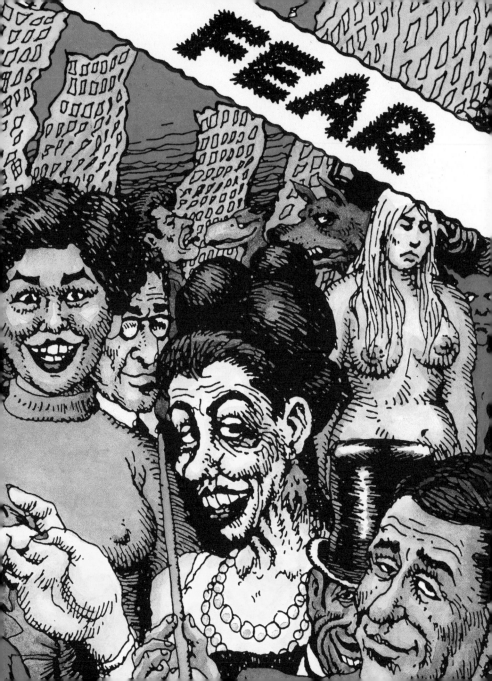

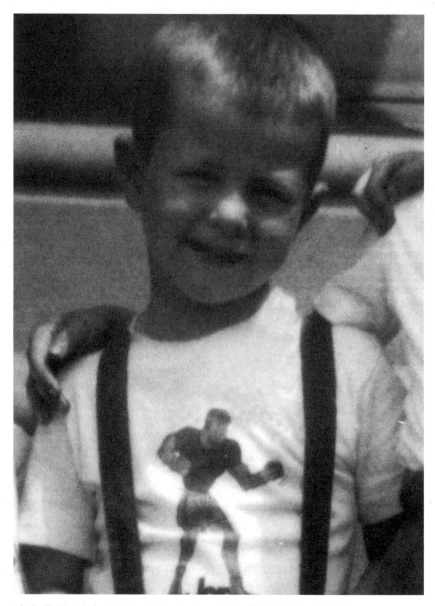

Little Bobby Crumb in Joe Palooka tee shirt, Philadelphia, 1948

Chapter 1

Poor Clod

As a kid growing up in the 1950s I became acutely aware of the changes taking place in American culture and I must say I didn't much like it. I witnessed the debasement of architecture, and I could see a decline in the quality of things like comic books and toys, things made for kids. Old things seemed to have more life, more substance, more humanity in them.

By the time I was nine years old I was a "collector"— a collector of cast off commodities. I collected match books, bottle caps, marbles, cardboard milk bottle tops (I had hundreds of these), old playing cards and, of course, comic books. It's surprising what you find if you're looking for stuff, so as a kid I was always looking down in the street for things I collected. Part of becoming a collector was religiously visiting secondhand stores like the Salvation Army.

Just walking into those stores and breathing in the musty smell of old shoes, old clothes, excited me. I would rush to the back to see what was there in the comic book section. We'd ask the old ladies there , *"Ya got any new funny books?"* That's what they called comics, "funny books," so we had to call them that.

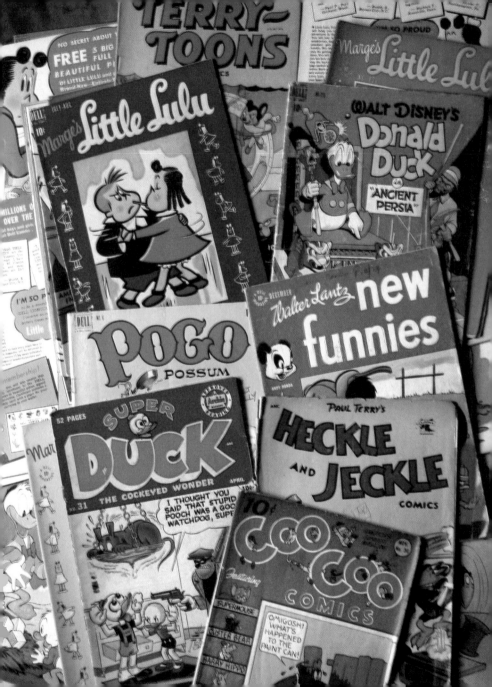

Those old ladies were always cranky with us. They frowned on our enthusiasm for old "funny books."

My father talked about being a kid on the farm and going out hunting and doing things connected with the earth. Real stuff that kids of his generation had to deal with, life and death stuff. We barely had contact with the real world. We were silly, wimpy, suburban kids playing games inspired by movies, television, and comic books. For us it was all filtered through the mass media. Everything came out of the mass media. We were children of the media, the first TV generation.

My vision of the world was very much influenced by my older brother Charles, who lived mostly in the world of imagination and fantasy. We were close in age and spent a lot of time together. Charles had a burning obsession with the Walt Disney animated cartoons, films and comic books, and so I too was swept up in that.

I really have no idea whether I would have become so interested in comics without Charles' influence. No idea. He had a very strong, forceful personality. His vision, his imagination was so powerful that he influenced everyone in the family.

I was the middle kid of five children. Carol and Charles were older than me, Sandra and Maxon were younger. I was born in 1943. My parents came from very different cultures. My father, Charles Crumb, Sr., was a farm boy from Minnesota. My mother, Bea, grew up in a working class section of Philadelphia. My father was one of fourteen kids—he was the fifth child of nine brothers and five sisters. They had big families in those days out on the farm. My mother was the oldest in her family, and had four younger brothers.

Left: **Some of Crumb's favorite childhood comic books, late 1940s to early 1950s**

The Crumbs of Minnesota were fairly successful farmers. They worked hard and they were very straight, strict, puritanical, respectable. It would be unthinkable to be dishonest, to lie or cheat in their business. They were completely upstanding people. And my mother's family was more or less the opposite, they were urban, a bit lumpen, dissolute, alcoholic, degenerate. Sexual weirdness, all that stuff.

My father didn't know that at all when he got involved with her. My mother used to tell the story of how she met my father, a career marine who had been in Shanghai in the late 1930s, and was then stationed at the Philadelphia Navy Yard. She was "slinging hash" in a hamburger joint nearby. In 1939 my father walked in, and years later she would rant and rave and holler, *"I was so stupid! I fell for the uniform! What did I know? I was a stupid kid!"* She'd go on and on.

They were both Catholic, but though neither was very religious, they sent us kids to Catholic school, and we attended church regularly. My parents tried to be proper middle class people. Honor, duty and responsibility were what my father was all about. He had left the farm and moved right into the military. He liked military life. It was elemental, simple, life and death. Post-war America was bewildering to him.

Culturally, my parents didn't have a clue. My father watched the fights and baseball on television, read the newspaper and that's about it. My mother was an indiscriminate reader of cheap popular movie, romance and detective magazines. They never cracked a book.

When my father came home to Philadelphia in 1947, after the war, it was very traumatic for me. I didn't like him. He was very strict and hard on us, and he had a violent temper. We were all afraid of him. My dad used to say that he could easily kill a man with his bare hands. He was a trained killer.

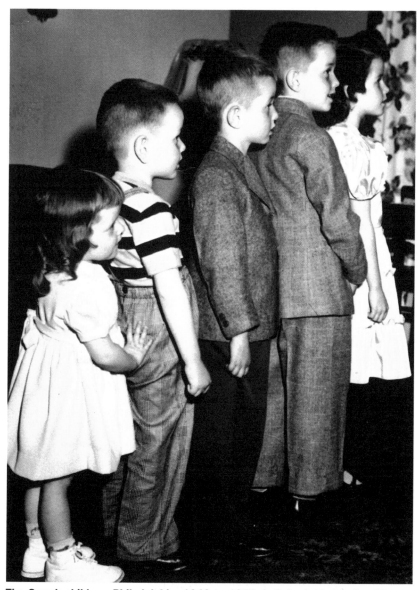

The Crumb children, Philadelphia, 1949 to 1950. Left to right: Sandra, Maxon, Robert, Charles, Carol.

Sometime in the late 1950s I asked him how many Japs he thought he'd killed during the war. *"Well,"* he told me, *"It's hard to say because we killed so many from a distance, but, that I know of ... Oh, 45 or 50."*

Wow! My dad the mass murderer! All of our dads were killers if they were in the war. They had that under their belt. They had killed other humans!

It's strange to think of our fathers going to war. The glory of war is as old as the human race. You proved your manhood by going out and fighting another tribe, being a brave warrior. Get out there and prove yourself—*kill somebody!*

All my natural compulsions are perverted and twisted. Instead of going out and challenging myself against other males, all those impulses are channeled into sex. That's why I want to ravage big women: that's how I get out all my aggressions, and fortunately I've found lots of women who like that! Oh thank the gods! Thank the forces that rule our destinies!

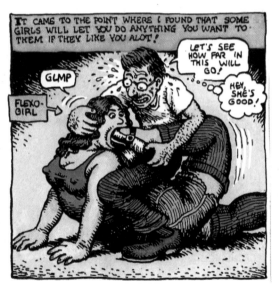

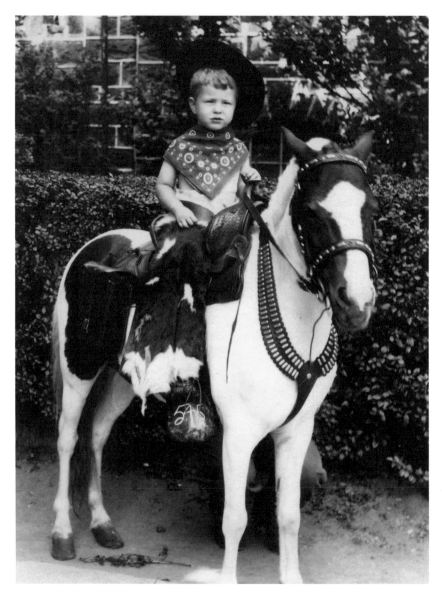

R. Crumb, Philadelphia, 1947: Every small boy in the 1940s had his picture taken on this pony

THE GUY WITH THE BASS DRUM

WHO USED TO COME THROUGH THE NEIGHBORHOOD, SLOWLY DOWN THE MIDDLE OF THE STREET... BOOM..... BOOM... YOU COULD HEAR HIM COMING TWO OR THREE BLOCKS AWAY. US LITTLE KIDS WERE TERRIFIED OF HIM AND WOULD RUN IN THE HOUSE 'TIL HE PASSED BY. I ONLY ACTUALLY SAW HIM ONCE... THE FIRST TIME WAS ENOUGH FOR ME. MY MOTHER SAID HE WAS WALKING THROUGH THE NEIGHBORHOODS BEATING THAT BASS DRUM WHEN SHE WAS A LITTLE GIRL.
— PHILADELPHIA, LATE '40s

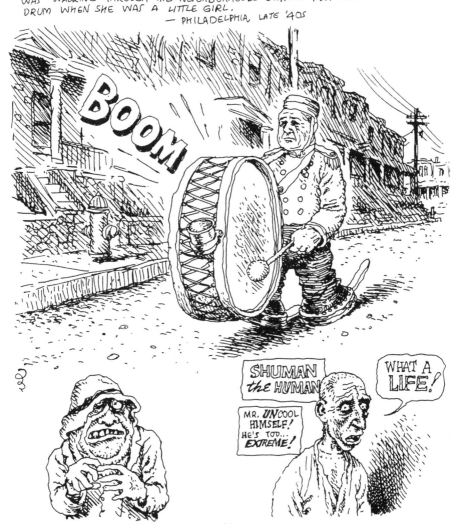

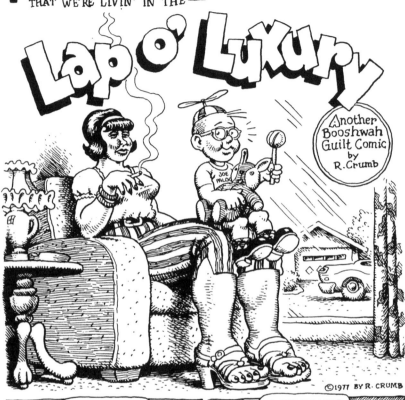

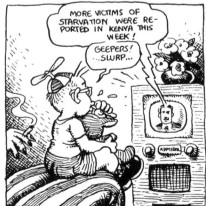

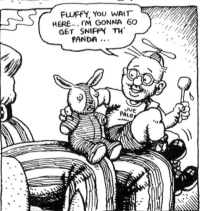

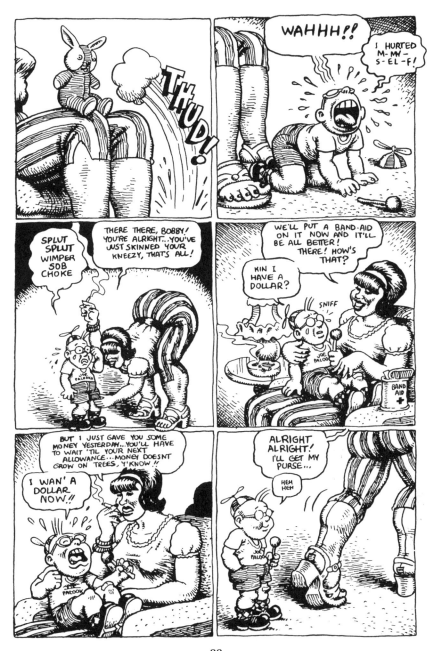

33

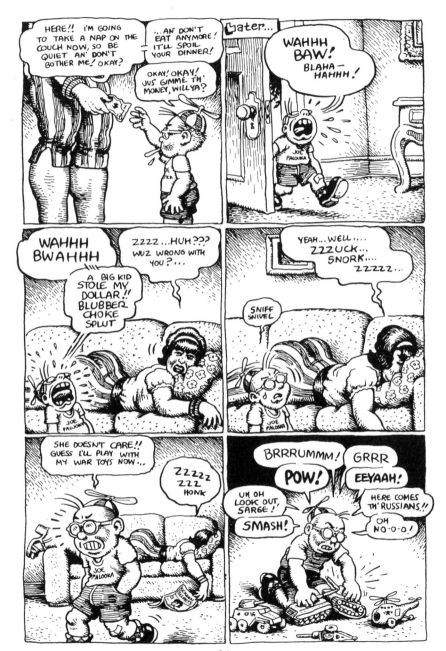

34

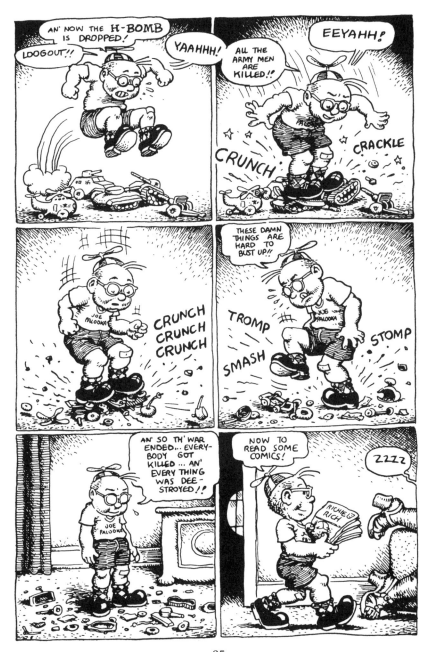

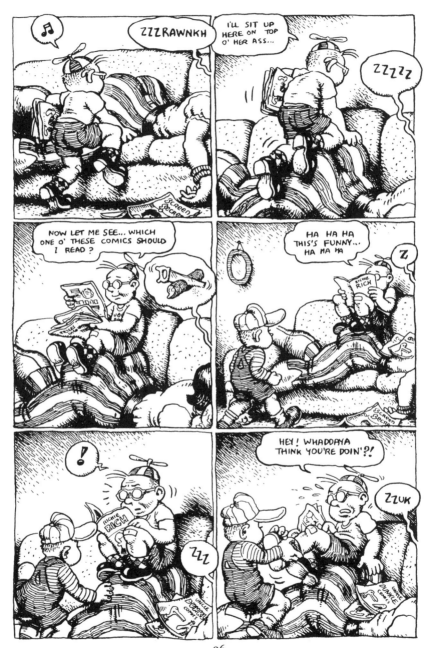

36

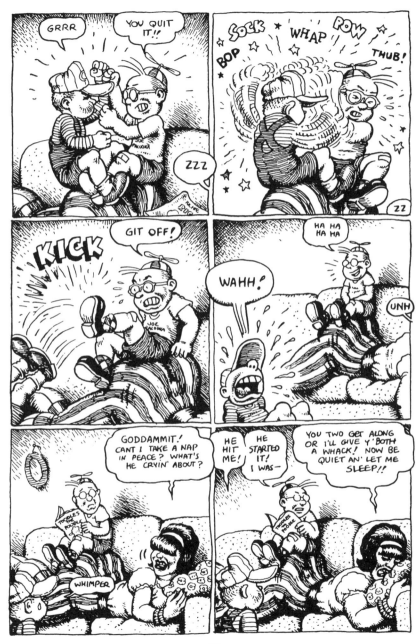

37

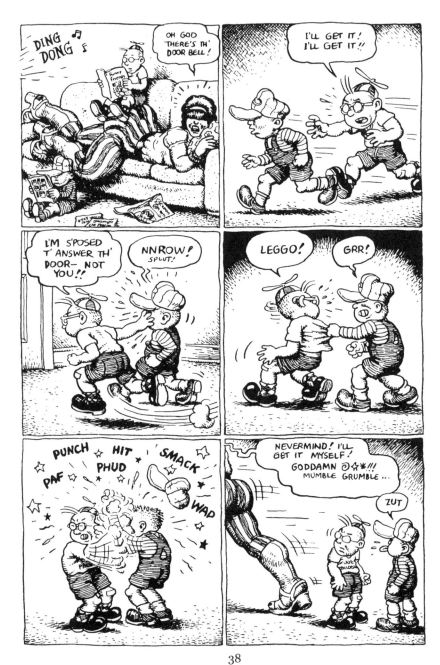

38

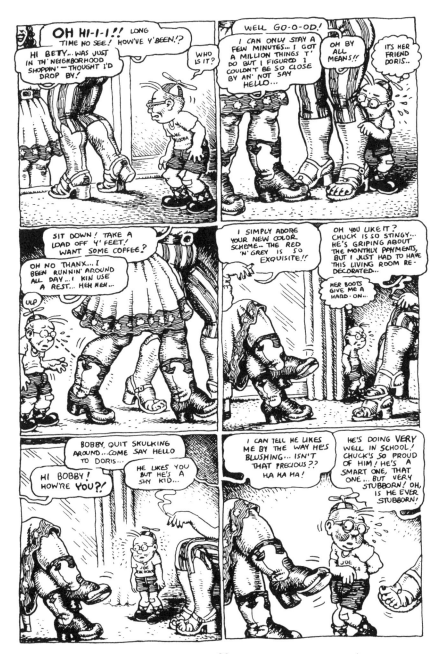

39

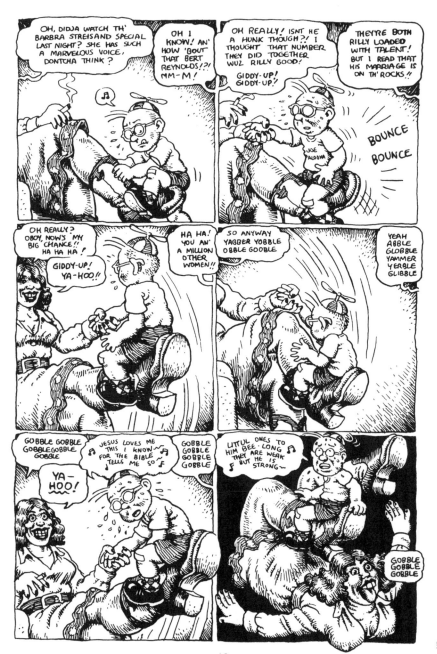

40

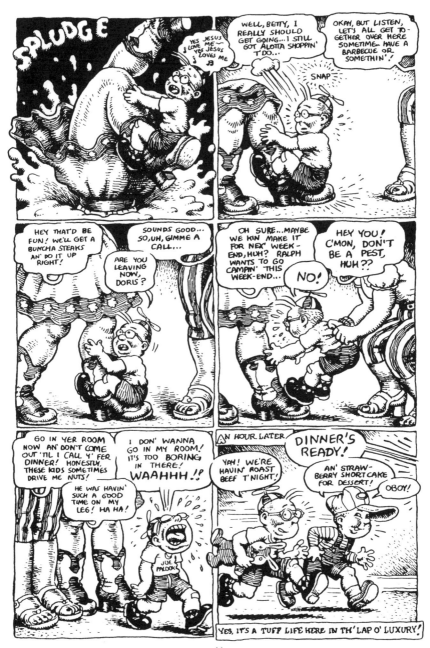

JUST US KIDS!!

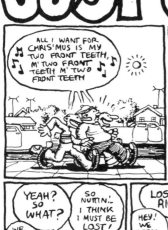

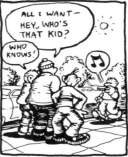

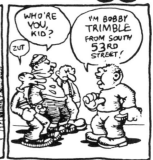

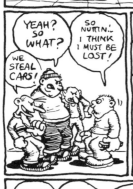

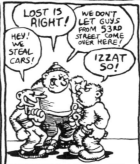

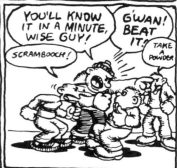

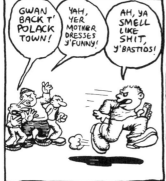

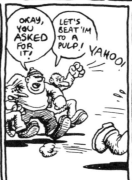

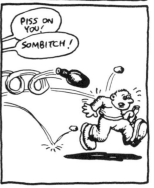

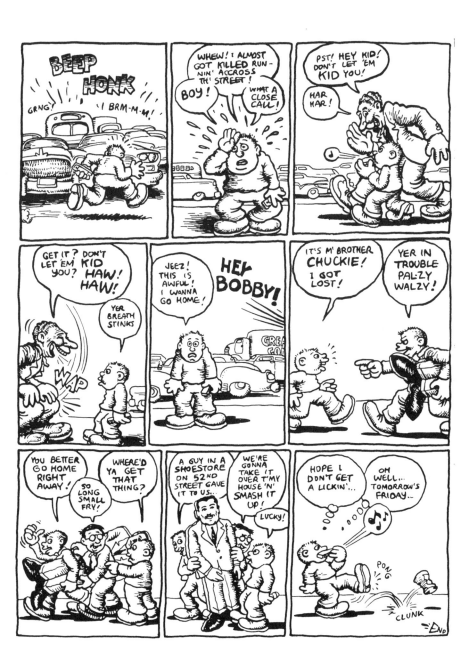

43

When I was a little kid, my mother said that I was always squinting, trying to see. I had a lot of accidents, bumping into things and falling down. When I was in the first grade I couldn't read the blackboard, and Sister Thomas Mary was beating me. I remember screaming, *"I can't see it! I can't see it!"* She stopped beating me.

A thought obviously dawned on her. She immediately made out a slip to my parents to send me to have an eye examination after school. I remember coming back on the subway from the eye doctor's with my mother, wearing my new glasses. I was looking around at everything, looking at people, looking at the little advertising signs above the windows. It was a revelation to suddenly be able to see things clearly and sharply.

"Oh, no wonder you were always so clumsy," my mother said. Everything had been sort of blurry up to that moment. Earlier when my mother brought home Disney comics for us kids, all I could see were big white round heads with orange ducks' bills, kind of vague.

I wasn't especially spiritual as a kid, but I wanted to be a good Catholic boy and go to heaven when I died. I made the sign of the cross every time I passed a church. I bowed my head whenever I heard the name of Jesus mentioned, just like the sisters told us to do. I've never known very many authentically spiritual people. I think my brother Charles struggled to achieve high spiritual states, and my brother Maxon still does, but both of them were crazy! Where do you draw the line between craziness and spirituality? I don't know. Especially as they are often embodied in the same person.

I was in the fourth grade when the concept of "the milk bottles of sin" was introduced from the *Baltimore Catechism*. The graphics in the catechism made a deep impression. When I was fifteen, both Charles and I became very fervent, devout

Actual Sin

SIN IS ANY ACT FORBIDDEN BY GOD

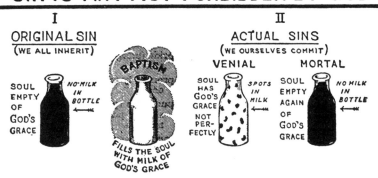

I

ORIGINAL SIN
(WE ALL INHERIT)

SOUL EMPTY OF GOD'S GRACE — NO MILK IN BOTTLE

BAPTISM

FILLS THE SOUL WITH MILK OF GOD'S GRACE

II

ACTUAL SINS
(WE OURSELVES COMMIT)

VENIAL

SOUL HAS GOD'S GRACE NOT PERFECTLY — SPOTS IN MILK

MORTAL

SOUL EMPTY AGAIN OF GOD'S GRACE — NO MILK IN BOTTLE

"Take Heed Thou Never Consent to Sin."—*Tobias* 4: 6.

Catholics. Then, after a couple of years, I stopped going to confession and praying and all that. Charles went on to become what he called "a failed mystic" in the last years before he killed himself, but it is hard to be a mystic when you are drugged all the time with mood elevators and tranquilizers. You can't make spiritual progress in a drugged state. You've got to be sober.

Around 1950, we started drawing our own home made comics. We drew our own coloring books—a whole line of *Animal Town* coloring books, all instigated by Charles.

Charles even developed an idea for a full length animated cartoon based on the fairy tale *The Fisherman and His Wife*. He and my sister Carol wrote songs for it. I helped him on the story boards and we created fake animation stills later because Charles kept *The Fisherman and His Wife* project going for years. He wanted to be like Walt Disney.

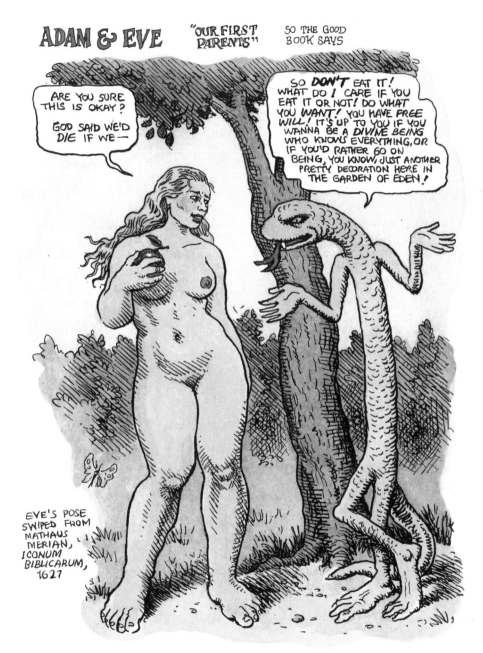

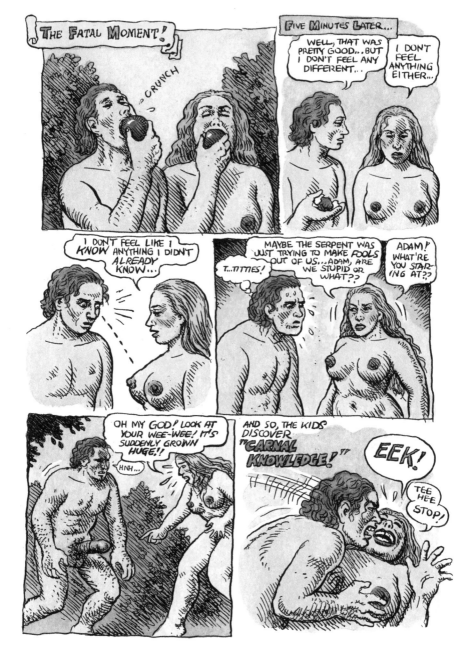

47

From 1950 to 1952, while my father was stationed in Ames, Iowa, we went often to visit his relatives in Minnesota. That's the only time I saw much of them. They were nice people, especially my grandmother, who seemed to be a kind, sweet person with a good sense of humor. My grandfather was sort of a distant patriarchal figure, smoking his pipe at the head of the table.

The Crumb Clan was so huge that at family reunions there would be fifty or sixty kids. They would line up the tables out in the yard heaped with food. All my cousins were rough and ready farm kids. They made fun of me because I'd be walking around holding my teddy bear. Well, I was already kind of eccentric by the age of ten, and I just accepted this about myself. I was "odd." I might even say I liked being odd.

Visiting the farm was like visiting a foreign country. Once at my uncle's farm, Charles and I wandered into the chicken coop. (Charles was always instigating mischief, he was the inspiration for my character, Eggs Ackley). *"Hey, look, there are eggs in here!"* Charles started throwing eggs against the wall, laughing. I remember wondering, *"Is this okay to do?"*. But eggs going splat against the wall seemed like fun, and so, we cleaned out several nests that way. Later, my father was so totally ashamed and embarrassed by our behavior that he reprimanded us. *"You boys know better than to do that! Why did you do it?"* We were town

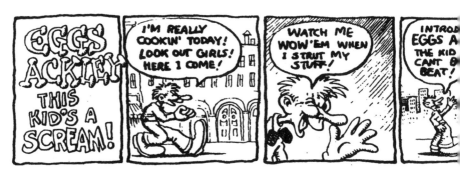

48

boys, it didn't occur to us that eggs for breakfast actually came from these chicken coops. I was only in the third grade.

I thought farm life had a certain easy going appeal, but my mother viewed the Crumbs as a bunch of rubes. When she fought with my father, she would make insulting remarks about his being a big hick from the sticks. Then he would come back with how stupid and worthless her relatives were, and so it went, the old "my family is just as good as your family" routine.

We moved to Oceanside, California in August 1952, just when I was turning nine years old. The pastel stucco houses, the palm trees, the light of the West Coast, the whole thing began having a depressing effect on me. I remember watching my mother working in the kitchen while listening to a plastic radio and the music coming from the radio seemed so dreary to me ... Rosemary Clooney, Perry Como ... even thinking about it now has a depressing effect!

I watched the tearing down of old pre-war downtown Oceanside and the putting up of modern, inferior architecture. Even as a kid I felt that this was all wrong. The old movie theatres, store fronts, nice streamlined Art Deco buildings from the 1920s and 1930s were replaced by squarish stucco boxes that had no character. My parents got a house in a brand new suburb, one of hundreds of houses that went on and on.

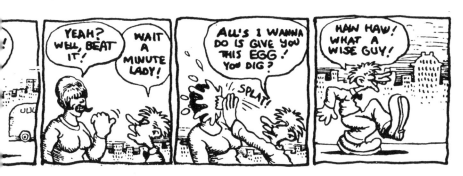

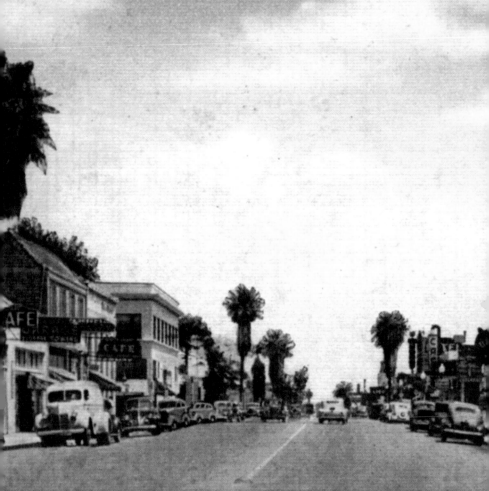

MAIN STREET, LOOKING

Postcard view, 1940s

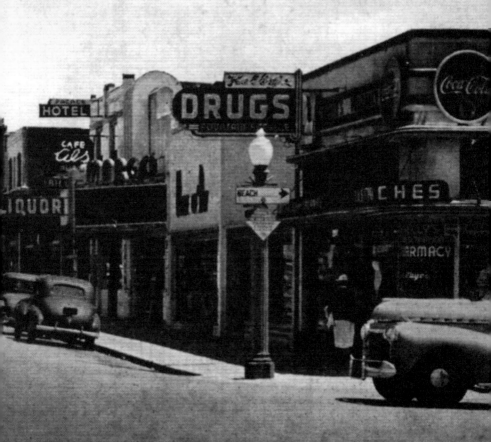

They were ticky-tacky boxes with no trees, just twigs planted in the front yard. The development was called "Francine Villas." I went back there in 1990 to look at it and there had been some individualization done of houses, but, the trees never made it.

There were no trees. The ground was just too barren in that place. God, it was bleak! There were no sidewalks because there was no place to walk to. To get to downtown Oceanside was a very long walk, might as well take the car.

We did a lot of TV watching when I was a kid. I'm sure TV had a profound effect on me from an early age. We watched all that cowboy crap—*Hopalong Cassidy, Roy Rogers, Gene Autry*. I remember the comedy relief sidekicks the best: Pat Buttrum, Pat Brady with his jeep called "Nellie Belle". I have a recurring dream about Gabby Hayes. I see old Gabby sitting around drinking at somebody's house.

"Incredible! Gabby, I watched you fifty years ago on TV and you look the same!" Gabby grins toothlessly. *"Well,"* he tells me, *"I just keep on puttin' this down!"* and he picks up a big bottle of whiskey and pours some in his glass.

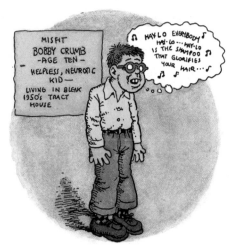

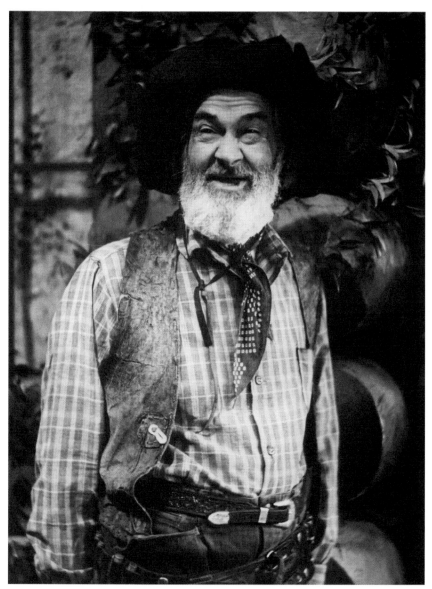

Gabby Hayes, popular old-time American movie and television cowboy character

There were a bunch of puppet and marionette kid shows on early TV that made a deep impression on me because, in spite of the adult assumption that these puppets were cute and lovable ... they were actually ... grotesque. Howdy Doody was an alien being, and the way the puppets moved was bizarre and dreamlike. Clarabell Clown was scary. My wife Aline tells of a "coming-of-age" moment in her life when she was eight years old and got to be a guest in the "Peanut Gallery" on *The Howdy Doody Show*. She saw the world the adults were trying to present to children, and the reality behind the scenes, were two different things. Buffalo Bob, the adult star of *The Howdy Doody Show,* off camera, was mean and scowling, but, as soon as the camera was on, he was all smiles, *"Hey kids! What time is it? It's Howdy Doody Time!"* Everybody off camera was sleazy and stressed out.

You had this uneasy feeling as a kid that something was going on that they were not showing you—something that was ugly.

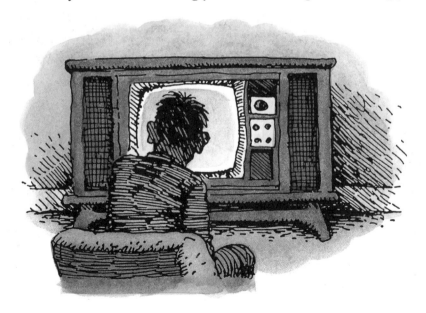

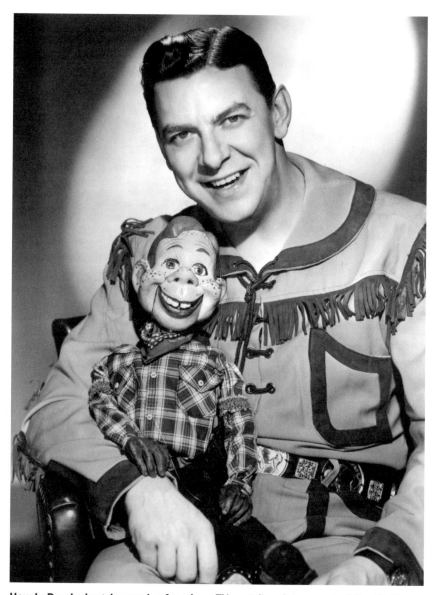

Howdy Doody, hugely popular American TV ventriloquist puppet of the 1940s and 1950s, with his creator, Buffalo Bob Smith

Adults were hiding something from us. And that's such a fascinating thing, the adult interpretation of the kid's world. A world artificially sweetened for kids, full of things kids were supposed to like and want. We sat in front of the television on Saturday mornings and looked at kids' stuff. The shows tried to tell kids that life could be fun and exciting, but the unconscious message was that the adult world is strange, twisted, perverse, threatening, sinister.

I think my brother Charles was hyper sensitive to this, and because his imagination was so active it was sometimes crippling for him. He was terrified of fire engines and police sirens. We used to go to an amusement park, Riverview Beach. There was one of those crazy house or scary house places with a mechanical laughing lady in a window that shook forward when she laughed, "*HA! HA! HA!*" and Charles would run screaming from her.

What we kids didn't understand was that we were living in a commercial, commodity culture. Everything in our environment had been bought and sold. As middle class Americans, we basically grew up on a movie set. The conscious values that are pushed are only part of the picture. The medium itself plays a much bigger part than anyone realizes: the creation of illusion. We are living surrounded by illusion, by professionally created fairy tales. We barely have contact with the real world.

Mass media is a fairly recent development, only as old as the Industrial Revolution, and it is spreading over the whole world and turning the last proud, independent, tribal populations into consumers. We are products of this industrial commodity culture. It's hard to make a value judgment about it, but certainly the world wasn't always like this.

I am perhaps more critical and more of a curmudgeon than a lot of people. Most people are very passive, they are like children. They just accept, they don't discriminate much at all.

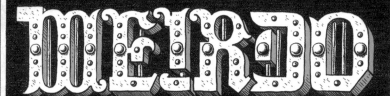

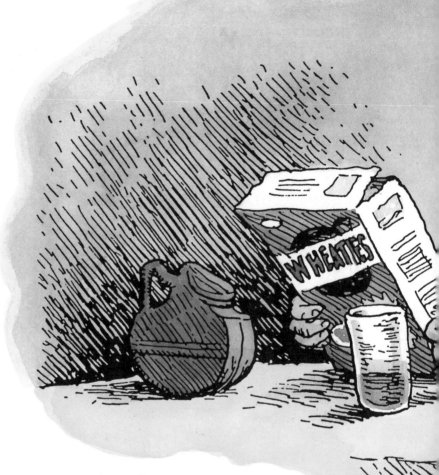

INNOCENCE BETRAYED
BY A PREDATORY ECO-
NOMIC SYSTEM. CHILDREN
ARE EASY PICKINGS...

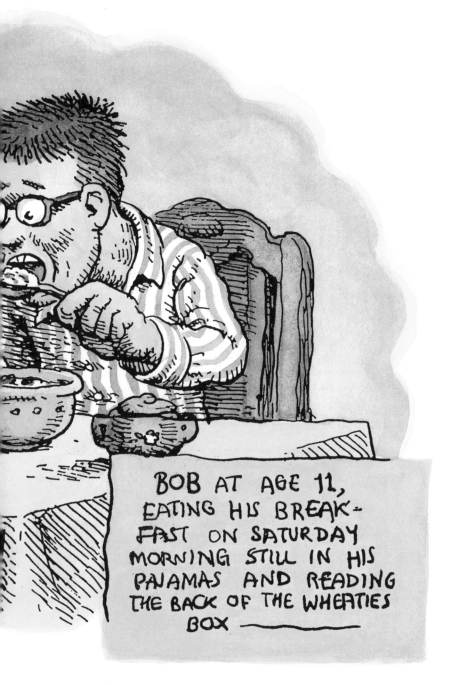

BOB AT AGE 11, EATING HIS BREAK-FAST ON SATURDAY MORNING STILL IN HIS PAJAMAS AND READING THE BACK OF THE WHEATIES BOX

About the only power you have is the power to discriminate. Living in a culture like this, you have to make choices, and search out what has the most authentic content or substance. In the 1960s, while on LSD, I realized that my mind was a garbage receptacle of mass media images and input. I spent my whole childhood absorbing so much crap that my personality and mind are saturated with it. God only knows if that affects you physically! As a kid I became increasingly interested in earlier periods of culture. I turned into a little nostalgia boy, and I became steeped in the *Our Gang* fantasy from watching them on TV. So much so, that my speech patterns were affected.

The style of those *Our Gang* comedies was so charming that I started acting and talking like Jackie Cooper and Alfalfa. They had these cute kid, artificial mannerisms. It must have been embarrassing for people to hear me talk like that. I made myself a kind of Jackie Cooper hat by trimming down the brim on a kid's cowboy hat. I walked around wearing that hat for a while.

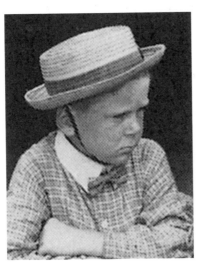

Jackie Cooper in Mal Roach's *Our Gang* comedies, early 1930s

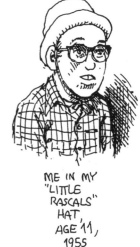

ME IN MY "LITTLE RASCALS" HAT, AGE 11, 1955

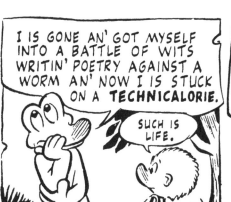

I IS GONE AN' GOT MYSELF INTO A BATTLE OF WITS WRITIN' POETRY AGAINST A WORM AN' NOW I IS STUCK ON A **TECHNICALORIE.**

SUCH IS LIFE.

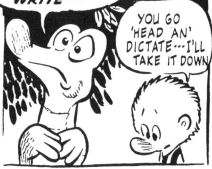

WHEN I **WRITES** IT'S HARD TO *READ* AT THE SAME TIME--- WHEN I **READS** I CAN'T SPELL SO GOOD *AND* WHEN I SPELLS GOOD I FERGETS HOW TO *WRITE---*

YOU GO 'HEAD 'AN' DICTATE---I'LL TAKE IT DOWN

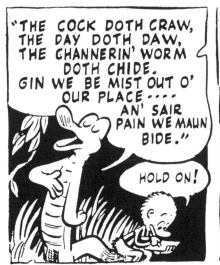

"THE COCK DOTH CRAW, THE DAY DOTH DAW, THE CHANNERIN' WORM DOTH CHIDE. GIN WE BE MIST OUT O' OUR PLACE---- AN' SAIR PAIN WE MAUN BIDE."

HOLD ON!

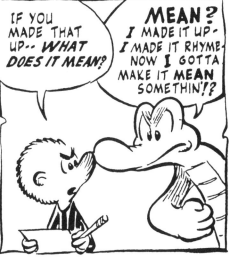

IF YOU MADE THAT UP-- *WHAT DOES IT MEAN?*

MEAN? I MADE IT UP- I MADE IT RHYME- NOW I GOTTA MAKE IT **MEAN** SOMETHIN'!?

Then, my friend, Freddy Martinez, a fat Mexican kid, liked it so much I gave it to him and he wore it around.

Then I started reading *Pogo* by Walt Kelly. I became so absorbed in Kelly's little world that I started talking with a fake Southern accent like Pogo and Albert the Alligator. Instead of saying: *"Are you going to the store today?"* I'd say: *"Is yo all goin' to dah sto' today?"* Embarrassing ...

I was an impressionable child. I saw *Samson and Delilah* in 1950 and the lurid, carnal quality of it made a powerful impression. The scene at the end where the Philistines are sitting in the arena watching the blind Samson being tortured and tormented: his great, powerful, courageous self is subjected to terrible humiliation as dwarfs poke him with sharp sticks. The crowd laughs at him. Somehow, Samson manages to get between the columns and pushes them apart. The huge idol topples and the whole arena collapses in a heap. The people who laughed at Samson are punished, crushed by giant stones.

This is powerful stuff, and Hollywood is so good at it. *Ivanhoe* in 1952 inspired us to play knights, all those battle scenes, those knights with broadswords bashing each other's shields, and the jousting tournaments. Every knight had his own bright color pattern. They were all different from each other, which was very appealing to me. I made a shield for myself and I painted a big checkered pattern on it. Charles and Maxon painted different patterns on theirs, and we jousted down the driveway with broom handles for lances.

Davy Crockett in 1955 really shocked me because—what?!—Davy actually loses the battle of the Alamo! I couldn't believe the good guy lost! All of Davy's friends and companions died: Jim Bowie, Davy's buddy George Russell, his gambler sidekick Hans Conried, the Indian friend. The hordes of Mexican soldiers just keep coming and coming, more and more of them, over the wall.

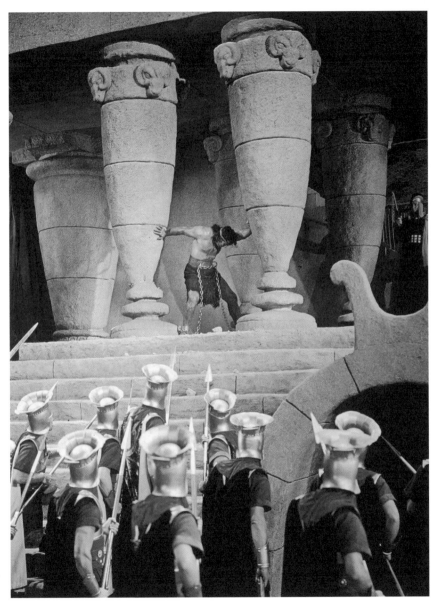

Scene from the 1949 Hollywood film *Samson and Delilah*

And Davy just keeps swinging his flintlock rifle, "Ol' Betsy," at them. Is it the end of Davy?

Oh my God, that's it! Davy's theme song starts playing while he's swinging his rifle: *"The story books tell they was all cut low, but the truth of it is, it just ain't so ... The miracle lives and the legend grows, As long as we remember the Alamo. Davy, Davy Crockett, fighting for liberty."* Everybody is killed in the end. These images from old movies stay with you for your whole life.

All the media at that time presented an image of a happy consumer America. Family life with all modern conveniences was pushed aggressively everywhere, creating a contradiction that was very stressful and very confusing. The illusion was the opposite of the sordid reality of everyday life, with stressed parents fighting each other, and worrying about paying the bills. There's a fantasy world created by the media. When we actually try to live it, we don't know why it's not working. The promise can never be fulfilled. It's just a sales pitch.

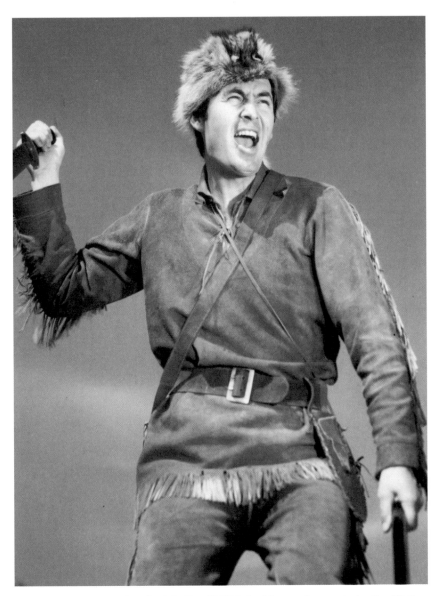

Fess Parker as Davy Crockett in the 1955 television series made by the Walt Disney Studios

KENNETH TYNAN
WRITER/DRAMA CRITIC

October 19, 1975: The most powerful influence on the arts in the West is—the cinema. Novels, plays and films are filled with references to, quotations from, parodies of—old movies. They dominate the cultural subconscious because we absorb them in our formative years (as we don't absorb books, for instance); and we see them again on TV when we grow up. The first two generations predominantly nourished on movies are now of an age when they rule the media: and it's already frightening to see how deeply—in their behavior as well as their work—the cinema has imprinted itself on them. Nobody took into account the tremendous impact that would be made by the fact that films are permanent and easily accessible from childhood onward. As the sheer number of films piles up, their influence will increase, until we have a civilization entirely molded by cinematic values and behavior patterns.

from *The Diaries of Kenneth Tynan,* 2001

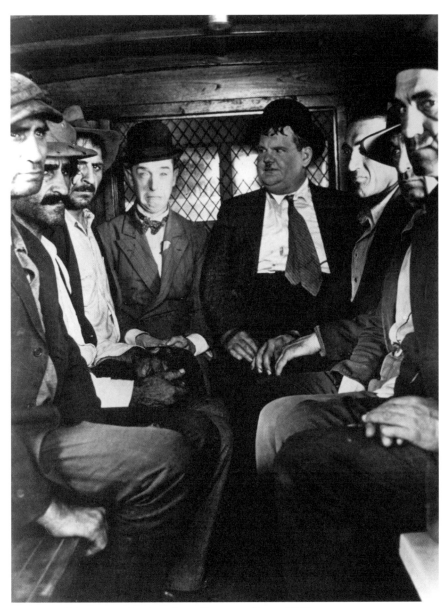

Laurel and Hardy, popular American film comedians, 1930s

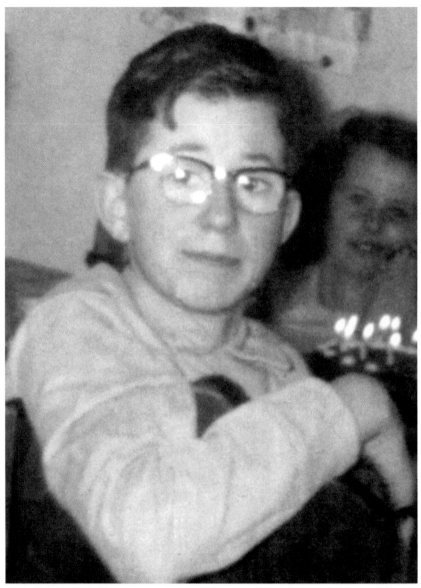

Above: R. Crumb, Milford, Delaware, 1957 with sister Sandra in the background
Following page: Italian poster of Cecil B. de Mille's *The Ten Commandments,* 1956

Chapter 2

Willful Ignorance

I was in the fifth grade when the Sister told our class, *"Some of you will fall away from the arms of the Holy Mother Church. Some of you will think you know more than the Church. You will think these beliefs are old fashioned and you will leave the security of the Mother Church."* I remember thinking, *"No! No! Not me! I never will! Why would I ever leave the Church and endanger my immortal soul? That's crazy! Why would anyone ever do that?"* And here I am today, excommunicated. I haven't been to Confession in ... gosh ... forty-five years. I had my last Confession when I was sixteen years old. If I went to Confession now, I'd be in there for hours, telling all the sins and perversions I've committed. Whoo! *"Bless me Father for I have sinned. I have drawn pornographic comics and I have foisted my perversions on the unsuspecting public."* I would have a really long Penance to say ... weeks and months of Our Fathers, Hail Marys, rosaries, Acts of Contrition ... everything.

I remember being curious about other boys my age. They didn't seem to be as impressionable as I was. They seemed more thick-skinned. Other boys didn't seem to be bothered when the nuns told us that if we said bad words we committed a mortal sin, and, if we died we'd go straight to hell. That affected me deeply. I avoided saying bad words for that reason.

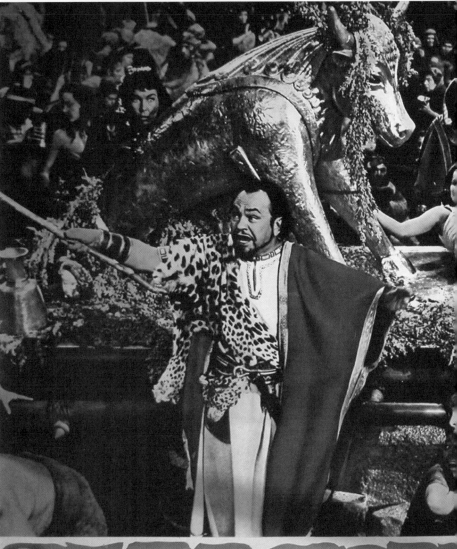

I dieci Coma

(THE TEN COMMANDMENTS)

Scritto per lo schermo da AENEAS MacKENZIE   JACK GARISS   JESSE L. LASKY, Jr.   FREDRIC M. FRANK   Basato sulla S

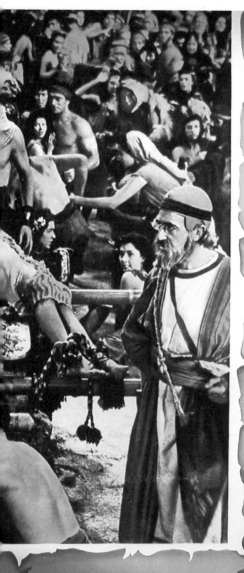

UNA PRODUZIONE DI

Cecil B. DeMille

in

VISTAVISION

CON

CHARLTON HESTON
YUL BRYNNER
ANNE BAXTER
EDWARD G. ROBINSON
YVONNE DE CARLO
DEBRA PAGET
JOHN DEREK

e

SIR CEDRIC HARDWICKE
NINA FOCH
MARTHA SCOTT
JUDITH ANDERSON
VINCENT PRICE

Diretto da CECIL B. DE MILLE

Colore della
TECHNICOLOR

È un film Paramount

damenti

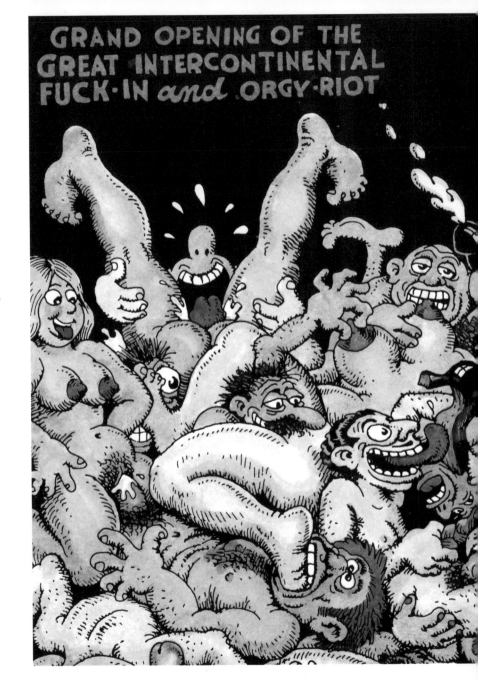

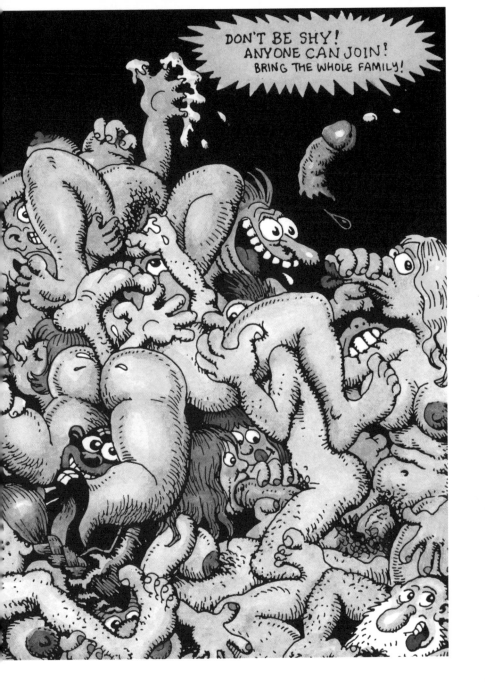

Other boys would just go ahead and use swear words. Weren't they afraid of going to hell?

I saw *The Ten Commandments* in 1956. There's a scene in which the children of Israel are worshipping the golden calf. A big orgy starts with all these gorgeous athletic bodies, young, well built movie extras, scantily clad, oiled up, rolling over each other, wrestling around in a big heap. I watched that in total amazement. It was kind of sexually arousing in some vague way. All these beautiful bodies crawling all over each other, humping each other. It was incredible! Then, Moses comes down from the mountain. He's just received the Ten Commandments from God and in great anger, he hurls them down at the feet of the idol worshippers, who now cower and cringe as lightning bolts rend the sky and a big chasm opens up. The beautiful bodies are falling in. Incredible! But I was not afraid, because I was a good Catholic boy. That had nothing to do with me, that's what happened to savage pagans.

In one of his stories Charles Bukowski describes how a schoolyard mentality affects the world we live in—meaning, everyone has to go through cruel hazing and testing rituals. You just can't be too goddam sensitive in this world. I was too fucking *s-e-n-s-i-t-i-v-e!*

My brother Charles never had much interest in typical boy's stuff, toys, or games, or weapons. He was more into performing. He liked play acting and drama. The high point of Charles' performing career was his imitation of Robert Newton as Long John Silver from Disney's movie version of *Treasure Island*. We had seen it in the theater in 1950, but after we saw it again on TV in 1955, Charles developed an elaborate Long John Silver act and even performed it for audiences at local affairs and for groups like the Kewannis Club. Charles *became* Long John Silver. This was an outgrowth of his obsession with Disney.

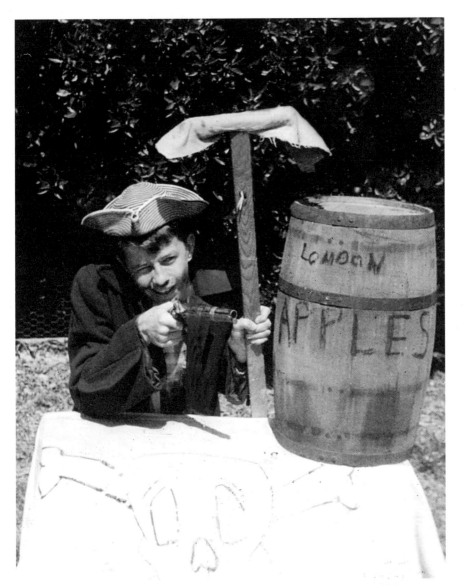

Above: Charles Crumb dressed as Long John Silver from *Treasure Island,* 1955
Next page: Treasure Island, 1950 Walt Disney film with Robert Newton as Long John Silver and Bobby Driscoll as Jim Hawkins

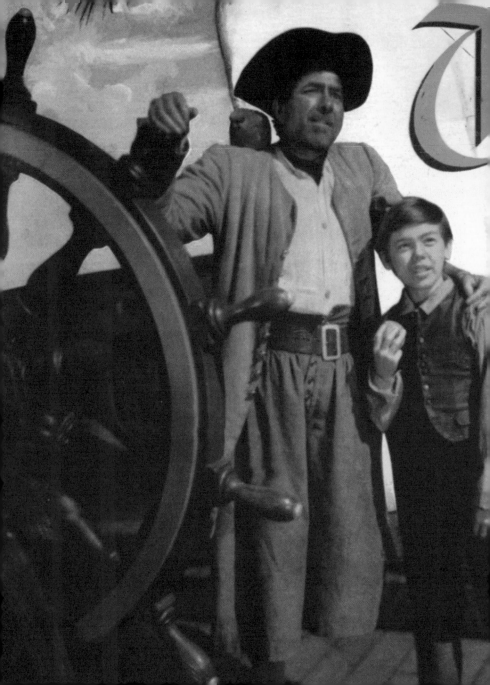

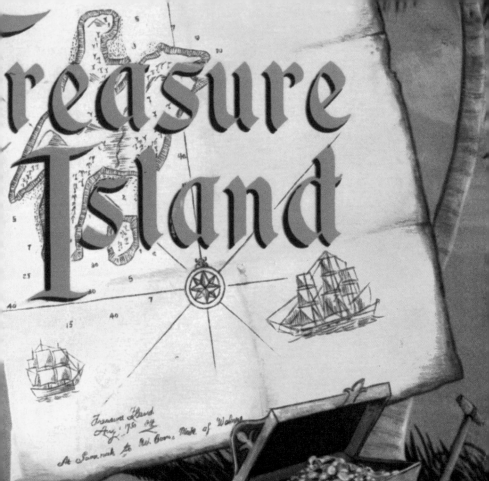

with
the original star of the Walt Disney Motion Picture

BOBBY DRISCOLL

AS JIM HAWKINS

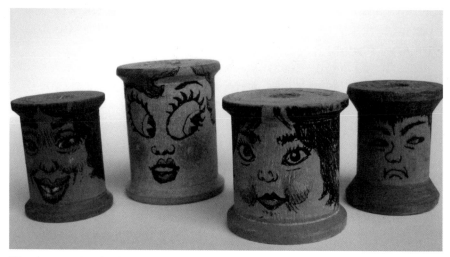

Wooden spools with faces drawn by R. Crumb

He created drama in his life all the time. We used to have games with our teddy bears and my sister's dolls, and we talked for them. Charles was really funny. He would take these stupid dolls and give them such wacky personalities that they became real to us. We would just watch the doll and forget that it was Charles putting the doll through it's wacky paces.

The funniest one was a stuffed clown my sister got from the Camp Fire Girls. He was called "Campfire Clown," and Charles invented a personality for him that was so nutty, so crazy, so funny, that he had us in stitches. He took a handful of little wooden spools and started drawing faces on them and created "the spool men." Fifty years later, I'm still making spoolmen!

I constantly marveled at Charles' devotion to the comics medium. His own comics, *Funny Friends* and other titles, were always tightly, patiently drawn, with carefully devised stories. He was much more prolific than I was. He was totally dedicated. He made hundreds and hundreds of well executed comic books as a kid and adolescent. He had no other interests. It was very intimidating for me. I always felt like such a second-rate artist compared to him.

I started drawing *Brombo the Panda* comics in January of 1952, and Charles made us pretend like we were working for the Dell Publishing Company, whose motto was: *"Dell Comics Are Good Comics."* We drew those home made comics throughout our childhood and adolescence, from 1952 right up until I left home in 1962: ten years solid of drawing comics with no let-up and no vacations.

I based *Brombo the Panda* on a teddy bear I was given on my seventh birthday in Ames, Iowa. I tried to make him be like the funny animal comics that we read, such as *Andy Panda*, or *Felix the Cat*. I turned out those comics every month, but I can't say that I enjoyed doing it all that much. Quantity was more important than quality. Just get those issues out, just fill the pages. Charles tried to shame me into doing a better job. I would then start out more carefully, lose patience, and get sloppier and sloppier as I went along. I just wanted to get it over with.

One day, when I was twelve years old, I noticed that both my teddy bears, Brombo and Sniff, were gone. I asked my mother about them and she didn't know anything. I asked my father and he just shrugged his shoulders, but my father was the kind of guy who would get rid of the family cat when you weren't looking. He'd "take them for a ride." My father was a hard guy, and he probably hoped I would "grow up" and become more manly if he got rid of my teddy bears.

He wasn't ready to accept the fact that he had a bunch of wimpy mama's boys for sons. I continued to draw *Brombo the Panda* until 1958. When I was nineteen, I took all those *Brombo the Panda* comics out in the backyard and burned them. No great loss, believe me, but it added up to a lot of "pencil mileage."

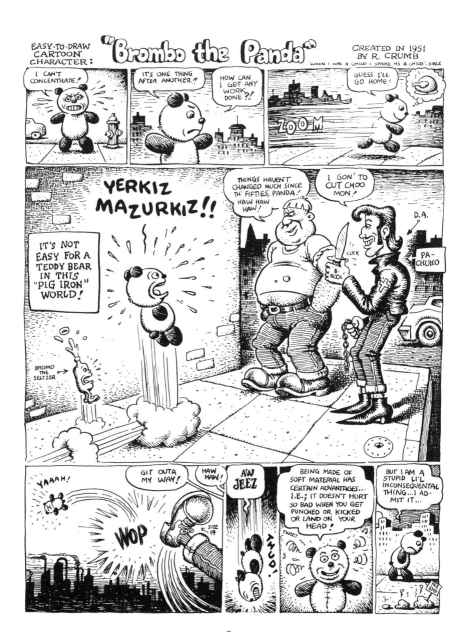

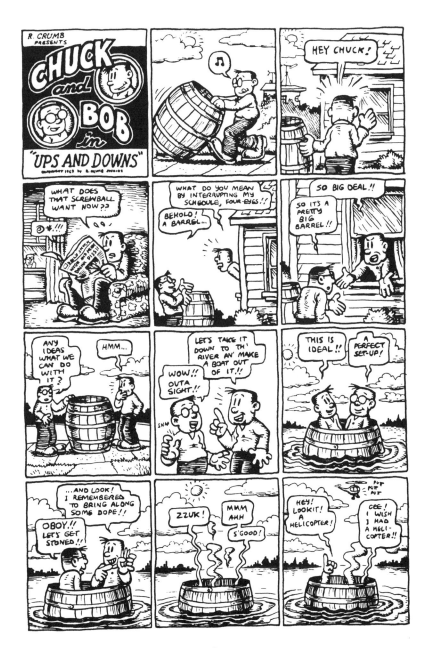

81

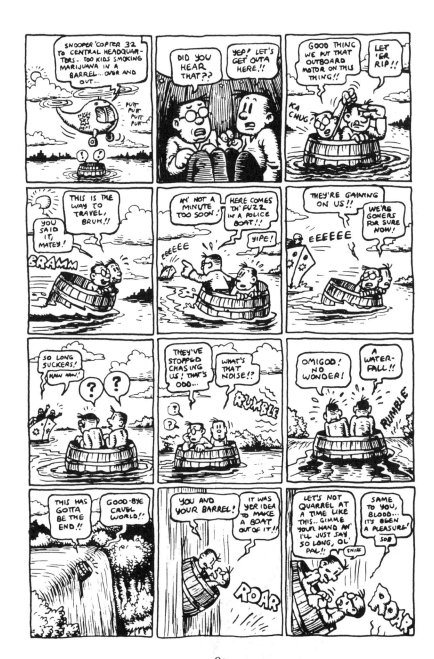

82

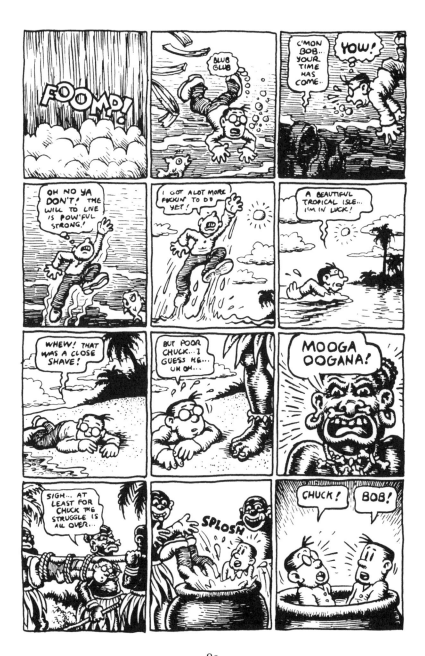

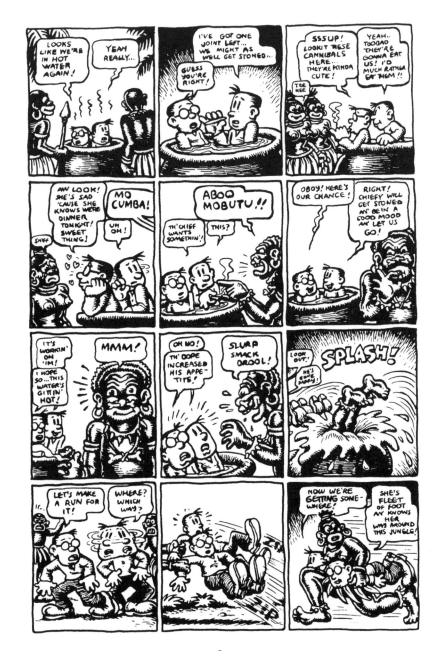

84

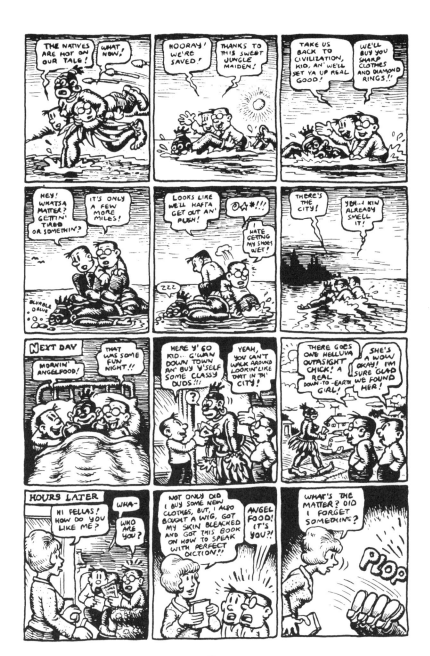

85

Charles had forced me to learn the language of comics very early.We tuned in to *The Mickey Mouse Club* on TV every day after school, and on Sundays our family always watched the *Disneyland* TV show. By this time I was getting old enough to perceive a change in the nature of the "Disney magic." It wasn't what it had been: it was becoming too cloyingly cute, conservative and corporate.

Charles and I were starting to get cynical about the media. There are studies that claim that children who watch a great deal of television with all those commercials become cynical at a young age. They become aware that they're being constantly hyped. Charles and I would watch TV in order to make fun of it and in the early years we anxiously looked forward to the "bloopers," which happened quite often, in fact. We'd shriek with laughter when they screwed up. That was one of the best things about early television!

But Disneyland itself was a truly magical place, created very meticulously and deliberately. The rides were like a fantastic dream come true. Afterwards, I remember often having dreams just like the Snow White ride, the Peter Pan ride, or the Mister Toad ride, in which you'd go inside a dark interior, similar to an old amusement park scary house, and the effects were very well done, lit with black light reflected on painted three dimensional surfaces, very dream like. Charles told me later that the first time our family went to Disneyland, when he was twelve years old, was the happiest day of his life.

My father retired from the Marine Corps with the rank of master sergeant in the summer of 1956, and we moved to Delaware, where my mother's relatives lived, and stayed there for the next six years. My father didn't really want to quit the Corps, my mother forced him to do it. He found himself adrift in the business world, working for a couple of companies in nebulous capacities that I was never quite clear about.

When we first arrived in Milford, Delaware, it was so old, quaint, and charming, after the modern, depressing, suburban world of southern California. I loved the way it looked. It was old-time America with almost no modern development. But it turned out to be socially backward, extremely racist and mean, with inbred families who had been there for generations. The locals seemed willfully and aggressively ignorant.

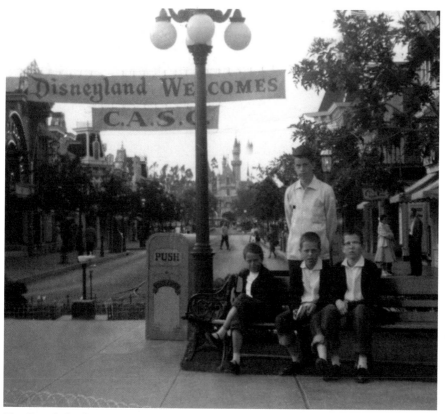

The Crumb family in Disneyland, 1955. Left to right: Sandra, Charles (standing), Maxon, Robert.

Milford was like the Deep South. The town made the national news on the issue of school integration in 1954, two years before we got there. There was an attempt to integrate the local school that caused a big race riot. Wayne Parker, a guy I knew in the tenth grade, bragged about how he had personally dragged two little black girls out of the school by their hair. Wayne was a very popular guy. All the girls liked him. He had a beautiful girlfriend, the magnificent Dolly Hensley. Oh, the injustice!

The kids in Milford often talked and joked about the "niggers." All the black people lived in an area known as "Jimtown," the poorest section of Milford. The school we went to was completely segregated. You did not see a black person on Main Street in that town. If I dared to assert that I didn't think negroes were inferior to white people, I was called a "black tail-licker" or a "nigger lover." That was just the social norm for white people there.

Milford traumatized the hell out of all us in my family, but especially Charles, who always had a lot of trouble in school. "Skutch" Kenton, George Welch, and all those guys broke Charles' spirit. Once I witnessed them publicly pound him in front of everybody, in a crowded hallway of the high school. The problem was that Charles was good looking. He was eccentric but girls liked him. So, the guys had to prove to the girls that Charles was not a man or a fighter.

Charles could have become a psychopathic criminal, because he was kind of going in that direction, but he was saved from that fate by his cultural interests. I, myself, was evolving into a bitter social reject. I was already looking back on my earlier childhood with a certain nostalgia, back to when I was still just a goofy, oblivious kid walking down the street reading a Pud comic and chewing "Dubble Bubble" gum. I didn't know what was going on or what anything was about. I was passive, mushy and vague when I was a kid.

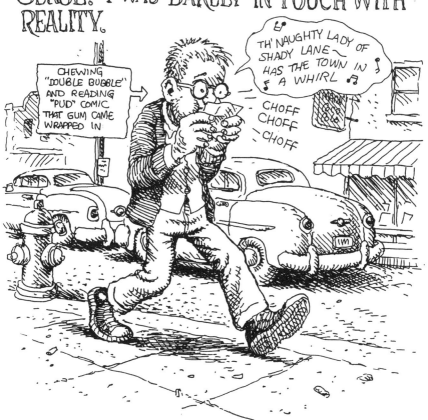

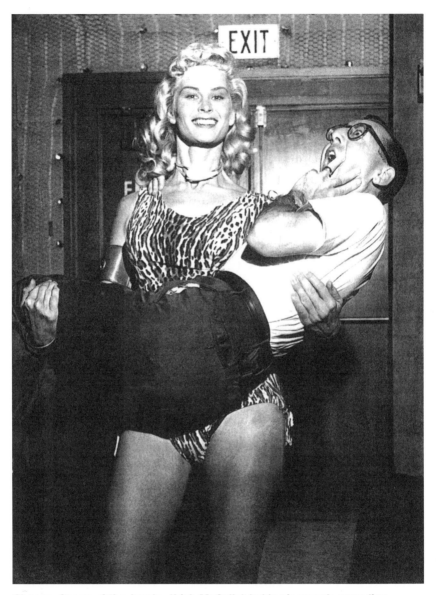

Sheena, Queen of the Jungle, (Irish McCalla) holds pipsqueak comedian Arnold Stang, mid-1950s

Then my sexuality began to kick in. Oh my God, was that painful! I was consumed with lust. I watched *Sheena, Queen of the Jungle* starring Irish McCalla on a hard-to-tune-in TV station in the summer of 1956. I couldn't wait to go to bed at night to fantasize about me and Sheena! In the TV show Sheena was always having to rescue the white explorer, "Bob," from some danger, usually some menacing black natives.

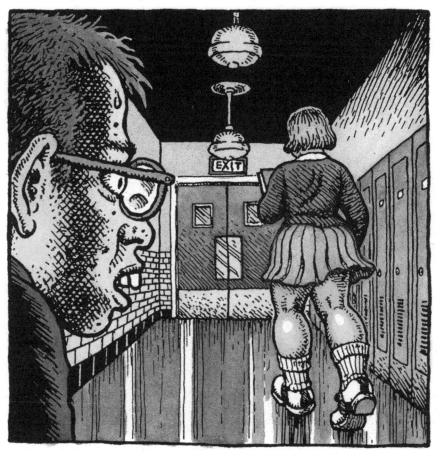

THE YOUNG R. CRUMB IN CATHOLIC SCHOOL

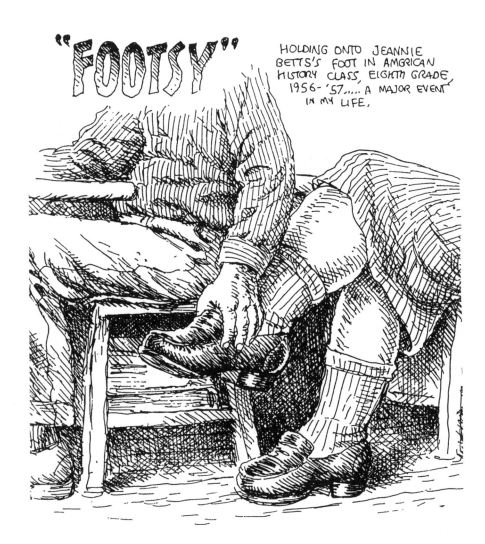

"FOOTSY"

HOLDING ONTO JEANNIE BETTS'S FOOT IN AMERICAN HISTORY CLASS, EIGHTH GRADE, 1956-'57..... A MAJOR EVENT IN MY LIFE.

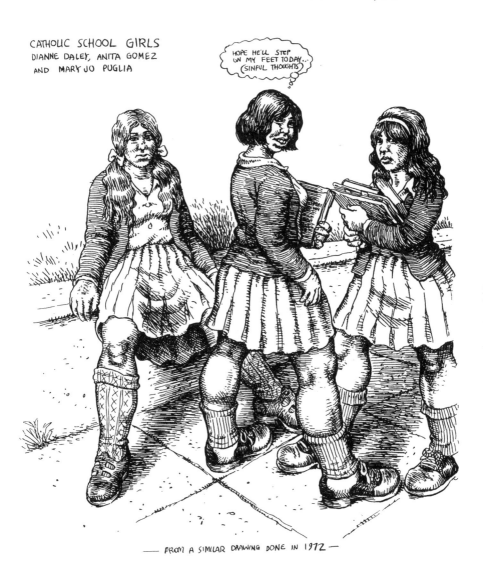

I dreamed of strong women. My sexuality has been rather quirky ever since, in a state of arrested development, and it makes me want to have my way with big, strong, powerful women. I don't know why, I just do.

My parents had to move every couple of years, since they created such a bad reputation for themselves in any neighborhood where they lived, with all their fighting and screaming! My mother was completely crazy. So they would just move, get out of there. I didn't figure this out until much later. We left Milford partially because my parents could see that their children weren't adjusting socially. We moved twenty miles north to Dover, which was a bit more cosmopolitan, what with the Air Force base and some small industrial plants such as the Latex Corporation, where my father worked for several years.

Today I saw a picture in the newspaper of Dover Air Force Base, because that's where the coffins of dead American soldiers are shipped from the Iraqi War. But I remember the Air Force base as the place where Charles and I tried to sell copies of our home made comic book, *FOO*, and failed. We printed 300 copies each of the three different issues, and it was so much work to sell them that we finally gave up and burned all the unsold copies.

It was a shattering disappointment when we couldn't sell *FOO* to the kids in our high school. We thought for sure that they would buy our little magazine—it only cost fifteen cents. But, because we were so unpopular with them, they wouldn't buy it. We tried selling *FOO* to the people in the housing developments in Dover, saying that it was an art project for the school. They asked, *"You drew this? Who's your art teacher over there? I'm going to call the school and ask him about this,"* all over a lousy dime (we'd reduced the cover price)! And, of course, my high school art teachers, Mr. Ferranto and Mr. Kunkle, both hated comics, and they didn't like me much either.

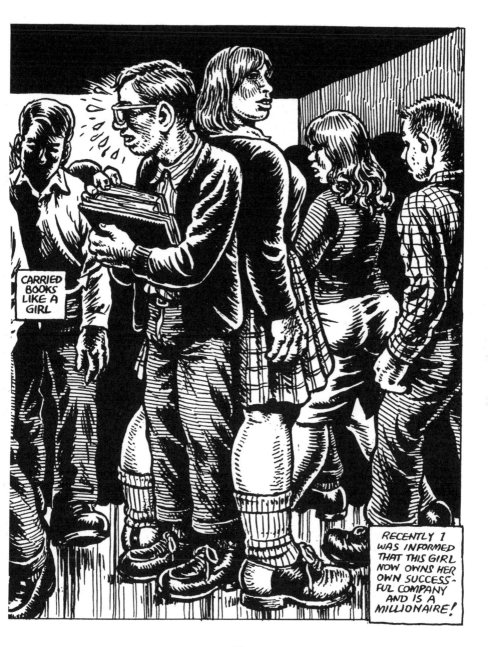

CARRIED BOOKS LIKE A GIRL

RECENTLY I WAS INFORMED THAT THIS GIRL NOW OWNS HER OWN SUCCESSFUL COMPANY AND IS A MILLIONAIRE!

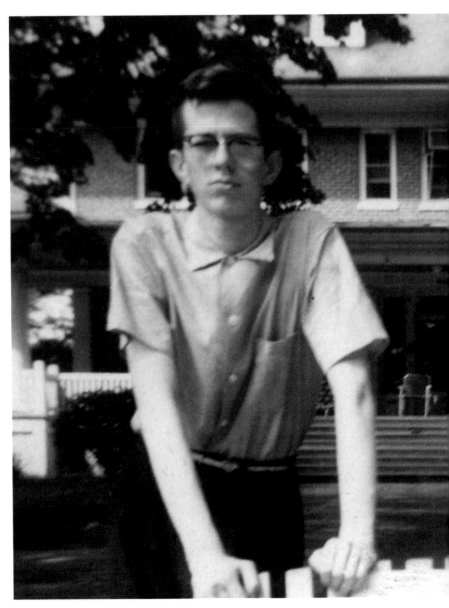

Robert and Charles Crumb, Milford, Delaware, summer 1959

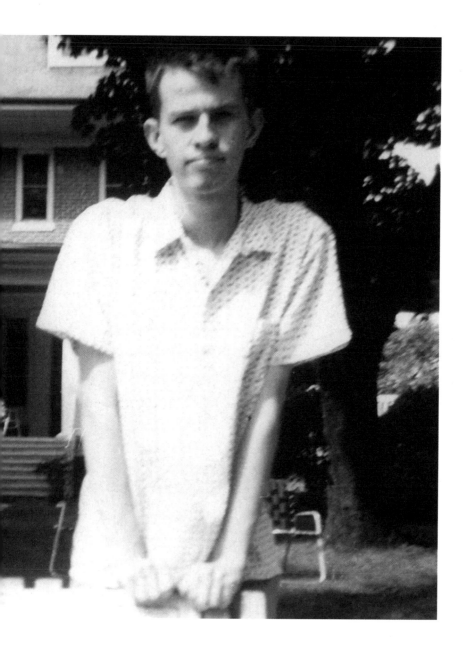

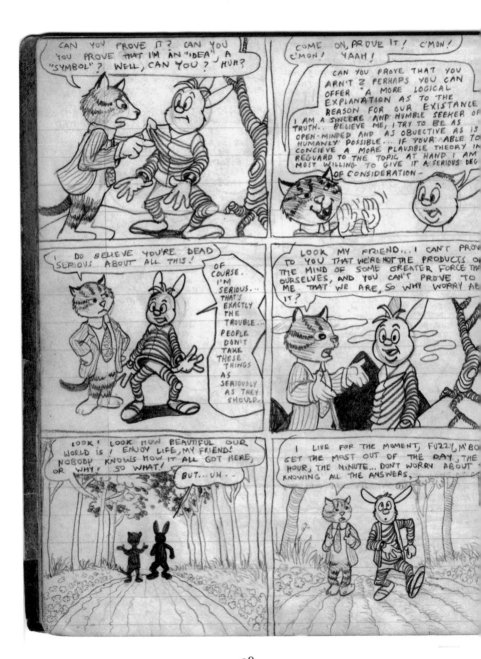

THE TROUBLE WITH YOU IS, YOU THINK TOO MUCH ABOUT ALL THIS STUFF! GET OUT AND DO THINGS, ANYTHING! EVERYTHING! AND DON'T WORRY ABOUT IT!

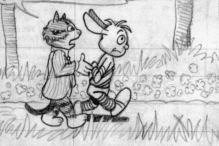

WHAT YOU NEED IS A GIRLFRIEND! SOME SWEET, CHARMING LITTLE BUNNY TO BRIGHTEN UP YOUR LIFE!

A MAN WHO'S LIFE IS PREOCCUPIED WITH SEX IS A MAN WHO IS TRYING TO EVADE THE TRUTH...

DON'T YOU SEE...! IN ORDER TO LIVE MORE WORTHWHILE AND PURPOSEFUL LIVES WE'VE GOT TO DIRECT OUR ENERGIES TOWARD THE DEVELOPMENT OF SELF-UNDERSTANDING AND ALL TRUTH IN GENERAL.... CAN'T YOU UNDERSTAND THAT? ARE YOU BLIND? YOUR A FAIRLY INTELLIGENT CHAP! YOU POSSESS AN ADEQUATE DEGREE OF PERCEPTION..... I'M SURE YOU HAVE THE MENTAL ABILITY TO PERCIEVE THAT WHAT I SAY HAS SOME AMOUNT OF SIGNIFICANCE..... BUT THEN AGAIN, PERHAPS YOU DON'T..... MAYBE I'M OVER-RATING YOUR MENTAL CAPACITIES. MAYBE YOU DON'T HAVE AS MUCH BETWEEN YOUR EARS AS I GIVE YOU CREDIT FOR... MAYBE YOU LACK THE MENTAL FACILITIES REQUIRED TO FULLY GRASP OR COMPREHEND MY PHILOSOPHICAL STATEMENTS.

NOW... OBSERVE SOME OF OUR MORE POPULAR AND WELL-KNOWN CONTEMPORARIES ..... BLONDIE AND DAGWOOD, MICKEY MOUSE, SMOKEY STOVER, WINNIE WINKLE, MANDRAKE THE MAGICIAN, NANCY, AND RIVETS, TO NAME A FEW... THERE ARE MORE... MANY MORE... HUNDREDS OF THEM... THESE CHARACTERS COMPLETELY AND UNQUESTIONINGLY CONFORM TO THE RULES AND CODES SET DOWN BY COMIC STRIP TRADITION.... THEY ALL DO EXACTLY WHAT THERE SUPPOSED TO DO... THEY DO PRECISELY WHAT THEY ARE EXPECTED TO DO. LET'S FACE IT! THAT'S THE WAY IT IS -- IT SIMPLY CANNOT BE DENIED. ANYBODY WHO TRYS TO DENY OR DISPROVE SOMETHING THAT IS SO UTTERLY APPARENT IS A DAMNED FOOL.....

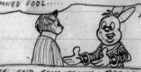

THEY MAKE DELIBERATE EFFORTS TO BE CUTE, FUNNY, SENTIMENTAL, EFFECTIVE, AND SO ON AND SO FORTH --- THEY CONTINUALLY ENGAGE IN THE SAME IDIOTIC REPITITIOUS ROUTINES, DAY AFTER DAY, WEEK AFTER WEEK, MONTH AFTER MONTH, YEAR AFTER YEAR... UNTIL THERE EVENTUAL DEATH... NEVER ONCE, AT ANY TIME... PAUSING.... TO ASK WHAT AM I? WHY AM I HERE? WHERE AM I GOING? THEY NEVER MAKE ANY EFFORT TO BECOME AS FULLY AWARE OF THEMSELVES AND THERE SITUATIONS AS POSSIBLE..... CONSEQUENTLY THEY LEAD SHALLOW, FUTILE LIVES, BECAUSE AWARENESS IS THE PARENT OF KNOWLEDGE.... KNOWLEDGE IS SELF-UNDERSTANDING. ONLY THROUGH SELF-UNDERSTANDING CAN WE LIVE HAPPIER AND MORE MEANINGFUL LIVES.... DO YOU SEE MY POINT...? AM I CARRYING MY IDEA OVER TO YOU CLEARLY AND EFFECTIVELY...?

IGNORANCE AND CONSISTENCY BREED BOREDOM..... AND IT'S PERFECTLY OBVIOUS THAT TODAY'S COMIC STRIP CHARACTERS ARE ALL BORED STIFF... ONLY THROUGH UNDERSTANDING CAN WE REALLY GET ANYTHING OUT OF LIFE..... WE MUST DIRECT OUR ENERGIES INTO THESE CHANNELS.... AND I'M POSTIVE THAT THE RESULTS OF THIS MOVEMENT WOULD BE MOST SATISFACTORY... COMIC STRIPS WOULD BECOME AN IMMENSELY STRONG INFLUENTIAL AND INTELLECTUAL FORCE IN THE WORLD. WE MIGHT EASILY BECOME A NEW AND IMPORTANT FORM OF ART!

WELL NOW I DON'T KNOW, UM...

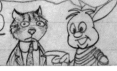

99

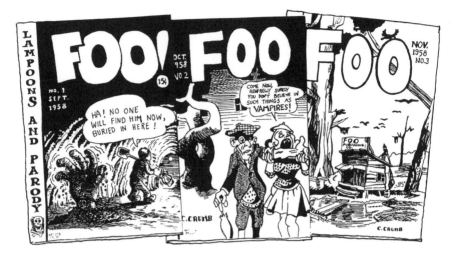

FOO was my first real experience with the business end of publishing. It's fine and dandy to create something, but somebody has to go out there and sell it, push it. The real importance of *FOO* was that it connected Charles and me with the national fanzine network, a whole comic book fan world that was just then sprouting up.

These comics fans were impressed with *FOO*. We received our first validation from the world, that maybe it was worthwhile doing these comics and that we might be good at it. It gave us a reason to hope we might have a career in that world.

My father, meanwhile, had me out drawing pictures of houses and trying to sell the drawings to the owners; and he got me a job doing an oil painting from a photo of a pair of hunting dogs of a friend of his from work. It turned out pretty good.

I was surprised, but I didn't pursue oil painting any further, because Charles had my nose to the grindstone drawing those comics. Charles said nothing about my oil painting. Art *per se* didn't interest him particularly. But there was another aspect of comic book fandom that was really great.

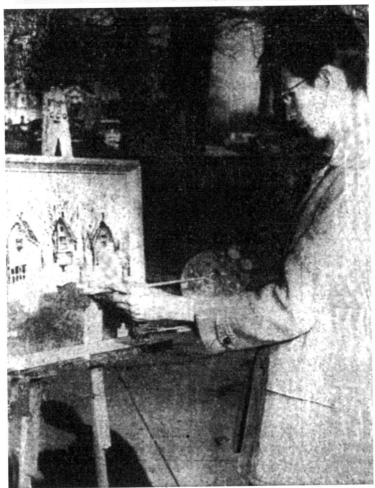

ROBERT DENNIS CRUMB, a senior at Dover High School has entered the Hallmark Cards and General Federation of Women's Clubs 1961 Art Talent Contest. The three top prizes are $600 scholarshihps to any art school or approved college. Crumb is sponsored in the contest by the Dover Century Club Fine Arts Committee: Mrs. Charles Conner, president; Mrs. Donald Quast, chairman; Mrs. Frederick Owen; Mrs. Carl R. Glines; Mrs. Frank Traynor; Mrs. Rowland Herdman; and Mrs. A. C. Bryson

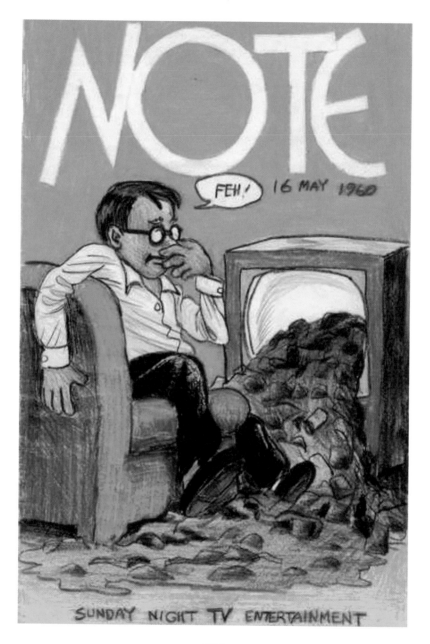

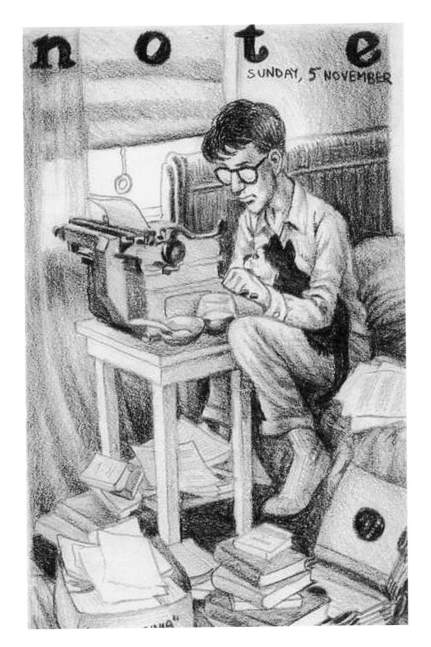

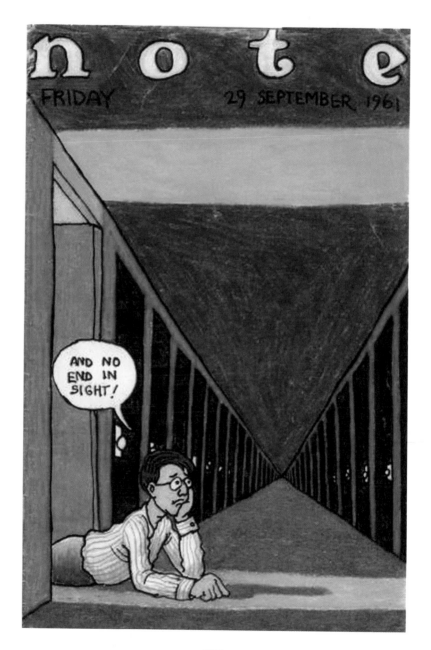

We discovered we could send away and buy old back issues of comics we needed to complete our collections. One of the most exciting days I ever had was coming home after school and opening a parcel containing old *Mad* comics!

In the summer of 1962 things were pretty bad at home. There was a lot of fighting going on, and during a particularly bad fight I slammed the cheap, flimsy door of our bedroom so hard, it came off its hinges! I decided I'd had it. I threw some clothes in a dinky little suitcase, and with my sketchbook and a few dollars, I started hitchhiking.

I had no plan. On the New Jersey turnpike I got picked up by the police, who said, *"Okay, where do you want to go? You can't hitchhike on the turnpike."* They were nice about it. I said, *"Well, I guess I'll go to my grandmother's house in Philadelphia,"* so the policemen dropped me off in Upper Darby. I had no intention of going back home, and I knew I couldn't stay at my grandmother's house. It was terrible there. My grandmother and old man O'Connell just sat around drinking all day.

So, I went looking for a job. I thought maybe I could get a job doing sign painting, so I walked into a discount store that had hand-painted signs hanging all over the place. I asked the manager if he could use another sign painter. He quoted me some low payment per sign, and gave me a long list of signs that he wanted done: *"$49.95/10% OFF!"*, *"SUMMER SALE ON SOCKS—HALF OFF!"*. I took the list back to my grandmother's, but I could not even bring myself to begin. I couldn't do one sign. I thought, *"If this is what I have to do, I'll just go home and be like Charles, be a bum."*

A few days later, my mother drove up to my grandmother's house. I had called my parents to let them know where I was. *"I'm fed up too,"* she told me. *"I want to run away too! Let's run away together!"* She opened the trunk of the car.

Her bags were in there, all packed. She was ready to run away. *"Nah, forget it! Let's just go home,"* I said. I didn't want to run away with my mother. I persuaded her to return to Dover with me. My father suggested quite strongly that Charles and I get our asses out, and get jobs. I had no plans to go to college and no prospects. I didn't know what the hell I was going to do.

In October of 1962 I left home forever. My friend Marty Pahls invited me to share an apartment with him in Cleveland, Ohio.

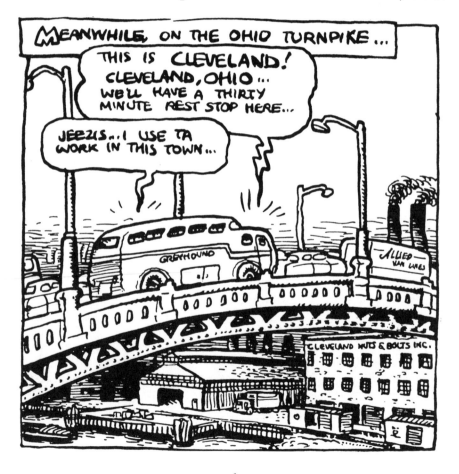

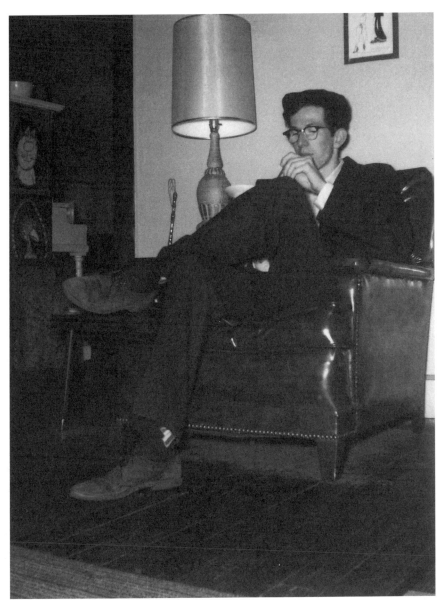

R. Crumb, age twenty, Cleveland, Ohio, 1964

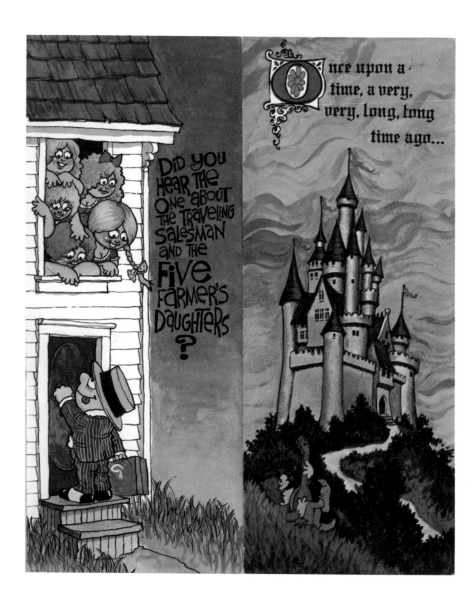

Marty Pahls was a guy who had liked our magazine *FOO* enough to get in contact with Charles and me, and eventually came and visited us in Delaware. He later even married my sister Sandra. Marty had only just graduated from Kent State. So, I got on a bus for Cleveland, and within a couple of weeks I had a job.

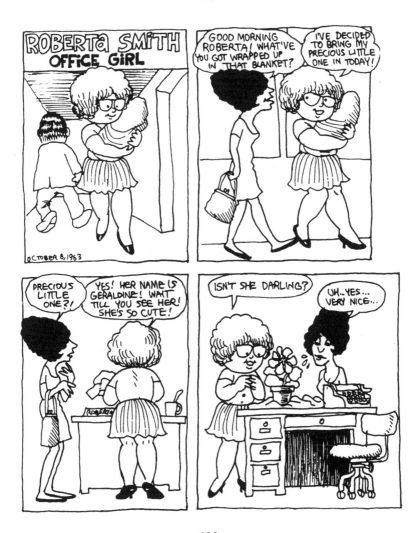

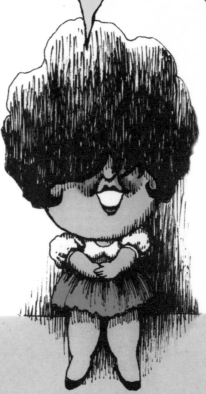
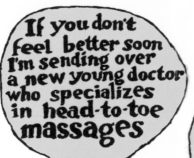

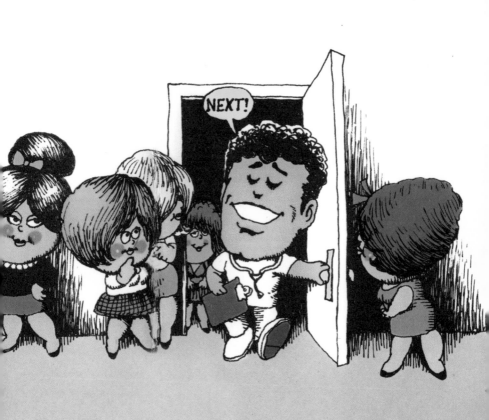

This was at American Greetings, a big greetings card company that hired a lot of young artists. American Greetings employed me as a color separator. After almost a year of this demanding and exacting work, I was about to crack under the pressure (I was too slow). But then I was promoted to the Hi-brow department, got a raise in pay, and was assigned to illustrate humorous "hip" cards. They trained me to develop a drawing style that was "cute."

I punched in at work every day, looking rather collegiate in my one charcoal grey suit that my parents had bought me for my high school graduation. There was a dress code at work, a suit and tie, polished shoes ... Two years after arriving in Cleveland I married my first wife, Dana Morgan, in September 1964.

At the age of twenty-one, I started asking myself, "Is this it? Is this my life now, until I grow old, and retire? I go to work at American Greetings, have a drink with the boys after work, go home to the wife, have an unsatisfying relationship, have a couple of kids, buy a house in Garfield Heights (Dana's parents had a line on a good deal) ... Oh my God ... Is this my life?"

That's why I ran away from home in January of 1967 to join the hippies. That seemed like a much more exciting prospect. I became good at running away! That was one of my main talents when I was young.

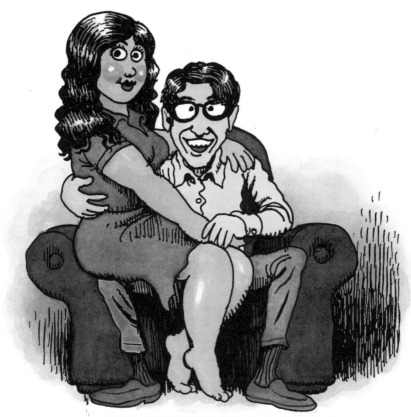

NOW THEY ARE MARRIED AND RESPECTABLE, AND DANIE IS AS SWEET AND GENTLE AS SHE ALWAYS WAS. THE HIP YOUNG ARTIST IS HAPPIER THAN HE EVER WAS BEFORE, COLOR HIM WELL ADJUSTED!!

CHARLES CRUMB
LETTER TO ROBERT, FEBRUARY 1989

THE LITANY OF FEAR

... It is wrong for parents to inspire their children with fear. Instead of inspiring them with terror they should inspire them with love. Gordon Liddy once said on television that when he was a little boy he was afraid of everything! That too can be said of me. When I was a little boy I was afraid of everything. I was afraid of teachers. I was afraid of nuns. I was afraid of priests. I was afraid of churches. I was afraid of the confessional booth. I was afraid of the statues and crucifixes in churches. I was afraid of negroes and jews and Mexicans. I was afraid of movies. I was afraid of the dark. I was afraid of insects and snakes. I was afraid of spiders. I was afraid of dogs and horses (just afraid of animals in general). I was afraid of cars and trucks (one of my greatest fears in childhood was that I might be killed in an automobile accident). I was afraid of atomic and hydrogen bombs (all through childhood I feared that World War Three was going to break out any day). I was afraid of airplanes. I was afraid of dirigibles. I was afraid of water. I was afraid of jellyfish. I was afraid of bridges. I was afraid of canyons. I was afraid of forests and woods. I was afraid to sleep (for fear I would have one of my terrible nightmares). I was afraid of the impression I might make on other people. I was afraid of mice, rats and bats. I was afraid of graveyards and hearses and funeral parlors. I was afraid of high places no less than I was afraid of low places. I was afraid of caves. I was afraid of basements and attics. I was afraid of houses and I was afraid of trains. I was afraid of politicians and policemen. I was afraid of taking my clothes off in front of other people. I was afraid of hospitals. I was afraid of doctors and dentists and nurses. I was afraid of criminals and murderers. I was afraid of sex. I was afraid of the bogeyman. I was afraid of elderly men and elderly women. I was afraid of God. I was afraid of Jesus Christ (though Jesus Christ himself never would have deliberately instilled fear into children. He has been used, and is used as a medium by others to instill fear in them). I was afraid of The Holy Ghost. I was afraid of The Blessed Virgin Mary and all the other saints. I was afraid of hell. I was afraid of the Devil. I was afraid of purgatory. I was afraid of girls. I was afraid of other boys. I was afraid of you and I was afraid of Carol. I was afraid of Mother, but chiefly and most of all, I was afraid of the Old Man! Perhaps all these things that I was afraid of were simply projections, as it were, of the Old Man.

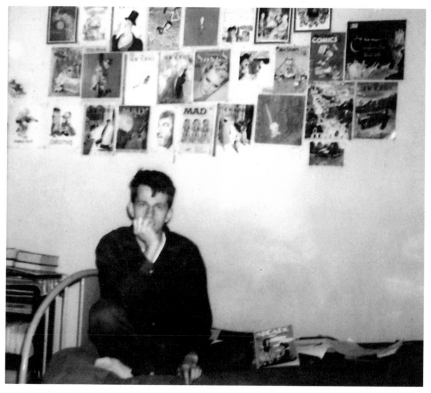

Charles Crumb, age nineteen, in his bedroom, Dover, Delaware, 1961

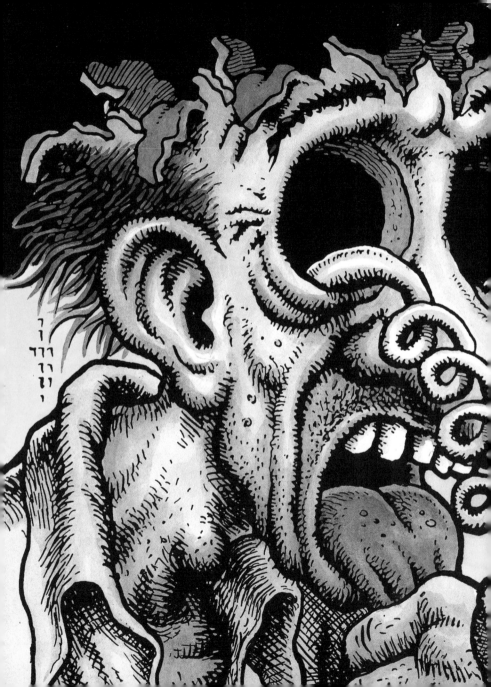

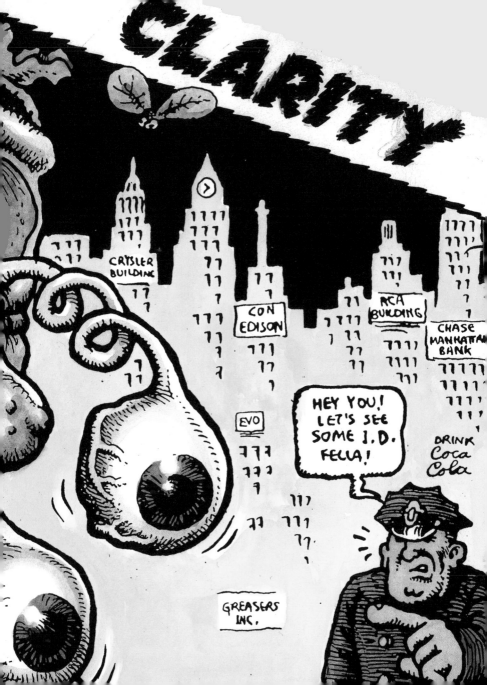

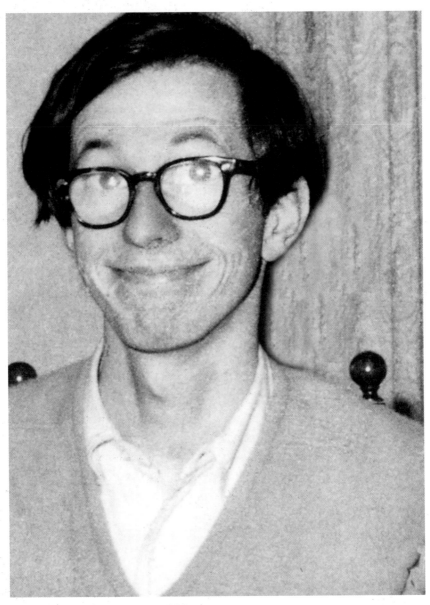

R. Crumb, age twenty-three, 1966

Chapter 3

In the Army of the Stoned

I was a young punk, I admit it. I was trying to run away from my marriage, my job, and a value system that was, for me, unbearable. I had just turned twenty-one when Dana and I got married, and as early as six weeks into our extended European honeymoon I started feeling trapped. At one point I had to leave Dana in Zurich for a few days, to travel down to southern Switzerland to look at an apartment for us in Locarno. As I was about to leave she suddenly started to cry like a child being abandoned. I remember gazing at her in shock and amazement, feeling both pity and fear at the level of her neediness.

We thought we could live in Europe and I could work for American Greetings through the mail, but we were just too young, too timid and untogether. And so we returned to Cleveland after starving in Copenhagen for several months.

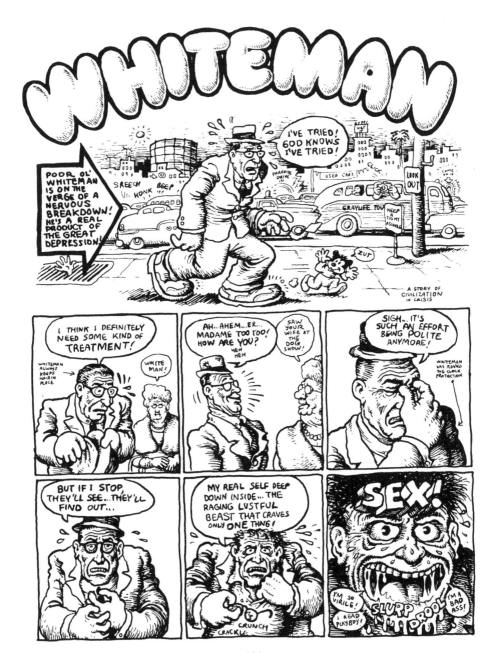

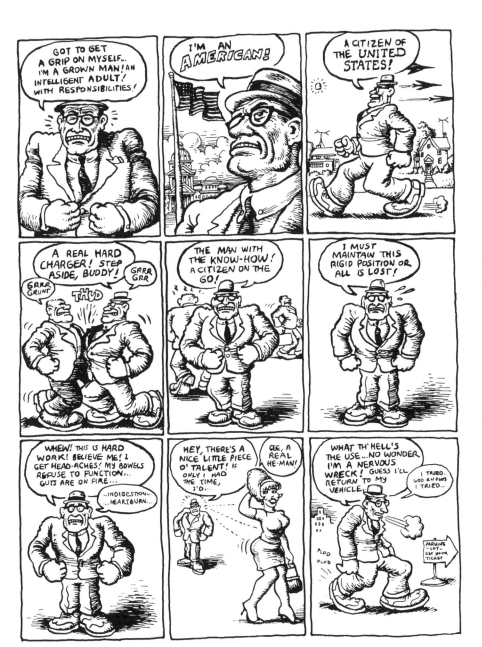

121

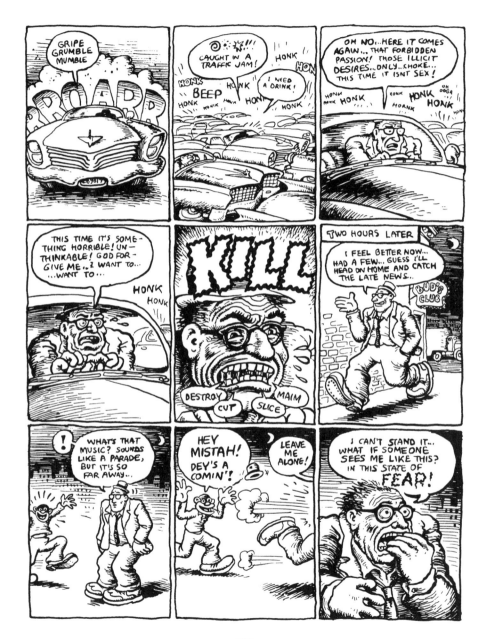

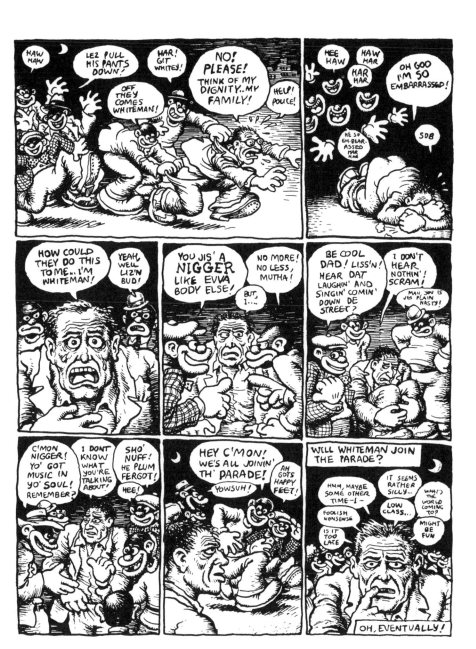

123

I returned to my job in the Hi-brow department at American Greetings. Almost everybody who worked there was depressed and alcoholic. At American Greetings I saw clearly that my talent and skills were being used by hard nosed businessmen whose only instincts were for making money. Still, I've always accepted the reality that the artist-dreamer needs the venal business guy, who takes the lion's share. That's the way it works ... nothing personal ...

Dana and I began experimenting with LSD, which was not yet illegal in 1965. I took LSD as a sort of substitute for committing suicide. Beginning in 1967 I became a regular daily smoker of marihuana. I was enlisted in the army of the stoned for a tour of duty that lasted eight years.

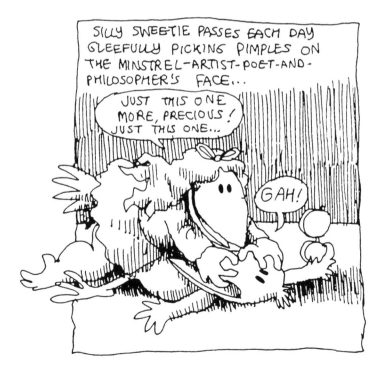

WHEN I WAS YOUNG I TOOK ALOT OF LSD

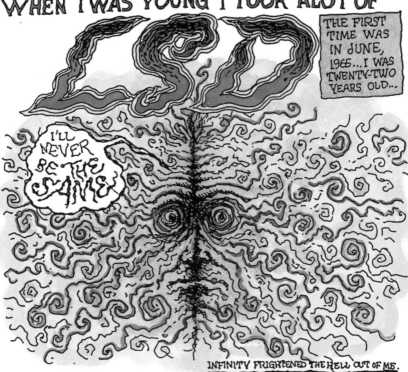

THE FIRST TIME WAS IN JUNE, 1965... I WAS TWENTY-TWO YEARS OLD...

I'LL NEVER BE THE SAME!

INFINITY FRIGHTENED THE HELL OUT OF ME.

WHOAAA

EVERYTHING POURED FROM A VERTICAL CRACK OR APERTURE, FLOWING TO THE LEFT AND TO THE RIGHT... ENERGY FLOWED FORTH FROM THIS CENTER LINE, EQUALLY TO ONE SIDE OR THE OTHER... BI-CAMERAL... TWO SIDES, VIBRATING AGAINST EACH OTHER... THE "TRICK" WAS TO GET BETWEEN THE TWO SIDES, TO OPEN THE CRACK, TO PENETRATE THE "COSMIC VAGINA"....

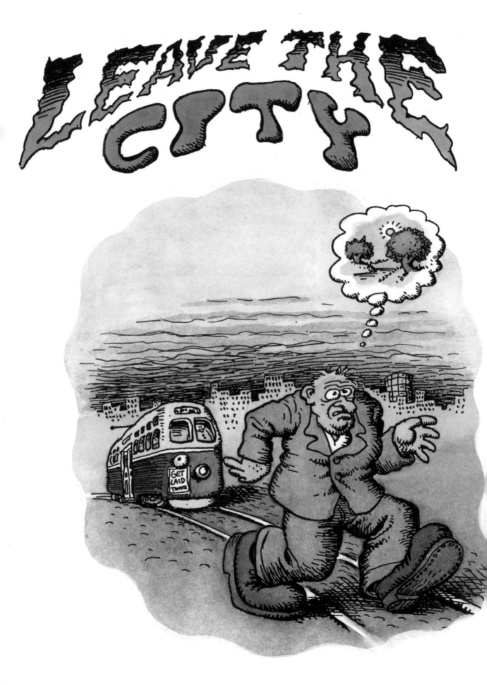

One night in January 1967, over drinks in a bar, two young guys I knew vaguely said they were driving to San Francisco that very night. *"Hey, got room for one more?"* I asked. *"Yeah, sure! Come with us,"* they said. So I went impulsively from the workaday world of Cleveland to the hippy Mecca of San Francisco, wearing the clothes I had on and with whatever money I had in my pocket. I didn't tell Dana. I just wanted my freedom ... and to get in on some of that "free love" we were hearing about in the midwest. I was selfish, I admit it.

In the pop culture world that I lived in, politics and literature were not discussed in any serious, intelligent way. They were not part of the dialogue of anybody I knew, until I met Marty Pahls. He was a real left wing intellectual, and read all the "heavy" tomes. Charles had begun reading the classic works of literature, but sociological and political concepts were out of his realm. Marty made us feel like ignoramuses. He urged Charles and me to read *Catcher In The Rye* by J. D. Salinger, *Junkie* by William Burroughs, and *On The Road* by Jack Kerouac.

The main feeling I remember from *On The Road* was, *"Oh my God, these guys are having so much fun! They're meeting girls! They're having adventures! They're footloose! They have no responsibilities! They don't worry about jobs, or money!"* The message of that book, that someone could actually be bold enough to live that way, was devastating for me. Kerouac was revolutionary because he told my generation that we didn't have to toe the mark. We could drop out of college and forget the whole responsibility thing that our parents had pounded into us: job, marriage and family.

The Kerouac dream was poetic and seductive, and after reading him both Charles and I talked about going "on the road," but we couldn't figure out a way to actually pull it off. First, neither of us could drive. Second, we were afraid of the world.

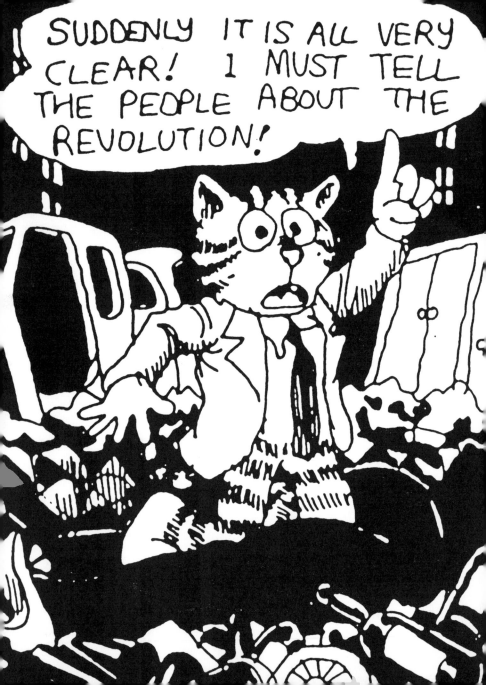

The Beat literature gave me an alternative point of view about living in America that we were not getting from our parents, from school, from television, or *Life* magazine. Before reading the Beats, the only alternative view I got was from Harvey Kurtzman's *Mad* and *Humbug* magazines, or from Stan Freberg's satirical records.

In those early strips such as *Fritz Bugs Out* I was making fun of the pseudo Jack Kerouac college boy (embodied in Richard Farina's ridiculous book, *Been Down So Long It Looks Like Up to Me)*—the black-turtle-neck-sweater kind of guy who contrived a worldly, vagabond hipster image that would attract young, romantic, middle class girls from fine homes. I was very bitter, observing how well this act went over with girls.

I knew, I was certain, that I was a much more interesting artist than this abstract expressionist painter I knew in Cleveland, who painted giant eight foot canvases that were nothing but ugly brown smears ... the worst! But he was a handsome, rugged, hale fellow who wore a big scarf around his neck over a shaggy sweater. He would stand there staring at his big muddy mess of a painting, while women brought him cups of coffee. There were always young, attractive women lounging around his studio waiting to get his attention. He had a swashbuckling aura around himself that made him supremely successful with women. It wasn't about his "art" at all.

When I was young, drawing comic books had no sex appeal whatsoever. Any silly assed poet attracted women more than drawing comics. There was just nothing romantic about being a cartoonist. I knew a couple of well meaning girls who urged me to forget about comics and pick up some paints and canvas and take up oil painting.

Maybe I should've taken their advice. I was still thinking vaguely in terms of being some sort of commercial artist then.

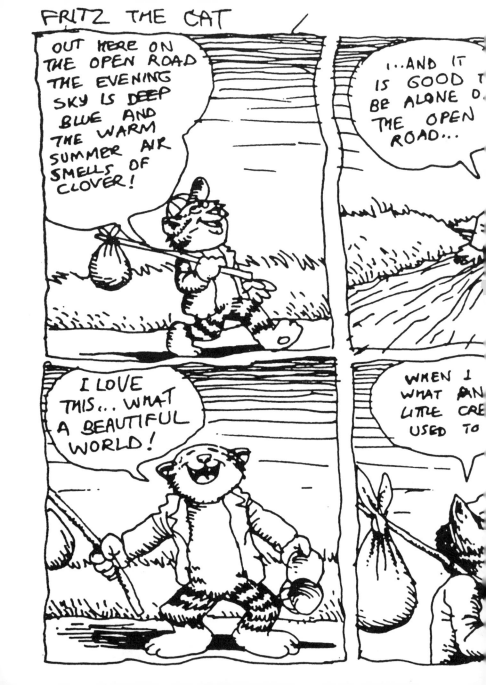

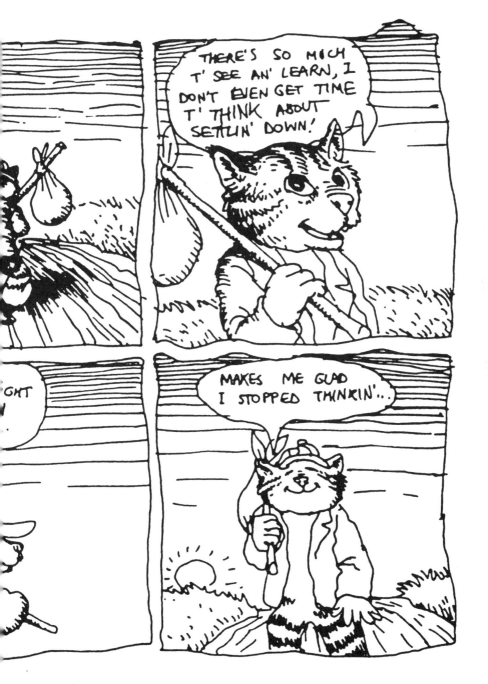

My experience working at American Greetings had given me certain technical skills and tools. When I drew *Fritz* it was simply for my own amusement. I thought I'd have to do straight commercial art for a living. The underground press was not yet a venue for comics.

I went to San Francisco, as a lot of young people did, looking for some ideal of complete freedom. Personally, I wanted to fuck a lot of girls, and in fact, ultimately, I got my share.

My direction in life was permanently altered by taking LSD! In a way, the rides at Disneyland kind of prepared me for my LSD experiences. But almost every time I took LSD, at some point I'd find myself on my hands and knees, puking my guts out and asking, *"What the hell does it all mean?"*

I took some bad acid in November of 1965, and the after effect left me crazy and helpless for six months. My mind would drift into a place that was very electrical and crackly, filled with harsh, abrasive, low grade, cartoony, tawdry carnival visions. There was a nightmarish mechanical aspect to everyday life. My ego was so shattered, so fragmented that it didn't get in the way during what was the most unself-conscious period of my life. I was kind of on automatic pilot and was still constantly drawing.

Most of my popular characters—Mr. Natural, Flaky Foont, Angelfood McSpade, Eggs Ackley, The Snoid, the Vulture Demonesses, Av' n' Gar, Shuman the Human, the Truckin' guys, Devil Girl—all suddenly appeared in the drawings in my sketchbook in this period, early 1966. Amazing! I was relieved when it was finally over, but I also immediately missed the egoless state of that strange interlude. LSD put me someplace else. I wasn't sure where. All I know is, it was a strange place. Psychedelic drugs broke me out of my social programming. It was a good thing for me, traumatic though, and I may have been permanently damaged by the whole thing, I'm not sure.

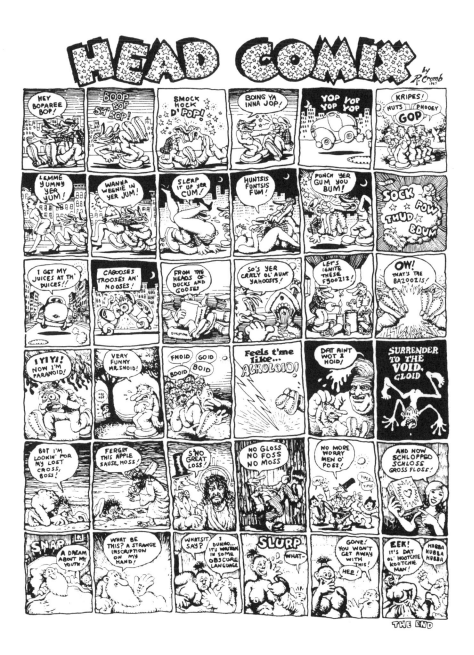

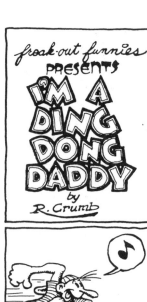

freak-out funnies PRESENTS

I'M A DING DONG DADDY

by R. Crumb

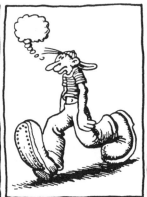

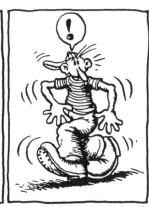

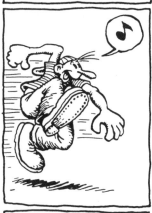

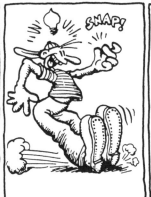

SNAP!

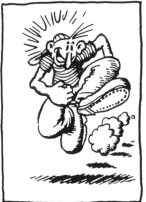

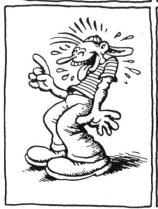

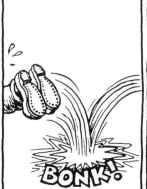

BONK!

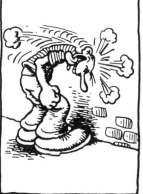

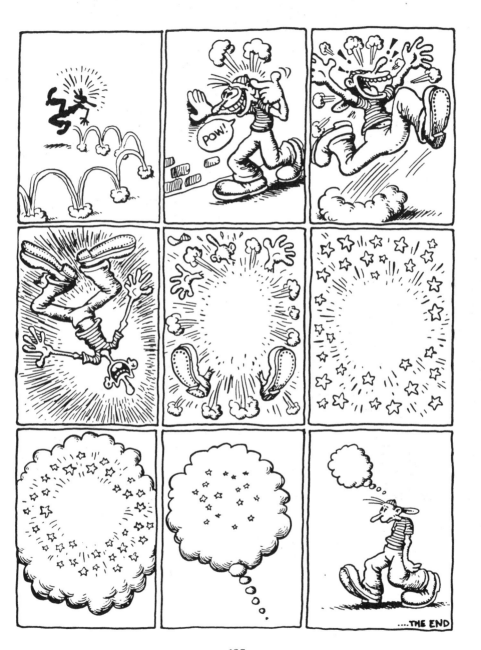

....THE END

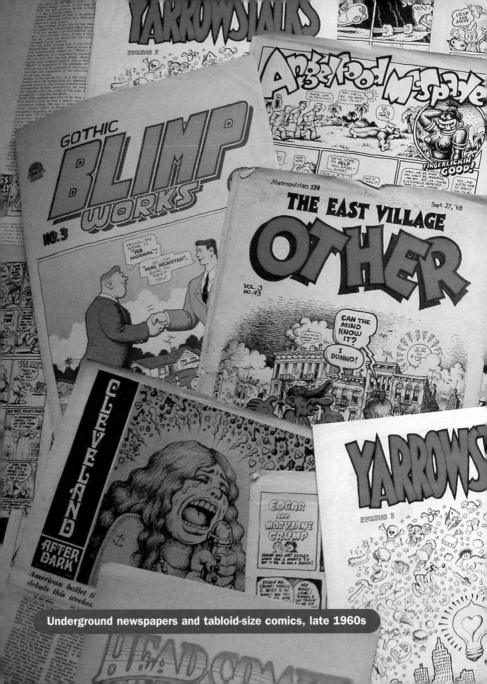

Underground newspapers and tabloid-size comics, late 1960s

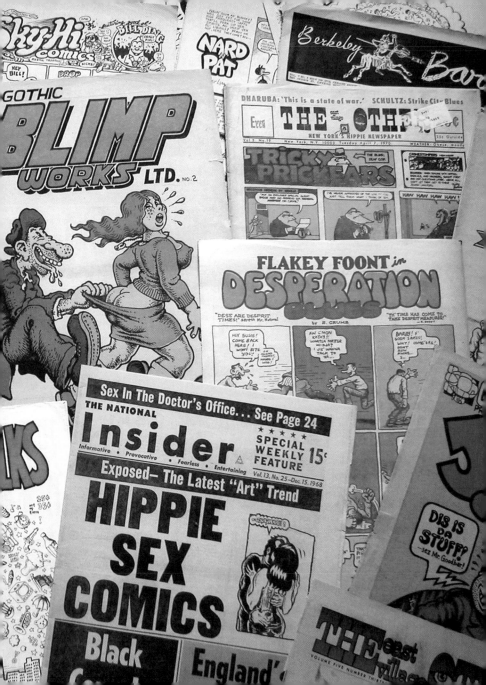

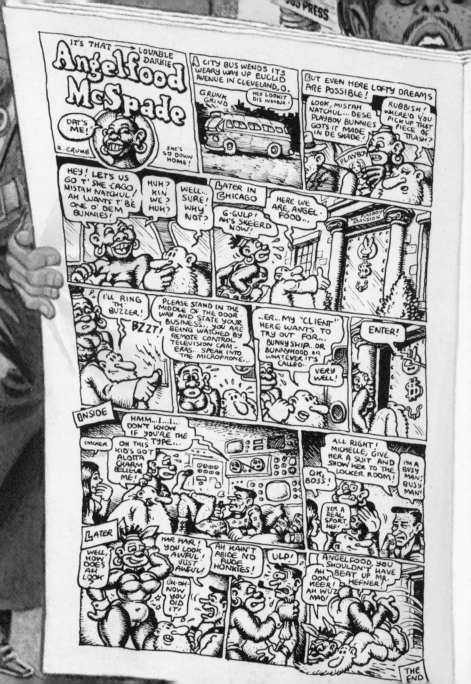

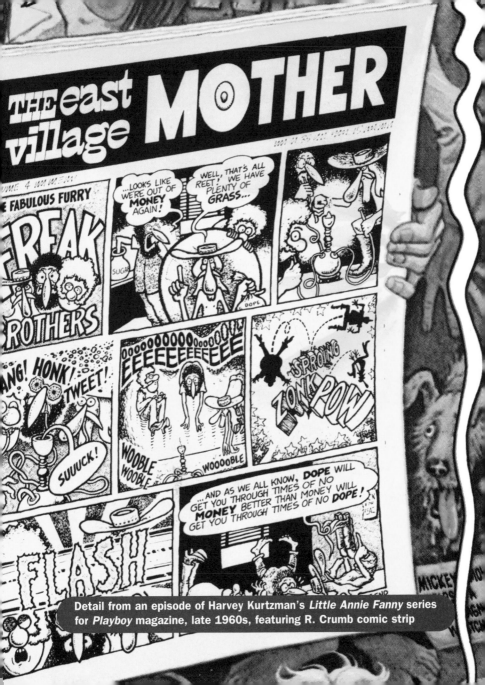

Detail from an episode of Harvey Kurtzman's *Little Annie Fanny* series for *Playboy* magazine, late 1960s, featuring R. Crumb comic strip

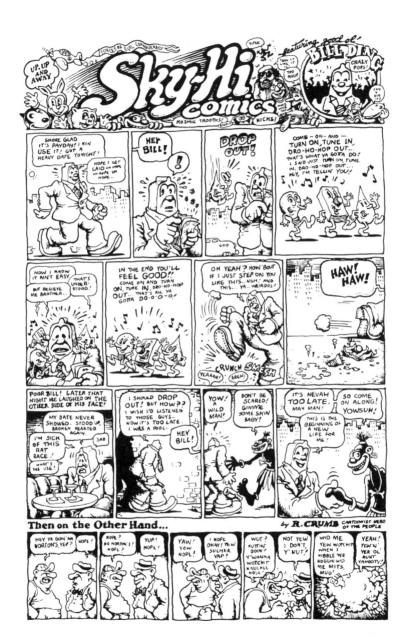

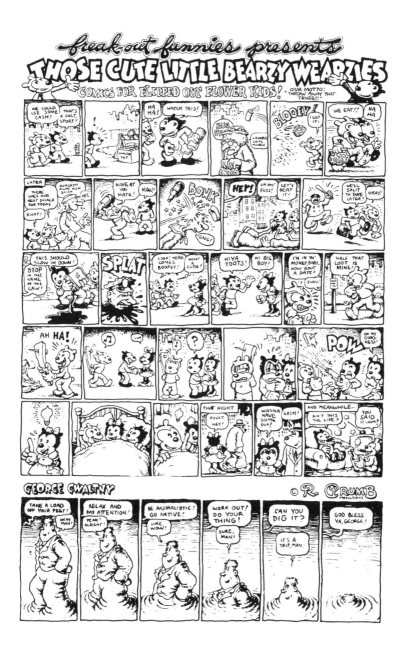

I see LSD as a positive, important life experience for me, but I certainly wouldn't recommend it to anyone else.

I guess 1967 was the year that my career as "America's Best Loved Underground Cartoonist" really began. I started to contribute work to underground newspapers like *Yarrowstalks* in Philadelphia for which I drew the entire third issue. I went to New York to drop off six pages of strips and a cover for Ralph Ginzburg's *Avant Garde* magazine, but Ginzburg didn't "get it" and rejected the whole thing, so I took the art down to the offices of *The East Village Other* and offered it to them. They loved the work and printed all of it. There was no payment, but it was a pleasure to have the space and the freedom to draw whatever you wanted and create something that resembled an old Sunday Comics page from the the 1930s. Plus, there was no censorship!

The big time syndicate cartoonists didn't even have those luxuries. The lack of restrictions in underground papers set the tone for the underground comics that were to follow. I went back to San Francisco inspired, and immediately set to work turning out the first issue of *Zap Comix*. I sent the original art to the publisher of *Yarrowstalks*, who disappeared with it. They told me he "went to India." It took me years to get that art back. (Luckily, I had made photocopies of the comic to show Viking Press. When I got those back one year later, I touched them up and published them as *Zap #0*).

In November I finished drawing the second issue of *Zap Comix*. Meanwhile, *Cavalier*, a men's magazine, had decided to serialize my *Fritz Bugs Out* story for nine issues. So, there was some sort of growing momentum of interest in my work.

The first issue of *Zap Comix* was published by Don Donahue and printed by Charles Plymell in late February of 1968. We sold *Zap* on the street in the Haight Ashbury district and a few hippy shops around San Francisco.

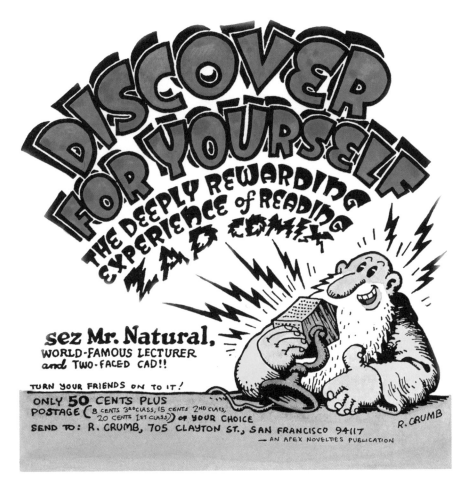

143

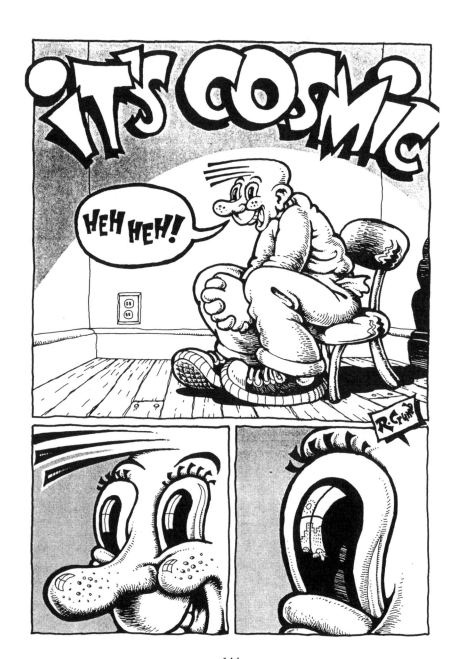

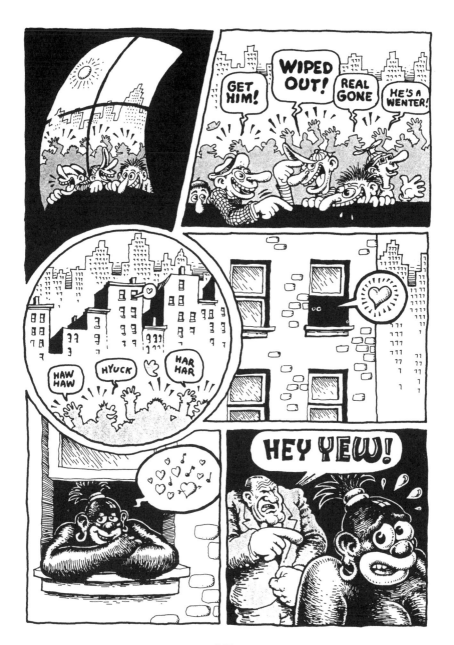

145

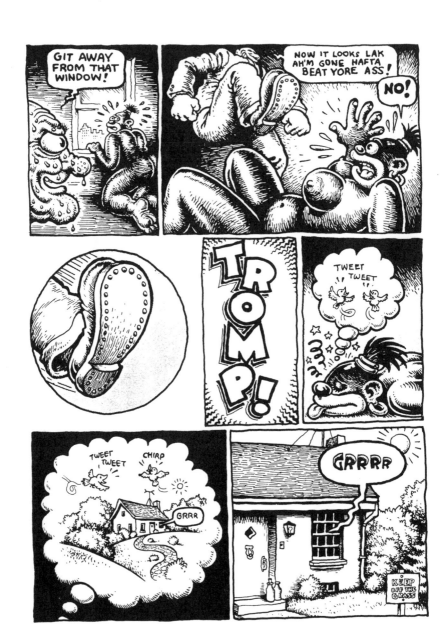

146

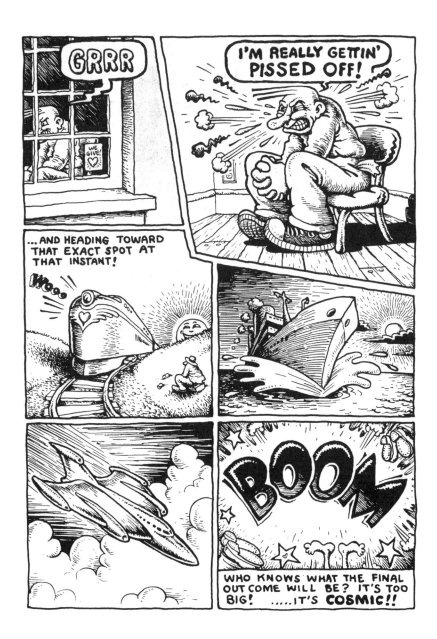

147

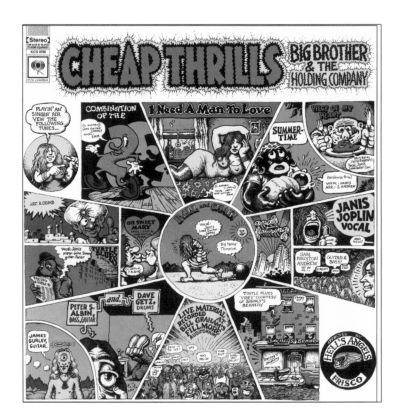

Dana was eight months pregnant with our son, Jesse, and we were living on welfare. *Fritz* was in *Cavalier*. My artwork was appearing in *The East Village Other*. I met other artists like S. Clay Wilson, Rick Griffin, and Victor Moscoso, who all joined me in the *Zap Comix* enterprise. *Yellow Dog,* a new comics newspaper, used a lot of my work. I went to Chicago and worked on *Bijou Funnies* with Jay Lynch, Skip Williamson and Jay Kinney. I did some art for the *Chicago Seed* while I was there, and went to the protest demonstrations during the Democratic National Convention. I did the *Cheap Thrills/Big Brother and the Holding Company* album cover for Janis Joplin.

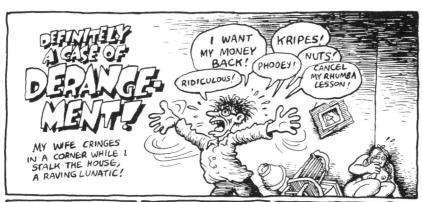

DEFINITELY A CASE OF DERANGEMENT!

I WANT MY MONEY BACK!

RIDICULOUS!

PHOOEY!

KRIPES!

NUTS! CANCEL MY RHUMBA LESSON!

MY WIFE CRINGES IN A CORNER WHILE I STALK THE HOUSE, A RAVING LUNATIC!

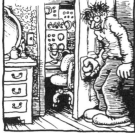

FROM THE BEDROOM CLOSET I OPERATE A HUGE NETWORK OF RADIOS, SENDING OUT INCANTATIONS, CURSES, VOODOO HOODOO!

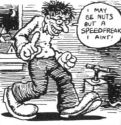

I'VE BEEN CALLED AN EVIL GENIUS BY CITIES OF ASS-HOLES... BUT I KNOW WHO THESE PEOPLE ARE! AND THEY'RE ON MY LIST!

I MAY BE NUTS BUT A SPEEDFREAK I AINT!

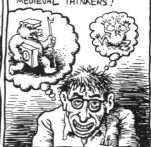

THE TRUTH IS, I'M ONE OF THE WORLD'S LAST GREAT MEDIEVAL THINKERS!

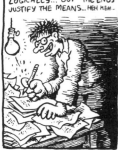

YOU MIGHT SAY I'M A MAD SCIENTIST, FOR MY PLANS HAVE ALL BEEN WORKED OUT QUITE METHODICALLY... LOGICALLY... BUT THE ENDS JUSTIFY THE MEANS... HEH HEH -

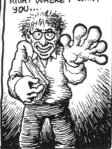

THIS COMIC BOOK IS PART OF THAT PLAN... BUT YOU'VE READ TOO MUCH ALREADY... I HAVE YOU RIGHT WHERE I WANT YOU...

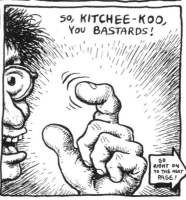

SO, KITCHEE-KOO, YOU BASTARDS!

GO RIGHT ON TO THE NEXT PAGE!

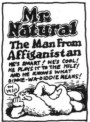
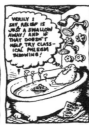
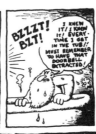
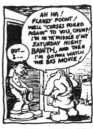
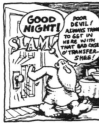
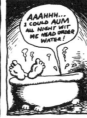
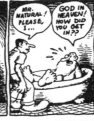
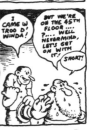
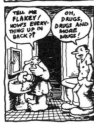
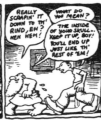
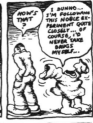
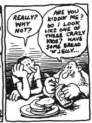
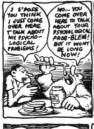
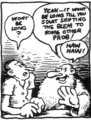
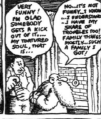
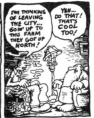
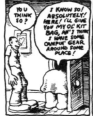
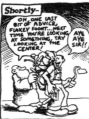
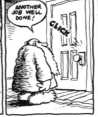
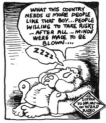

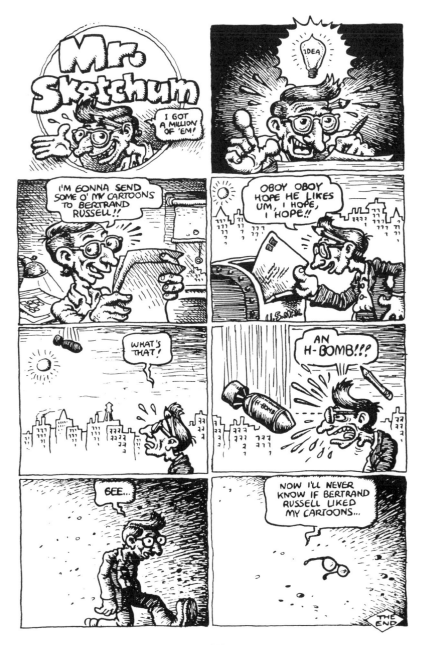

151

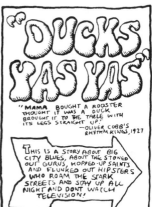

"DUCKS YAS YAS"

"MAMA BOUGHT A ROOSTER THOUGHT IT WAS A DUCK BROUGHT IT TO THE TABLE WITH ITS LEGS STRAIGHT UP."
—OLIVER COBB'S RHYTHM KINGS, 1927

THIS IS A STORY ABOUT BIG CITY BLUES, ABOUT THE STONED OUT GURUS, HOPPED-UP SAINTS AND FLUNKED OUT HIPSTERS WHO ROAM THE STARK STREETS AND STAY UP ALL NIGHT AND DON'T WATCH TELEVISION!

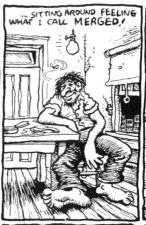

...SITTING AROUND FEELING WHAT I CALL MERGED!

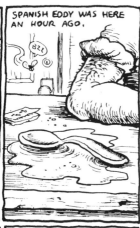

SPANISH EDDY WAS HERE AN HOUR AGO.

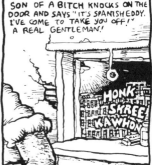

SON OF A BITCH KNOCKS ON THE DOOR AND SAYS "IT'S SPANISH EDDY. I'VE COME TO TAKE YOU OFF!" A REAL GENTLEMAN!

HONK STREE KAWHON

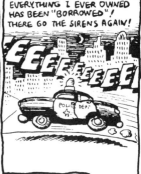

EVERYTHING I EVER OWNED HAS BEEN "BORROWED"! THERE GO THE SIRENS AGAIN!

EEEEEEEEE!

POLICE DEPT

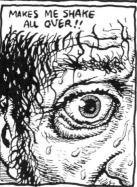

MAKES ME SHAKE ALL OVER!!

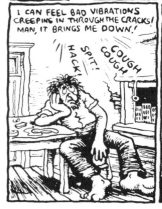

I CAN FEEL BAD VIBRATIONS CREEPING IN THROUGH THE CRACKS! MAN, IT BRINGS ME DOWN!

COUGH COUGH! SPIT! HACK!

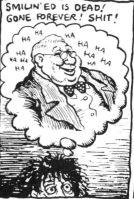

SMILIN' ED IS DEAD! GONE FOREVER! SHIT!

HA HA HA HA HA HA HA HA HA HA HA

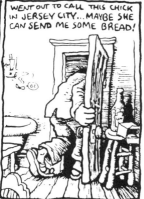

WENT OUT TO CALL THIS CHICK IN JERSEY CITY...MAYBE SHE CAN SEND ME SOME BREAD!

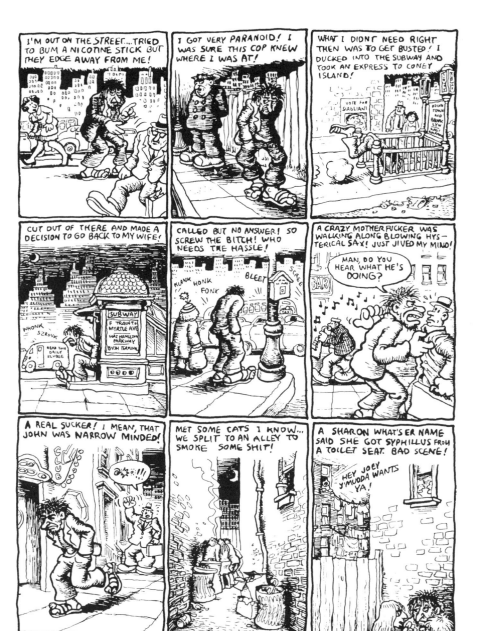

153

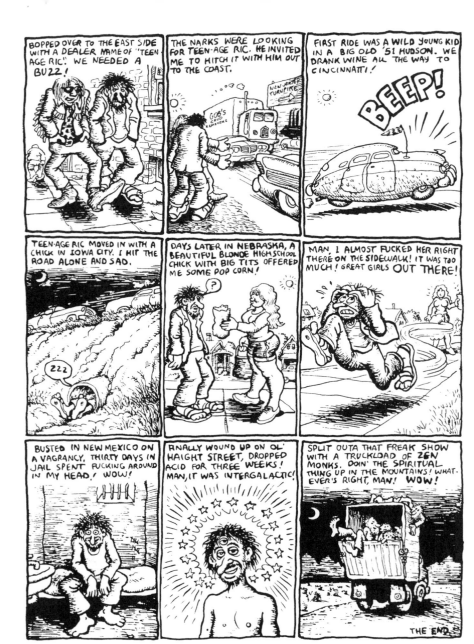

154

HELP BUILD A BETTER AMERICA!

NOW, YOU DON'T NEED A "SHRINK" TO FLUSH OUT KARMIC CONJESTION!

GET STONED! a Modern Miracle!

Here's How!

SMOKE AT LEAST TWO OF THESE EVERY DAY FOR ONE YEAR! THIS METHOD CAN'T FAIL!!

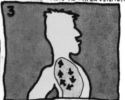

FIRST TAKE A GOOD LONG "DRAG" ON YOUR "JOINT" OR "MUGGLE".

PULL ALL THAT GOOD SMOKE DOWN INTO YOUR LUNGS. DO NOT EXHALE!!

HOLD THE SMOKE DOWN THERE IN YOUR LUNGS, USING THE PROCESS KNOW AS HYPERVENTILATION.

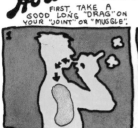

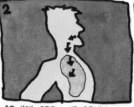

EXHALE VERY SLOWLY THROUGH THE NOSE, MAKING SURE THE "STUFF" IS GOING TO THE HEAD!

AS YOU BEGIN TO RELAX AND BREATH NORMALLY AGAIN, THE PROCESS WILL BEGIN TO TAKE EFFECT.

WHEN THE MIRACLE MOLECULES HIT THE CENTER OF THE BRAIN, YOU WILL FIND YOURSELF IN A NEW WORLD!

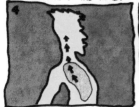

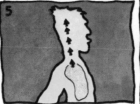

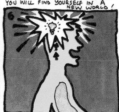

155

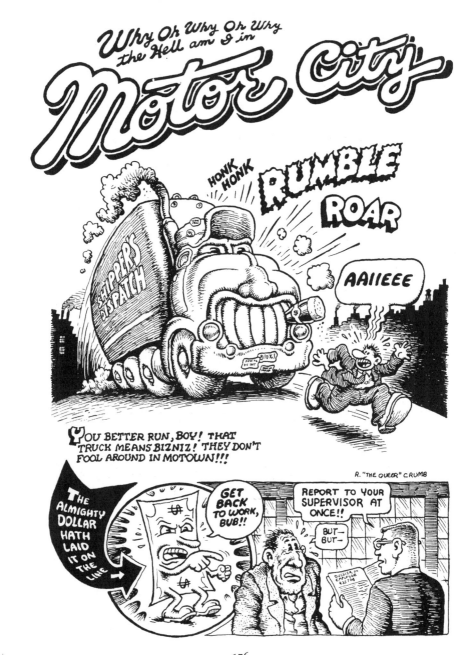

WHAT'S ONE MAN TO THE KING of MOTOR CITY?

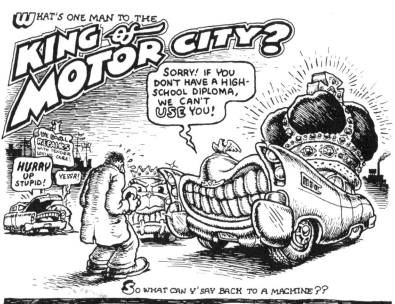

SORRY! IF YOU DON'T HAVE A HIGH-SCHOOL DIPLOMA, WE CAN'T **USE** YOU!

WE DO ALL REPAIRS WITH TENDER LOVING CARE!

HURRY UP STUPID!

YESSR!

$o WHAT CAN Y'SAY BACK TO A MACHINE??

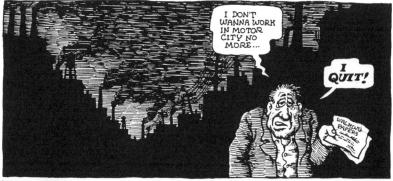

I DON'T WANNA WORK IN MOTOR CITY NO MORE...

I QUIT!

WALKING PAPERS

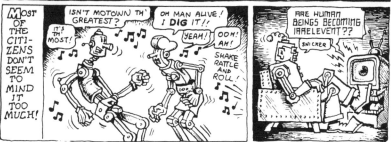

MOST OF THE CITIZENS DON'T SEEM TO MIND IT TOO MUCH!

ISN'T MOTOWN TH' GREATEST?

IT'S TH' MOST!

OH MAN ALIVE! I DIG IT!!

YEAH!

OOH! AH!

SHAKE RATTLE AND ROLL!

ARE HUMAN BEINGS BECOMING IRRELEVENT??

SNICKER

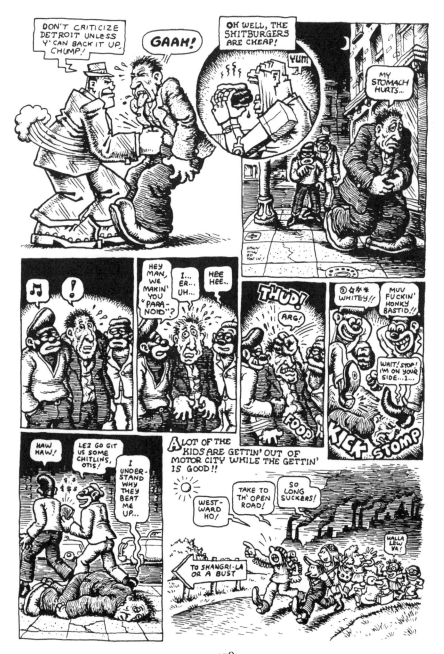

158

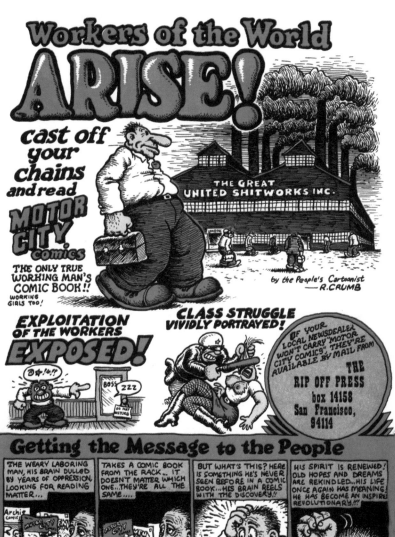

Workers of the World ARISE!

cast off your chains and read **MOTOR CITY comics**

THE ONLY TRUE WORKING MAN'S COMIC BOOK!!

WORKING GIRLS TOO!

THE GREAT UNITED SHITWORKS INC.

by the People's Cartoonist — R. CRUMB

EXPLOITATION OF THE WORKERS EXPOSED!

CLASS STRUGGLE VIVIDLY PORTRAYED!

IF YOUR LOCAL NEWSDEALER WON'T CARRY "MOTOR CITY COMICS", THEY'RE AVAILABLE BY MAIL FROM

THE RIP OFF PRESS box 14158 San Francisco, 94114

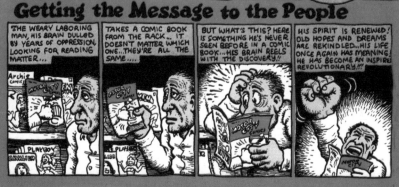

Getting the Message to the People

THE WEARY LABORING MAN, HIS BRAIN DULLED BY YEARS OF OPPRESSION, LOOKING FOR READING MATTER....

TAKES A COMIC BOOK FROM THE RACK... IT DOESN'T MATTER WHICH ONE...THEY'RE ALL THE SAME.....

BUT WHAT'S THIS? HERE IS SOMETHING HE'S NEVER SEEN BEFORE IN A COMIC BOOK!...HIS BRAIN REELS WITH THE DISCOVERY!!

HIS SPIRIT IS RENEWED! OLD HOPES AND DREAMS ARE REKINDLED...HIS LIFE ONCE AGAIN HAS MEANING, HE HAS BECOME AN INSPIRED REVOLUTIONARY.!!!

Viking Press published *Head Comix*. I did *Snatch Comix*. *Zap 2* and *Zap 0* came out at the end of 1968. It all seemed to happen so thick and fast, it made my head spin. I was young enough to be flattered, *"Oh boy, now I have arrived!"* People started coming over to the house all the time. They wanted me to do work. They wanted me to do interviews, *Rolling Stone*, *Playboy* ... A little bit of money was coming in, not a lot.

The underground comix thing began to mushroom over the next couple of years, and all of a sudden there were five little publishing companies putting out underground comix. My work and Gilbert Shelton's *The Fabulous Furry Freak Brothers* sold the best. The page rate was $35, and some paid $50.

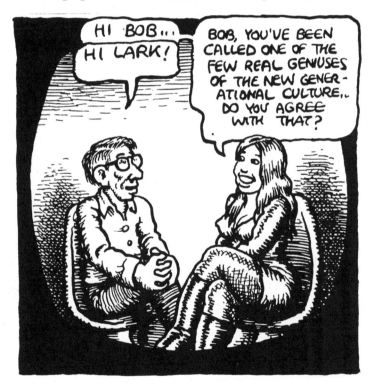

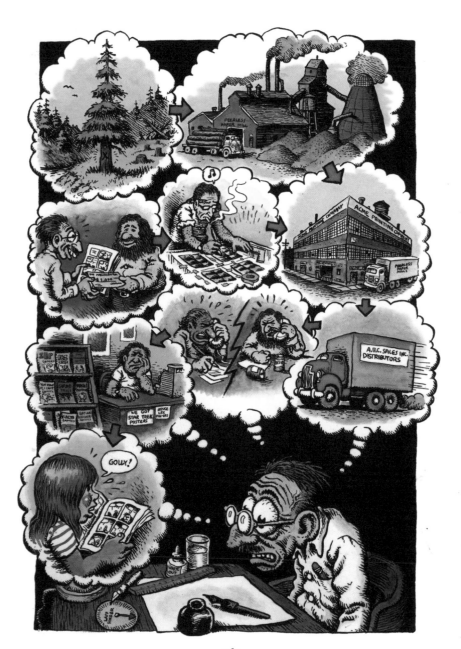

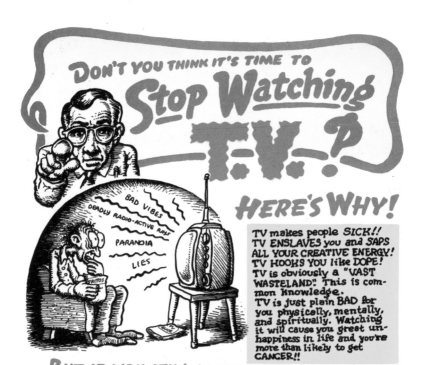

DON'T YOU THINK IT'S TIME TO Stop Watching T.V.?

HERE'S WHY!

TV makes people SICK!! TV ENSLAVES you and SAPS ALL YOUR CREATIVE ENERGY! TV HOOKS YOU like DOPE! TV is obviously a "VAST WASTELAND" This is common knowledge. TV is just plain BAD for you physically, mentally, and spiritually. Watching it will cause you great unhappiness in life and you're more than likely to get CANCER!!

BUT IF YOU STILL MUST HAVE YOUR MEDIA INJECTION, THEN READ

MOTOR CITY COMICS

IT'S THE COMIC THAT **ANSWERS TO NO ONE!!** Motor City Comics is the Last outspoken Bastion of TRUTH left in America today. Read it and you shall be FREE! Contained within these pages are mind-blowing glimpses of REALITY as it REALLY IS! These comics BREAK THROUGH the TV-INDUCED STUPOR, for this is ANTI-MEDIA! It's got the MEDICINE for the BLUES, and has been known to turn MENTALLY ILL persons into HEALTHY, GOOD-HUMORED FREE-THINKERS. You, too, will benefit from reading MOTOR CITY COMICS!!

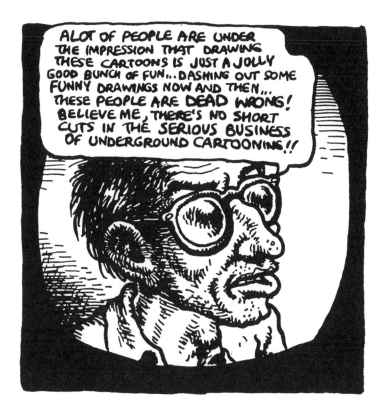

These small, independent, "underground" comix were not big money-makers. Their publishers were after me all the time to give them something. Some publishers stayed around for a few years, many came and went. I was totally amazed. This little home made underground comix thing was turning into a business before my eyes. It went from us going around Haight Street trying to sell these things we had folded and stapled ourselves to suddenly being a business with distributors, lawyers, contracts, and money talk. The comix were now being printed on big web presses just like any commercial newspaper or magazine. The whole thing began to take on a heaviness that I believe had a negative effect on my work.

I was only twenty-five years old when all this happened. It was a case of "too much too soon," I think. I became acutely self-conscious about what I was doing. Was I now a "spokesman" for the hippies or what? I had no idea how to handle my new position in society! I'm still working on it, truth to tell. Like in this "handbook" for instance ...

Take *Keep On Truckin'* ... for example. *Keep On Truckin'* ... is the curse of my life. This stupid little cartoon caught on hugely. There was a D.J. on the radio in the seventies who would yell out every ten minutes: *"And don't forget to KEEP ON TR-R-RUCKIN'!"* Boy, was that obnoxious! Big feet equals collective optimism. You're a walkin' boy! You're movin' on down the line! It's proletarian. It's populist.

I was thrown off track! I didn't want to turn into a greeting card artist for the counter-culture! I didn't want to do 'shtick'— the thing Lenny Bruce warned against. That's when I started to let out all my perverse sex fantasies. It was the only way out of being "America's Best Loved Hippy Cartoonist." And it worked. *Snatch* and *Big Ass Comics* made most of them back off fast!

From 1968 to 1973 I worked like a dog! I did so many comics! Man, I was prolific! After my work got to be well known, crowds of people were always hanging around in my studio all day. I would work at night when the ne'er-do-wells were sleeping, then I could get something done. But that was part of the hippie lifestyle. If you had a house, you couldn't turn people away who needed a place to "crash." And they would stay for six months and just hang out! I didn't have the courage, the nerve, to kick people out. Eventually, the wife had to be the ogre and do the hard thing. I couldn't do it, I was too weak.

As my fame grew, my work got darker and darker. In 1969 I was shifting around a lot, working on *Snatch* and *Big Ass Comics*, turning out weird *Vulture Demoness* stories and all that.

164

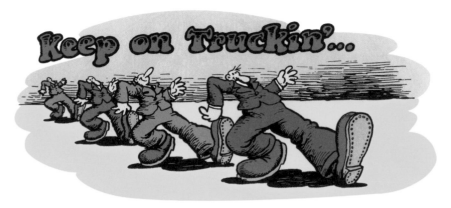

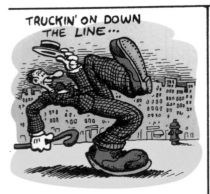

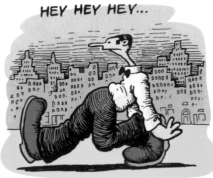

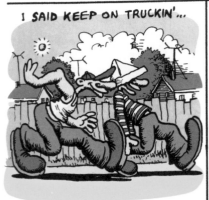

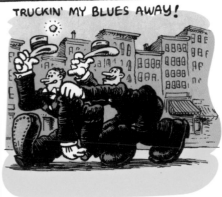

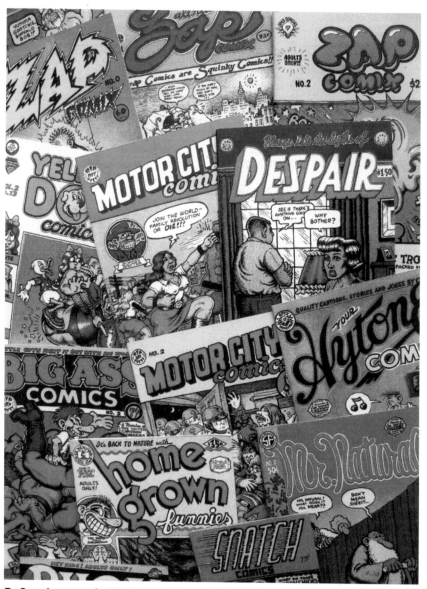

R. Crumb covers for Underground comics of the late 1960s and early 1970s

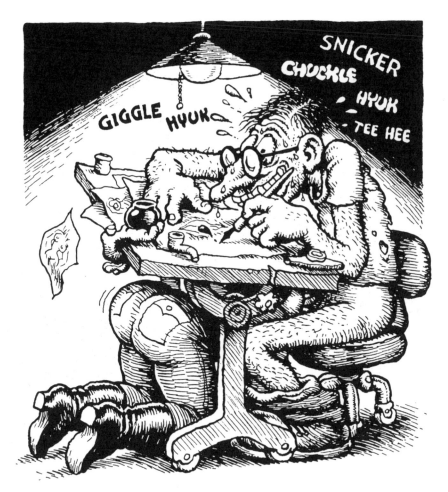

THE PLEASURE IS OURS, FOLKS!

WE REALLY *LIKE* DRAWING DIRTY CARTOONS! IT HELPS US GET RID OF PENT-UP ANXIETIES AND REPRESSIONS AND ALL THAT KINDA STUFF... WE HOPE **YOU** ENJOY LOOKIN' AT 'EM AS MUCH AS WE ENJOY *DRAWIN'* EM !!

"WHAT THIS WORLD NEEDS IS MORE SATISFIED CUSTOMERS!"

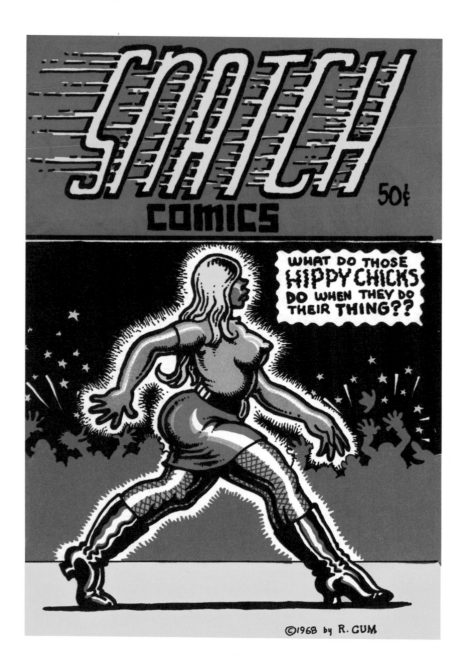

THE NATIONAL
Insider

Informative • Provocative • Fearless • Entertaining

★ ★ ★ ★ ★
SPECIAL **15¢**
WEEKLY
FEATURE
Vol. 14, No.4 — Jan. 26, 1969

Exclusive Interview With Artist!

COPS SNATCH HIPPIE SEX COMIC!

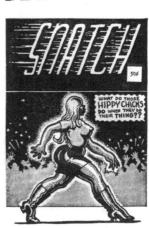

Sex Change Tells All!

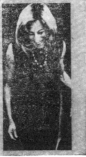

Exclusive Interview With Mrs. Eldridge Cleaver!

I lived in a cheap hotel in the Mission district for a while, then I stayed down in Venice, California at a place Gilbert Shelton and some friends—a big gang of wild young Texans—had on a canal there. They partied really hard, drank beer, and smoked dope day and night. I had a room in that place for about a month and I just stayed up there working on *Big Ass Comics*. I didn't show it to anybody. I was in my own strange twilight world, getting off drawing my own bizarre sexual fantasies.

By 1973, my whole situation started to grind to a halt. My life had become so crazy, complicated and confusing that I essentially ran out of creative energy. I was "burned out." It's probably better not to have that kind of success when you're young. If it happens when you're older, you're likely to be better able to cope with it.

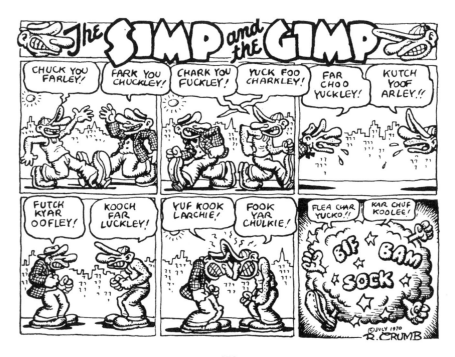

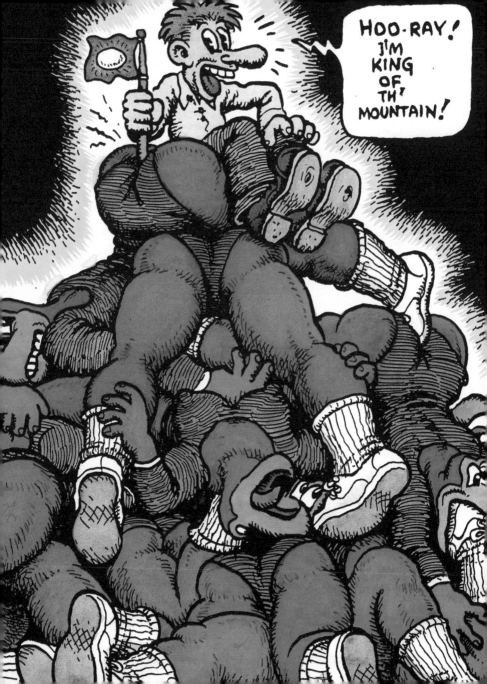

The poet Charles Bukowski's career and work are a good example. I met him through Robert Williams at a party in LA in the early 1970s. He gave me a piece of advice. He said, *"Your stuff is good, kid. Just stay away from the cocktail parties!"* He was right. Bukowski had observed that successful artists and writers get spoiled by all the lavish attention, especially from rich people, bourgeois people, and then they don't have anything to say any more. They get bought off, basically. The last thing I want to be is someone who is constantly being gawked at, and trotted out like some fucking celebrity. Horrible! Sure, I always wanted to get recognition for my work, but I prefer to be the anonymous observer on the sidelines. I never had any desire to be "America's Best Loved Underground Cartoonist." That was supposed to be a joke, not my life.

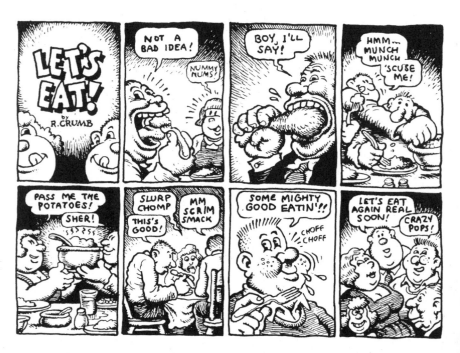

STEVE MARTIN
COMEDIAN

If there was an influence measuring machine, I'm sure it would register a very high reading in regard to Robert Crumb's effect on my comedy. As much as Laurel and Hardy and Jack Benny and Jerry Lewis, who made me love comedy, Crumb taught me how to walk. One look at his famous "Keep on Truckin'" drawing, with its exaggerated profiles of three characters strutting, and I realize that some of my own exaggerated body movements on stage in the late 1970s can be traced back to Crumb. I still walk down the street today and see Crumb caricatures everywhere, except they are living, breathing humans. In some way, we are all Robert Crumb caricatures, as we parade in our fashions and hairdos. I remember being dumbstruck on the fifth reading of a Crumb comic book in the late 1960s, discovering that his work was more complex and serious than I had allowed. The one word that entered my brain was the era's equivalent of "aloha," an all purpose exclamation that described everything from a doorknob to the universe: Wow.

from *Kindly Lent Their Owner,* 2001

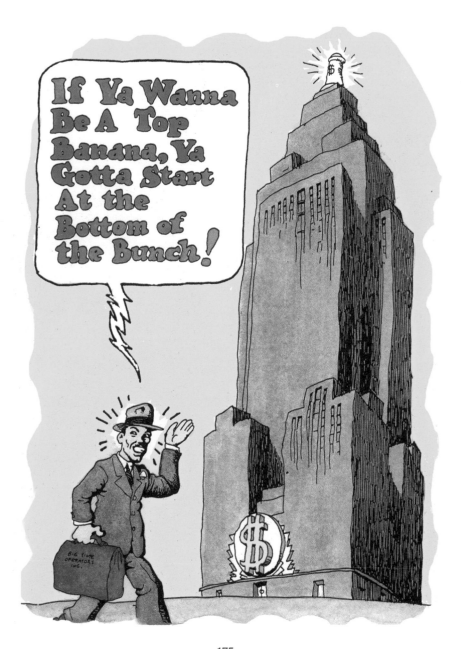

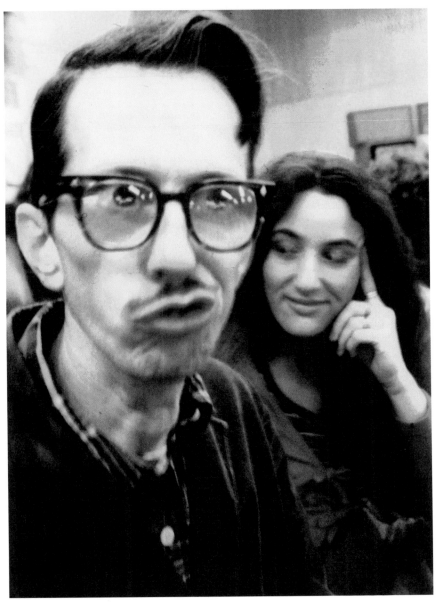

R. Crumb and Aline Kominsky, late 1970s

Chapter 4

The Meat
and the Butcher

Almost all of our mass culture is "mouth feel," a calculated manipulation of the pleasure impulse, and if it has any real nutritional, authentic value, that's mere happenstance, a side effect. At the Cannes Film Festival I saw thousands of people gawking at movie stars. The worshipful behavior of the crowd was deeply disgusting to behold. You'd have thought that Brad Pitt really was the Greek hero Achilles come to Earth.

Brad did a good warrior act in the movie *Troy,* but he's an actor, not a mythological demi-God. He is just the "meat." He might be well paid, but it's the "butcher" behind the scenes who is really raking it in!

The way the world works, it's much smarter to be the butcher, but no one tells you this. Glamor and glory aside, there are vast amounts of money to be made in the film industry and in the music business. The film industry is a filthy, rotten business, and

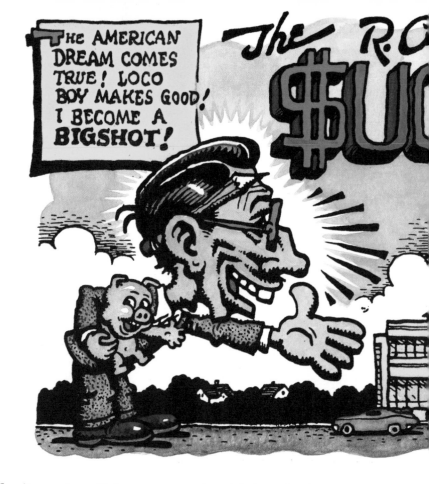

I don't want anything more to do with it. I don't want to be the "meat." But, of course, who am I kidding, I *am* the meat. I let the butchers go at me, chop me up in little pieces and put me on the counter! I didn't know what I was doing when I first got myself into this situation.

Before the fame thing happened, I hadn't really experienced the butchers up close. Now it's too late! Before anybody had heard of me, I used to wander aimlessly up and down a five block

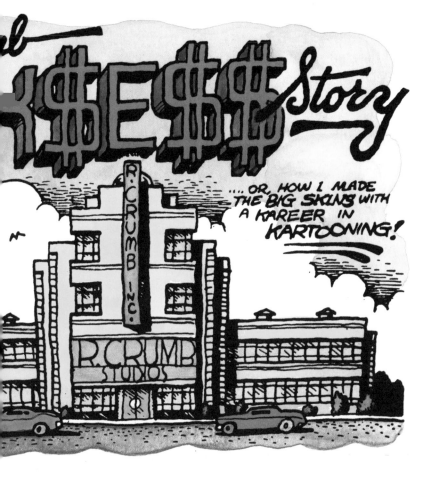

stretch of Haight Street, ogling all the beautiful young hippie girls, full of self-pity. Then, in 1968, when *Zap Comix* came out, my life changed completely. I started getting phone calls and people coming to the door wanting to get high with me. Oh, how my pathetic ego ate it up! I was the center of a kind of attention I'd never experienced before. I found I had a lot less time on my hands. Practically overnight I went from being ignored to being pestered all the time.

But then, too, fame put me over with beautiful, attractive girls for the first time in my life. Up till then, I was just another desperate loser-schmuck with nothing going for me. Now, all of a sudden I had this mysterious aura of attractiveness! Fame also brought media attention. The media is a big hungry beast. I've known a few who have died from too much of it, like Janis Joplin and Jim Morrison. (I was discussing this with Aline once, and her comment was, "I almost died from lack of media attention!").

All the people who work in the commercial culture are part of a conspiracy against the average man to get his money. They are not concerned with what effect their product might ultimately have, physically or spiritually. They are always looking for the lowest common denominator, the broadest possible market. They don't care what that might be. If Jesus movies are putting butts in theater seats, they'll make Jesus movies. If ultra-violence appeals to a certain segment of the population, the butchers are happy to provide it for them. Basically, the commercial media culture is a cold, merciless mechanism that is there to feed money to the people who perpetuate it.

Before industrial civilization, local and regional communities made their own music, their own entertainment. The esthetics were based on traditions that went far back in time—i.e. folklore. But part of the con of mass culture is to make you forget history, disconnect you from tradition and the past. Sometimes that can be a good thing. Sometimes it can even be revolutionary. But tradition can also keep culture on an authentic human level, the homespun as opposed to the mass produced.

Industrial civilization figured out how to manufacture popular culture and sell it back to the people. You have to marvel at the ingenuity of it! The problem is that the longer this buying and selling goes on, the more hollow and bankrupt the culture becomes. It loses its fertility, like worn out, ravaged farmland.

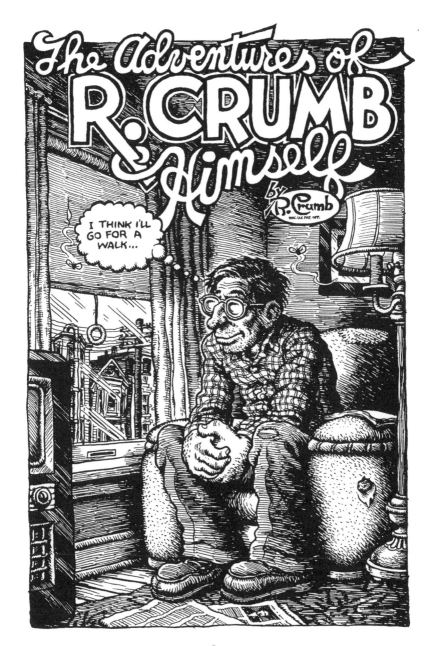

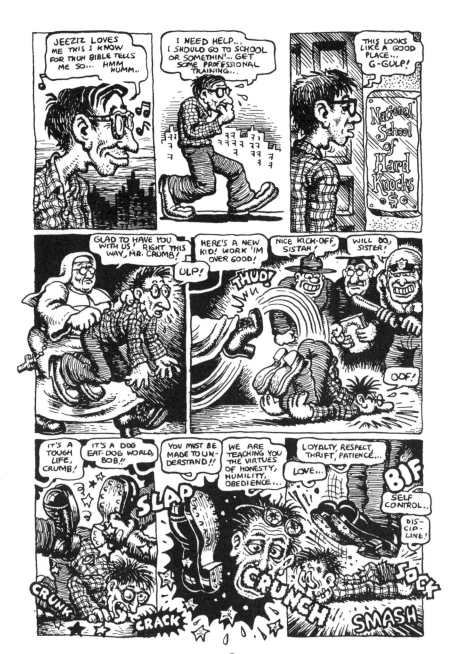

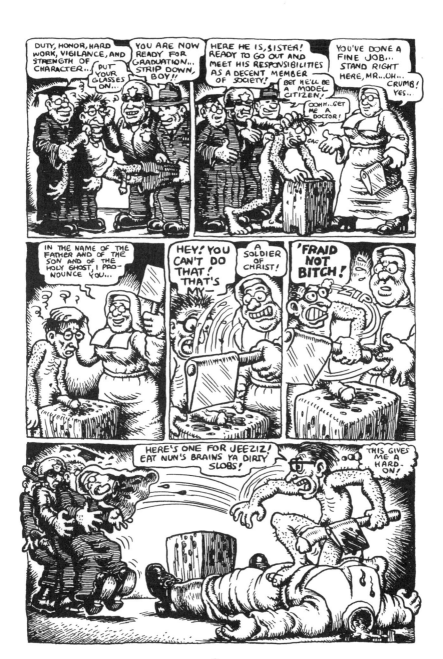

183

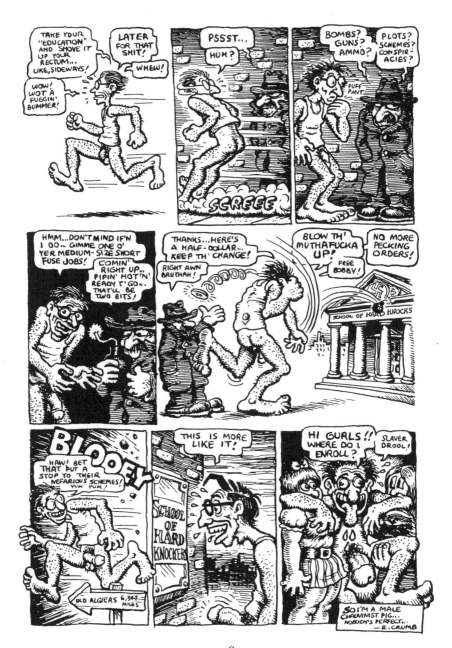

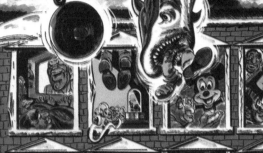

THE NATIONAL

SHEEP CHEEP SHEEP

AMERICA'S NEWEST HEADACHE

CRUMB

AUGUST

50¢

CDC

00134

A CRUMB IN EVERY POT

GOD BLESS OUR CRUMB

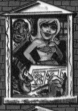

HOME OF THE NATIONAL CRUMB
(EVERY LITTLE CRUMB COUNTS)

BUILDING CONDEMNED

BLACKLIST
NATIONAL CRUMB

THIS ISSUE:
TOWERING EARTHQUAKE
CRUMB OF THE MONTH

CRUMB

CRUMB

CRUMB

00134

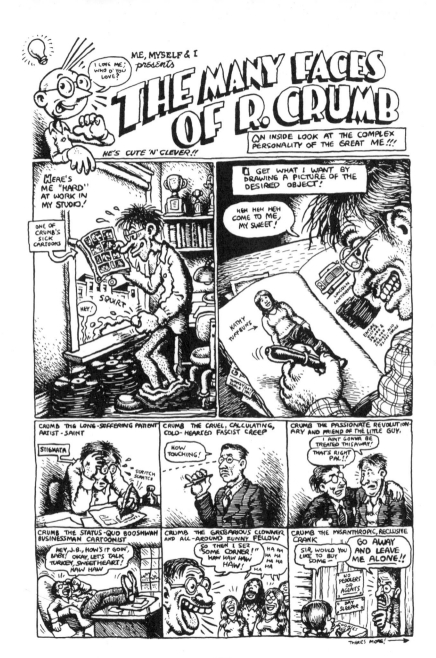

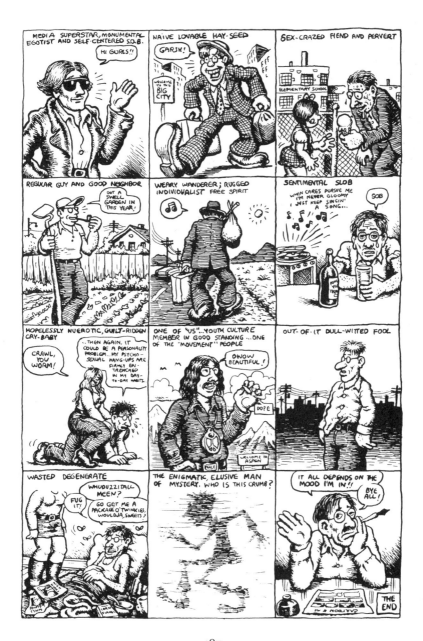

187

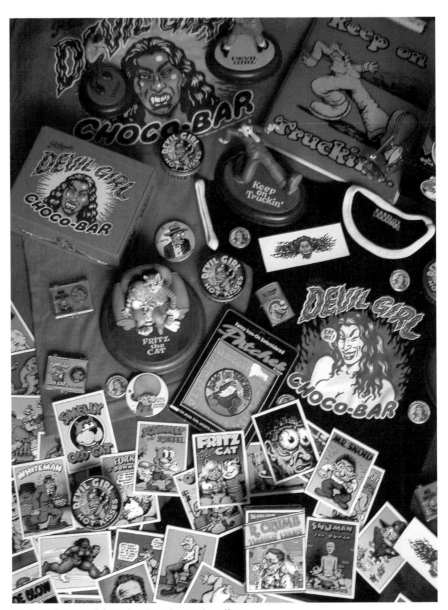

Various items of Crumb-related merchandise

Eventually, the yokels who bought the hype, the pitch, they want in on the game. When there are no more naive hicks left, you have a culture where everybody is conning each other all the time. There are no more earnest "squares" left—everybody's "hip," everybody is cynical.

Recently, I was watching a documentary film about the heavy metal rock band Metallica, and I thought, *"Oh my God, the culture is totally fucked!"* The film shows scenes of concerts where thousands of young men stand with their shirts off, raising their fists in the air, screaming and cheering to this shrieking heavy metal music. I felt like I'd just arrived from another planet. *"What in God's name is this about?"* I wondered. It seemed to be about everybody thinking they're a rebel, thinking they're hip and angry against some square culture that barely even exists any more.

The moment that my name became known to the larger world, I had to start dealing with lots of these enterprising hustlers. There is a constant pressure to make products based on my characters. Some of it comes from earnest, sincere people who love my work, and want to make a quality item, a limited edition art print, or a figurine. On the other hand, there are the *schlock-meisters* who want to make tee shirts, patches, magnets, key chains, lighters, posters, postcards, candy bars, cigarette papers, all that crap. That junk is very hard to control, and has never brought me a lot of money. Schlock will happen whether I give my consent or not. That's just the nature of business.

Steven Krantz and Ralph Bakshi just rolled over me like a freight train when they wanted to make *Fritz the Cat* into a movie. I couldn't cope with their aggressiveness. I ran away. My first wife, Dana, signed the contract and got ten thousand dollars on the spot. On two other occasions, we received large sums of money from the film's producers, Steve Krantz Productions.

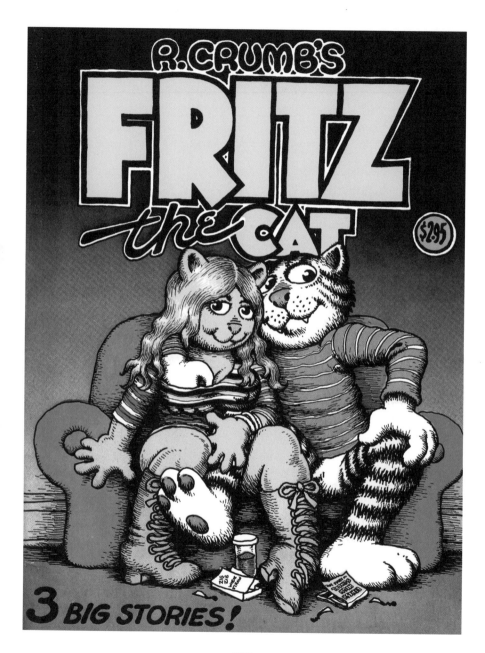

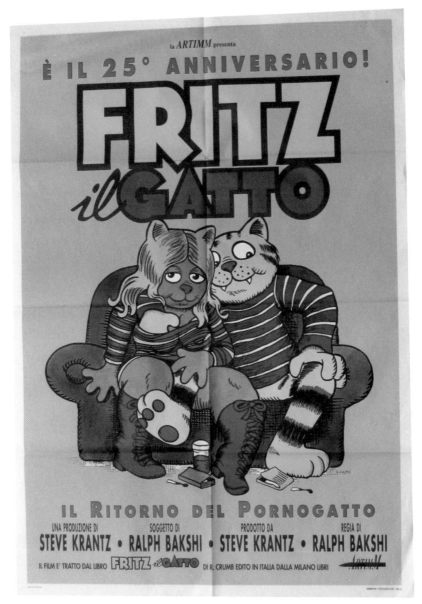

Above and next page: Italian movie posters for *Fritz the Cat*

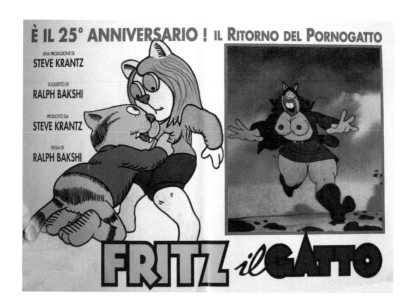

I barely remember the movie. It's one of those experiences I sort of block out. The last time I saw it was when I was making an appearance at a German art school in the mid-1980s, and I was forced to watch it with the students. It was an excruciating ordeal, a humiliating embarrassment. I recall Victor Moscoso was the only one who warned me, *"If you don't stop this film from being made,"* he told me, *"you are going to regret it for the rest of your life!"*—and he was right. But Dana, all the lawyers, everybody wanted me to make that film. *"It will be great! Think of the exposure! It will bring your character and your vision to the whole world!"*

I tried to tell them I really didn't think that Krantz and company had the background to make a high quality film. They were Saturday morning cartoon hacks! But I was twenty-five years old. I had no idea how to stop them. I couldn't confront all of them. I still can't confront people.

Ralph Bakshi, the director of the film, was a guy who really wanted to become the hip Walt Disney. He was energetic, neurotic and high strung. I kind of felt sorry for him in a way. He really wanted to do this thing, make the first X-Rated, full length animated cartoon. But when it came down to vision and content, he just didn't have any original ideas. As soon as he strayed away from my story, Bakshi's movie fell apart. Ultimately, he was just another one of those media jockeys trying to cash in on the hippy culture without actually being a part of it.

The producer, Steve Krantz, was a hard, slick, cynical character. When I tried to confide to him all my doubts and anxieties about the project, Krantz put his arm around my shoulders and said, *"Robert, if I could, I would keep you from any possible harm. I would protect you from the world,"* etc.

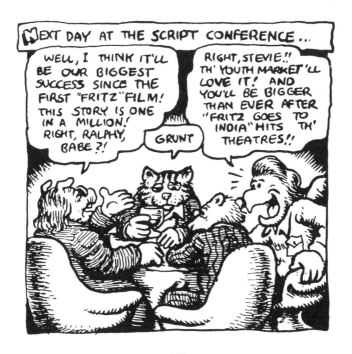

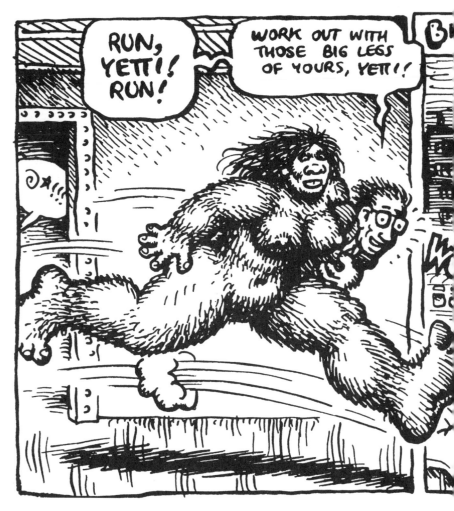

Well, what a shark! He was the Butcher. And I was the Meat. Small time theater people were much easier to deal with than the movie makers. When a couple of these little theater companies chose something of mine to make into a play, my main interest was to see how they would handle the wacky sex element. That surely did arouse my curiosity!

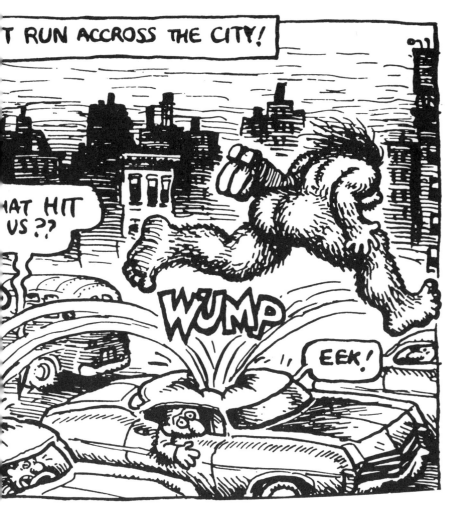

The Dell'Arte Players Company of northern California amazed me with their adaptation of *Whiteman Meets Bigfoot* in the late 1970s. I was fascinated to see how they were going to pull off the blatant sexual element of the story. *"Oh boy! Oh boy!"* I thought. *"What about Yeti? Are they going to find some giant big girl to play the part? Wow!"*

THE DAILY CALIFORNIAN 9

FRIDAY, OCTOBER 10, 1980

theater/charles burress

Bigfoot Lands in S.F.

BACK IN THE "New Age," circa 1965-1975, the nation's hunger for spiritual guidance found relief in an underground comic book. The top guru of that domain was a cagey, _____ "Mr.

his wife and two kids into the Winnebago and heads out for two weeks of camping in the woods. Out one night for a hike, Whiteman is snatched up by a giant female bigfoot named Yetti. Yetti _____ him back to her hairy tribe,

side the costume.) But what made it one of those Don't-Miss-It events was the addition of the fine-executed circus high jinks and music of the Dell' Arte Players, a hard-working collective of actors from Blue Lake, California, whose _____ them invite.

INDEPENDENT COAST OBSERVER

OCTOBER 25, 1985

'Bigfoot' Meets With Big Success

By Rob Wells

The Dell' Arte did it again Friday night with the hilarious performance of "Whiteman Meets Bigfoot."

On several levels Dell' Arte delivered a splendid evening of entertainment with carefully thought out and ingenious costumes, acting, set design and script adaptation.

Jael Weisman did a marvelous, job of creating the character Whiteman, a bumbling General Dynamics executive out on vacation. In a word, Whiteman is the perfect nerd; more on this character later.

Louise Whiteman, created by Joan Schirle, is the quintessential middle-class nightmare. Adorned in garish polyester, _____

Winnebago comfort, for all the cliche reasons we so well _____ love. (The design

cing.

Back to the story. The scared and shivering executive _____ escape

amorous bigfoot make the supermarket tabloids, and 60 Minutes.

The medical and scientific _____

videos and cure-all water; as bandleader and all-around prankster.

Mr. Natural's humorous monologues smoothed tran-

Entertainment

Comic-inspired beastly lust

By DAN TAYLOR

GUALALA — What happens when a hairy, lusty Abominable Snowgirl abducts a suburban husband? More to the point, what happens when his wife finds out?

You guessed it. The fur flies. "Whiteman Meets Bigfoot," is a furry, funny, rowdy, bawdy musical comedy that will shock some but delight most. The _____

Review

show also adds another character from other Crumb comics — a bald, bearded, bogus guru, Mr. Natural.

Mr. Natural _____ _____

ers and the clinical, cynical doctor — fit this format. And the Dell' Arte Players' masks and costumes are impressive, particularly those for a whole family of bigfeet (Bigfoots?)

Jael Weisman _____ _____

animal grunts and growls are convincing but still just intelligible enough to allow him a solid one-liner on occasion. His body language is lusty, funny and even moving, when the yeti mourns the loss of a friend.

_____ Whiteman, _____b's carica-_____an's por-_____ in a wild _____nough to _____ther, and _____ moving, _____d a Bay _____ t.

The Dell' Arte Players company of Blue Lake will present "Whiteman Meets Bigfoot," at 8 tonight at Vintage High School Theater in Napa. Tickets _____ People _____

Comedy is the nature of the beasts

By Barbara Shulgasser
EXAMINER THEATER CRITIC

"WHITEMAN Meets Bigfoot," the Dell'Arte Players Company revival, is a hilarious example of how far into sublimely hysterical humor a company can go when placed in the hands of a Not R_____ for Prime Time costume design.

Too many names are listed in the program to individually pr_____ all the costume "constructors," their work certainly supplies _____ basis for the show's funniest scen_____

"Bigfoot," inspired by the adven-tures of cartoonist R. Crumb's dis-penser of unstinting wisdom, Mr. Natural, is two hours of high silli-ness. Somewhere amid the duc_____ _____lks and tasteless humor a me_____ _____pens when cit_____

fectionately known, is played by the bouncy Michael Fields, an actor whose face, for all we know, might be as featureless as an ice skating rink. Wags _____

er's notions about fashion. Has it already been observed that clothes make the Bigfoot?

Mr. _____

THEATER
DELL'ARTE PLAYERS

A Cartoon-Style Bigfoot Stomps Out a Message

_____RD WEINER

The DELL' ARTE Players Company presents
their stage adaptation of R. CRUMB's

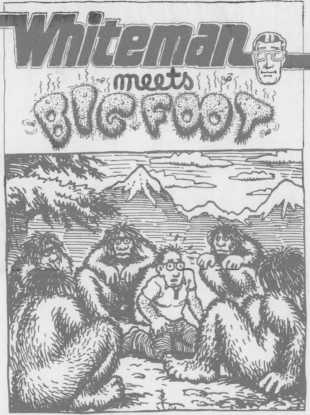

Whiteman meets BIGFOOT

The most incredible encounter ever!

JULIA MORGAN THEATRE

2640 College Avenue (at Derby), Berkeley

November 21 – December 8

All shows 8pm Thurs-Sun • No performance November 28 (Thanksgiving Day)

TICKETS

Thursday & Sunday – $7 • Friday & Saturday $9
$1 discount to students, seniors & TCCBA members
$2 discount to groups of 10 or more

Box Office: 548-7234 Open 10am-1pm daily & at Derby Market, 2705 College, 9am-7pm

TICKETS AVAILABLE AT ALL BASS OUTLETS:
DIAL "TELE-TIX"

FLAKEY FOONT Says!

SUGGESTED FOR MATURE AUDIENCES!!

Tour funded by the California Arts Council Theatre Touring Program and the National Endowment For The Arts

ALAIN SCHONS
THEATER DIRECTOR, ON THE THEATRICAL ADAPTATION OF *WHITEMAN MEETS BIGFOOT*

In 1980, The Dell'Arte Players Company adapted Robert Crumb's comic, "Whiteman Meets Bigfoot" for the stage and toured California. The show was very successful and later on, in 1986, the Bigfoot production was invited to be performed at the American Pavilion of the World's Fair in Vancouver, EXPO '86.

The Dell'Arte Players Company was a theater group co-founded by Jael Weisman, Joan Schirle, Donald Forrest, Michael Fields, Jon Paul Cook and myself in 1976, to do theater that was relevant to our lives and to the place that we were living. We would develop productions and "tour the sticks" of northern California. It was natural for us to want to adapt Robert's work for a show, and once he saw us work, he said okay. Robert gave us carte blanche.

"Whiteman Meets Bigfoot" was performed and revived in three slightly different versions over several years. The show probably brought The Dell'Arte Players a wider audience than any other show. We were reviewed by Variety, which brought us Hollywood people who would come to the show every night and take notes. We knew these guys would never do Robert's stuff as he had written it because there were no "family values." Eventually, Harry And The Hendersons came out of it for the suburban audience—very uninteresting.

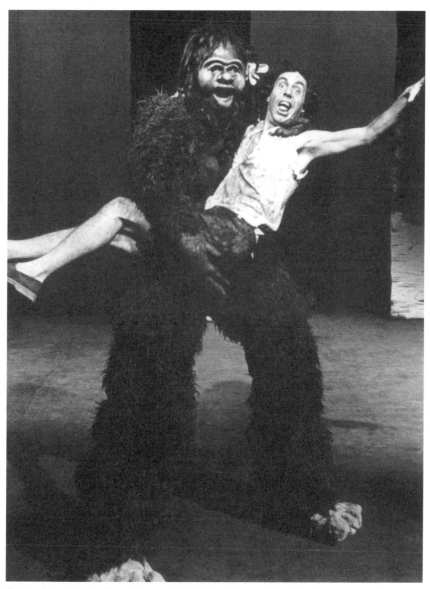

Scene from the California-based Dell Arte Players' live theater version of
R. Crumb's comic story "Whiteman meets Bigfoot," early 1980s

Guess what? Yeti was played by a guy in a costume. That was a bit disappointing, but Dell'Arte pulled it off. It was great! ... Funny, like the old time burlesque comedy, but more so. I give them credit for that, and they didn't flinch from the grossest sex scenes that are in the original comic.

The Hip Pocket Theater from Fort Worth, Texas, created *The R. Crumb Comix Show* and performed it in the 1980s and 1990s. Again, I rushed down there to see how they were going to handle the sex stuff. The head of the theater, Johnny Simons, told me they were going to put in all the girls, the sex, everything! Simons was kind of a randy guy himself and perfectly willing to have plenty of scenes of creepy characters manhandling women and pulling them about in a funny, low comedy spirit.

I was relieved when I saw the Texas audience laugh raucously at the nutty sex bits. Simons wanted to take the show to New York. I warned him not to. *"They'll run you out of town!"* I told him. He took my advice to heart and stayed away from New York. But while the audience generally seemed to enjoy the R. Crumb hi-jinx, the show in Texas received several disapproving reviews complaining of its misogyny. One review said, *"Crumb is an uncomfortable combination of the meek and mean spirited."*

I was portrayed by three different actors for the runs of these Hip Pocket shows. The actor in the first production was a dentist by the name John Murphy, who went so far as to create false buck teeth to make himself look uglier. He was a tall, skinny guy who played a creepy, scowling, hunched-over pervert R. Crumb. I thought Murphy played me much funnier than the professional performer Avner Eisenberg, who starred in the production they did in Durham, North Carolina a few years later.

Avner tried to portray R. Crumb as this aweshucks, shy, lovable eccentric character that I didn't think really fit with the action of the play. Avner is good when he does his own thing.

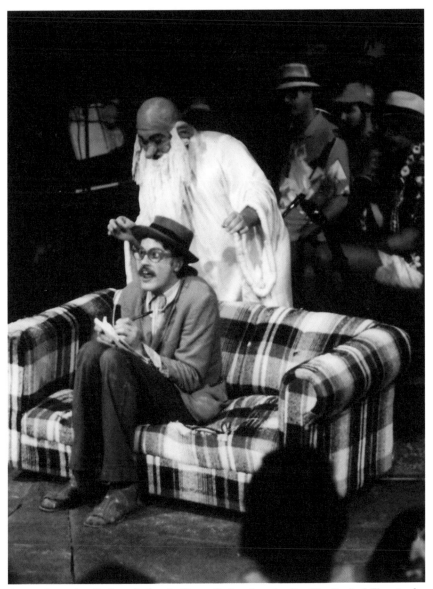

Scene from the *R. Crumb Comix Show,* first put on by the Hip Pocket Theater in Fort Worth, Texas, 1985. Dentist John Murphy plays R. Crumb.

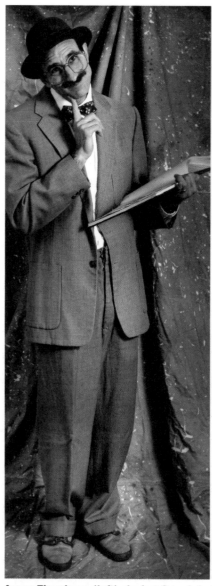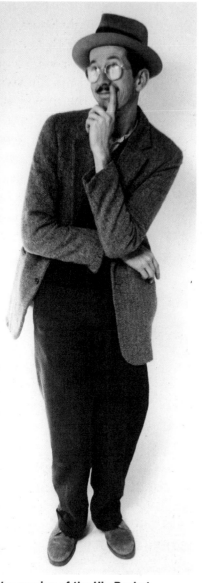

Avner Eisenburg *(left)* playing Crumb in later version of the Hip Pocket Theater's *R. Crumb Comix Show,* 1990, and R. Crumb *(right)* early 1980s

In my opinion he was a flop playing R. Crumb. But the dentist—he was truly hilarious in the part.

Another actor has played me recently, the guy in Harvey Pekar's *American Splendor* movie. Aline and I saw it in New York, and she told me afterward that if I was like the actor had portrayed me in the movie, she never would have married me. She hated his rendition of me.

As I said earlier, I will never work in the film industry again. I've wasted so much time on big schemes connected with optioning the rights or developing a film script from, for instance, *Whiteman Meets Bigfoot,* the long 1971 comic story. There was a guy from the San Francisco Bay area who pursued me for years about doing a film based on that story. I got endless pestering phone calls and visits from him.

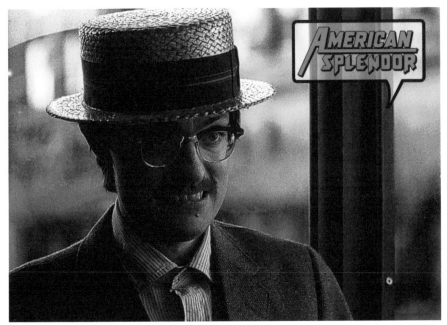

James Urbaniak, the actor who played R. Crumb in the film *American Splendor*, 2003

I dreaded to hear his voice on the phone, but then he got cancer and died. I hate to say it, but the truth is, I was relieved.

Another time, I got a contract which was so unfair I called up the law firm that sent it to me and asked, *"What is this? This contract doesn't seem fair to me at all!"* The lawyer just laughed at me. *"What do you mean fair? This isn't about fairness. You get your lawyers and we get our lawyers and we hammer it out. That's how it works."* The guy couldn't believe how naive I was. But I couldn't afford to hire lawyers.

Then the Mitchell Brothers wanted to do *Bigfoot* with explicit sex, a pornographic version. Terry Zwigoff wanted to get his career off the ground after his documentary *Louie Bluie*, and we worked for months on a script we called *Sassy*. Of course the Mitchell Brothers got cold feet over the millions it was going to cost and lost interest. I learned a lot about storytelling from that script writing experience, so it wasn't a complete waste of time. Terry and I took that script down to Hollywood and took a bunch of pitch meetings. I thought we had a pretty damn good story worked out there with lots of funny bits in it. The reaction was always, *"Hey, me, I love it, but it's way too negative and uncommercial! So, what else ya got?"*

Buck Henry, a comedy writer and sometime *Saturday Night Live* performer, gave us an audience of forty-five minutes and said he'd read our script. We dropped it off at his house in the Hollywood Hills. *"Look guys,"* Buck Henry said to us as we were leaving, *"Before you go I want to show you something!"* He opened his garage door and in one corner were hundreds of movie scripts thrown in a random heap about four feet high. *"And that's just the last few months,"* he said. *"Are any of them any good?"* I asked. *"Hey, you wanna read some a'them? Go ahead, take some!"*, he urged me. Terry and I called him two days later. He had read our script.

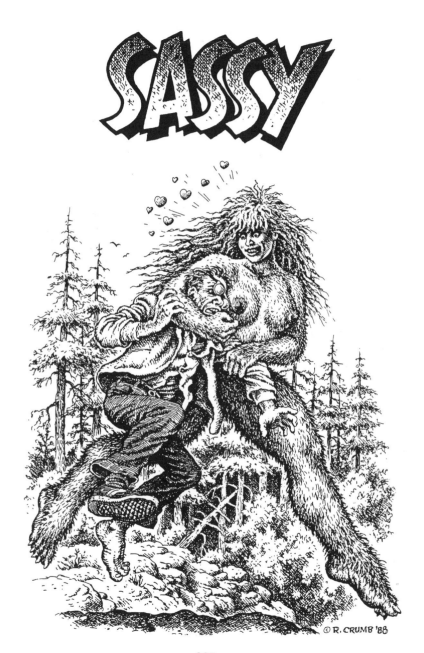

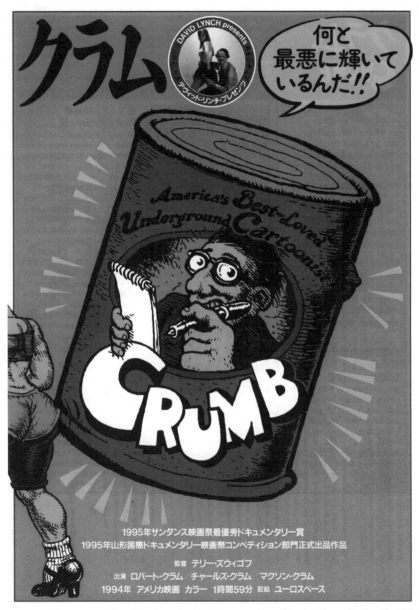

Japanese film promotion for *Crumb*, the documentary film by Terry Zwigoff, 1994

He couldn't judge whether it was good or bad. He said he just couldn't tell any more. In fact, nobody in Hollywood can tell if a script is good or bad. So nothing ever came of our *Sassy* script.

Terry really wanted to make movies. But since our script collaboration was dead in the water, he decided instead to make that documentary about me. His first film, *Louie Bluie,* had been well received. And there I was, ready-to-hand. I was his old friend, I was easy, accommodating. I gave him complete access to my life. Neither Aline nor I ever thought this thing would get the wide circulation and media attention that it did. It was a big surprise to all of us, Terry included!

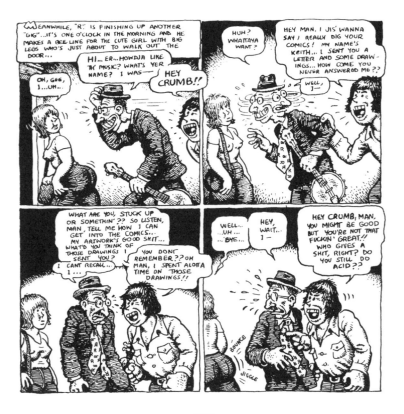

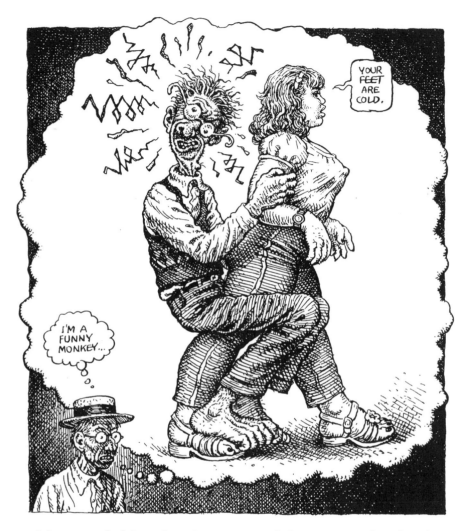

It's a good thing that I was out of the country by the time *Crumb* came out! Living in France afforded me some refuge from the media and other kinds of unwanted attention.

But I'm a slave to immortality. I wanted it from the very beginning. I just didn't know what I was getting myself into.

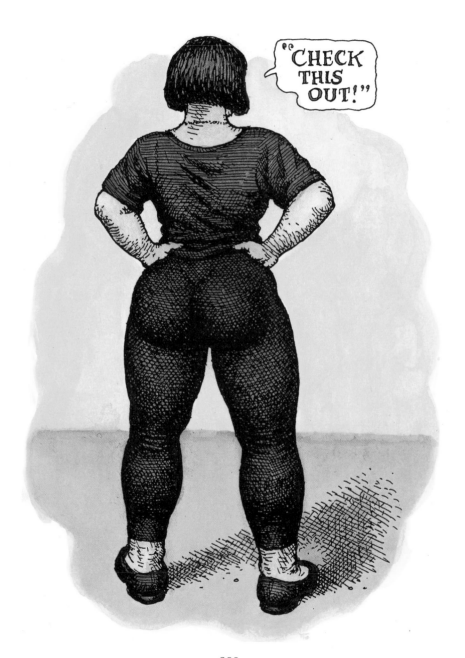

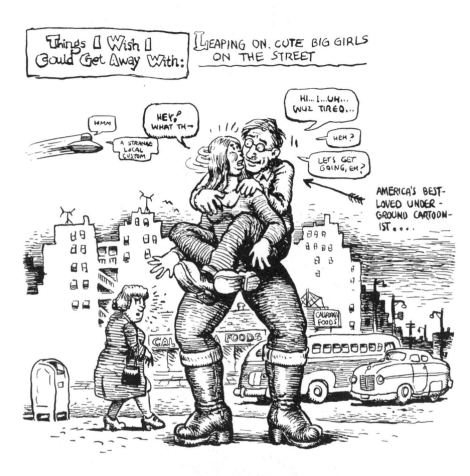

I was a fool. There is something in us that is always looking for the hard-to-find ultimate experience. We wade through a lot of shit to get to the fulfilment of our dreams.

In my case, all my life I've been a slave to that butt. Yes, the motion of a big, round, human female butt while she's walking has the same effect that the blossom has on the bee. To see is to desire! It's primal. It's an animal reflex.

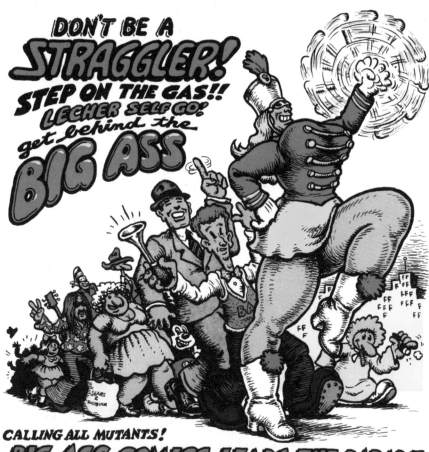

DON'T BE A STRAGGLER! STEP ON THE GAS!! LECHER SELF GO! get behind the BIG ASS

CALLING ALL MUTANTS!

BIG ASS COMICS LEADS THE PARADE

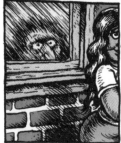

THIS GUY MAKES HIMSELF SICK!

AND WHY? BECAUSE HE WAS SOLD A BILL OF GOODS SOMEWHERE ALONG THE LINE AND LIKE A SAP HE BELIEVED THEM! IS IT ANY WONDER HE HAS AN UNHEALTHY ATTITUDE? WHO'S TO BLAME FOR HIS ABNORMAL BEHAVIOR? CAN HE EVER HOPE TO BECOME WELL-ADJUSTED? OR IS HIS HIDDEN ANXIETY A SIGN OF LATENT PERVERSE TENDENCIES BEYOND HIS POWER TO COPE WITH? THE ANSWERS TO THESE BURNING QUESTIONS ARE FULLY EXPLAINED IN EASY-TO-GRASP TERMS IN THE PAGES OF BIG ASS COMICS!

READ Big Ass comics and SEE FOR YOURSELF!

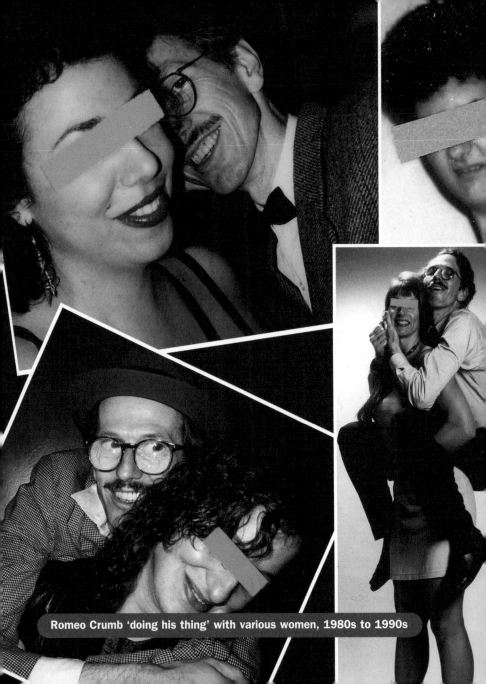

Romeo Crumb 'doing his thing' with various women, 1980s to 1990s

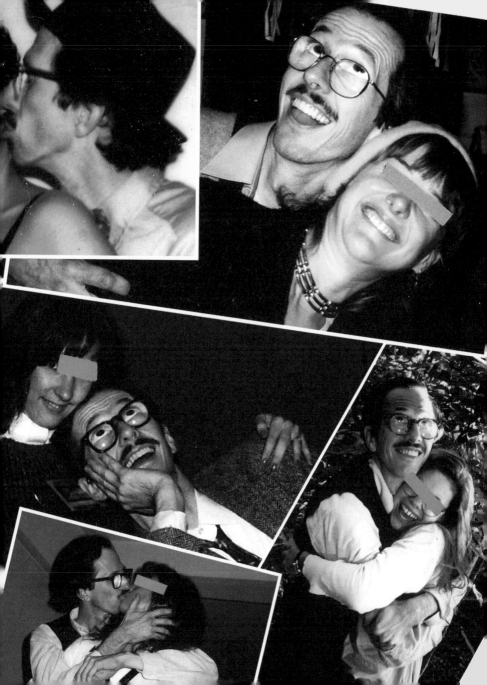

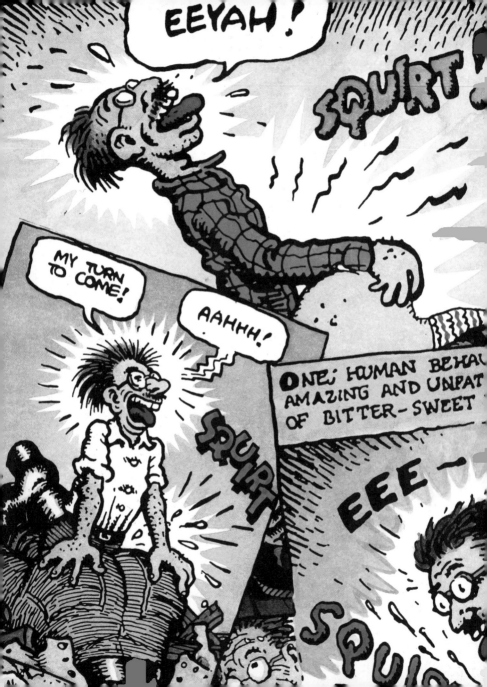

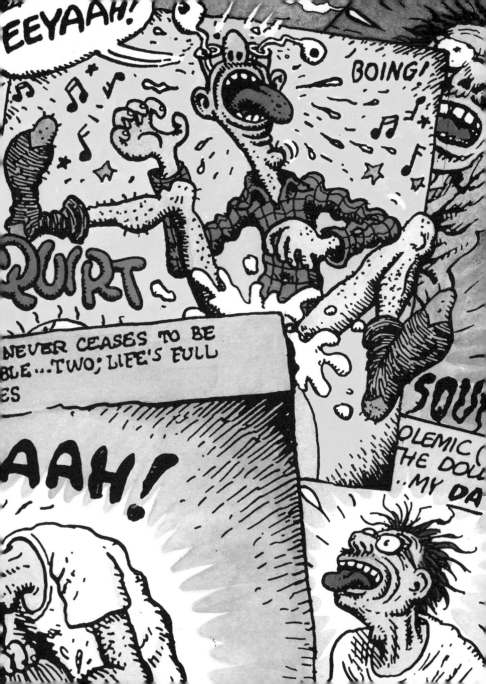

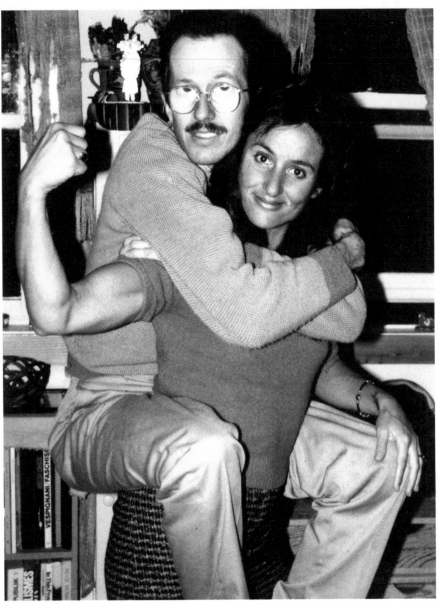

Crumb with his powerful wife Aline, Winters, California, late 1980s

The truth is, my sexuality is very quirky and eccentric. Out of all the women I've been intimate with, only a few were truly exciting partners. A lot of them, in fact, were real fiascos. Sad, but true ... It wasn't necessarily their fault. I can be turned off by petty and seemingly insignificant things. My sexual desire is highly particularized. Everything has to be just so, or the whole operation starts to seem sordid and pathetic.

On the other hand, when the circumstances are right, when the chemistry works, then sex is the most profoundly thrilling experience imaginable. But, you can't have that on a routine basis. At least, I can't. It's just the nature of the game! Deprivation enhances the desired object—*every* desired object! If heaven meant having everything you desired in life, whenever you wanted it, eventually it would become meaningless. And then what? Where do you go from there? What do we really want? What is this yearning, this "fire in our bellies?"

Being a Mama's boy, the woman is important to me for more than just sex. I needed somebody to save me from all the life threatening ravages connected with fame, and my second wife Aline has been very helpful in that regard. She saved my life! I'm not kidding! Aline is a very powerful woman, a formidable force. She is also a very funny cartoonist.

By 1973, the scene in the place in the country that Dana and I bought with the *Fritz the Cat* movie advance was so crazy, Aline finally got disgusted, and left. Soon after, I also left the "commune" and went to seek her out. The tragic part was that I got cut off from my son Jesse for seven years, but back then I wasn't ready for the responsibilities of fatherhood. I was weak! Aline is strong. She's a dynamo. That's why I'm married to her. When my daughter Sophie was born in 1981, I changed. I became more conservative. I believe in law, order, stability! You gotta have it for the protection of the children!

THE CRUMB FAMILY

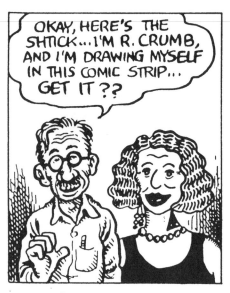

OKAY, HERE'S THE SHTICK...I'M R. CRUMB, AND I'M DRAWING MYSELF IN THIS COMIC STRIP... GET IT??

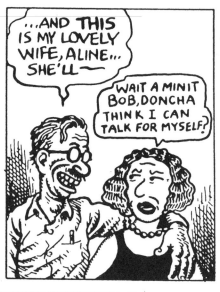

...AND **THIS** IS MY LOVELY WIFE, ALINE... SHE'LL—

WAIT A MINIT BOB, DONCHA THINK I CAN TALK FOR MYSELF?

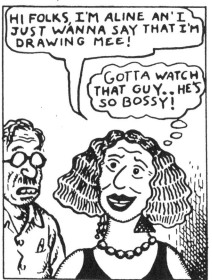

HI FOLKS, I'M ALINE AN' I JUST WANNA SAY THAT I'M DRAWING MEE!

GOTTA WATCH THAT GUY.. HE'S SO BOSSY!

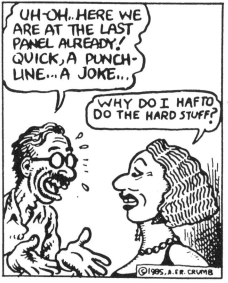

UH-OH.. HERE WE ARE AT THE LAST PANEL ALREADY! QUICK, A PUNCH-LINE...A JOKE...

WHY DO I HAFTO DO THE HARD STUFF?

© 1985, A. ER. CRUMB

218

THE CRUMB FAMILY

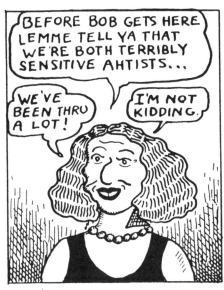

BEFORE BOB GETS HERE LEMME TELL YA THAT WE'RE BOTH TERRIBLY SENSITIVE AHTISTS...

WE'VE BEEN THRU A LOT!

I'M NOT KIDDING.

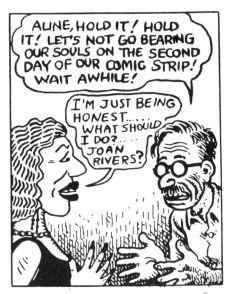

ALINE, HOLD IT! HOLD IT! LET'S NOT GO BEARING OUR SOULS ON THE SECOND DAY OF OUR COMIC STRIP! WAIT AWHILE!

I'M JUST BEING HONEST...... WHAT SHOULD I DO?... JOAN RIVERS?

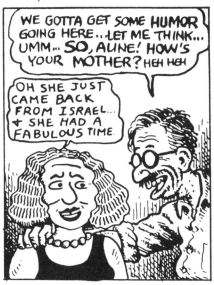

WE GOTTA GET SOME **HUMOR** GOING HERE... LET ME THINK... UMM... **SO, ALINE! HOW'S YOUR MOTHER?** HEH HEH

OH SHE JUST CAME BACK FROM ISRAEL... + SHE HAD A FABULOUS TIME.

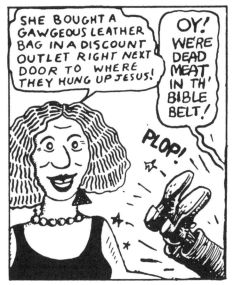

SHE BOUGHT A GAWGEOUS LEATHER BAG IN A DISCOUNT OUTLET RIGHT NEXT DOOR TO WHERE THEY HUNG UP JESUS!

OY! WE'RE DEAD MEAT IN TH' BIBLE BELT!

PLOP!

THE CRUMB FAMILY

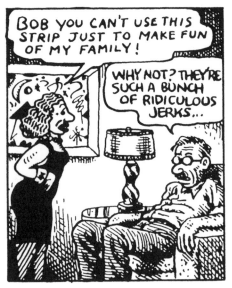

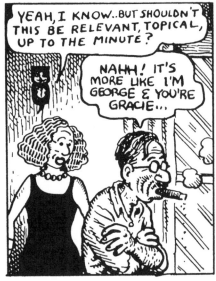

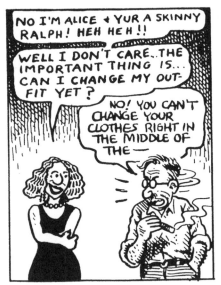

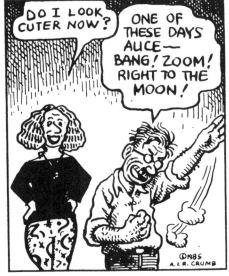

THE CRUMB FAMILY

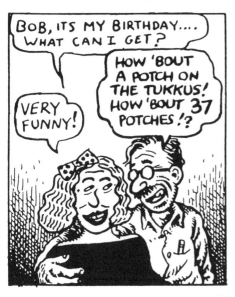

BOB, ITS MY BIRTHDAY.... WHAT CAN I GET?

HOW 'BOUT A POTCH ON THE TUKKUS! HOW 'BOUT 37 POTCHES!?

VERY FUNNY!

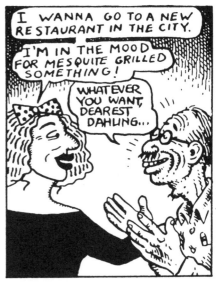

I WANNA GO TO A NEW RESTAURANT IN THE CITY.

I'M IN THE MOOD FOR MESQUITE GRILLED SOMETHING!

WHATEVER YOU WANT, DEAREST DAHLING...

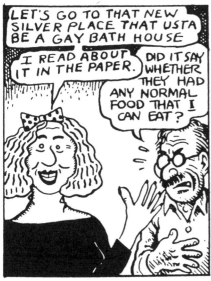

LET'S GO TO THAT NEW SILVER PLACE THAT USTA BE A GAY BATH HOUSE

I READ ABOUT IT IN THE PAPER.

DID IT SAY WHETHER THEY HAD ANY NORMAL FOOD THAT I CAN EAT?

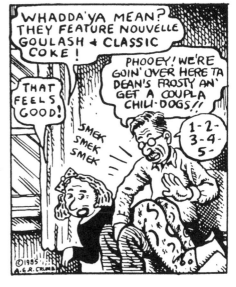

WHADDA'YA MEAN? THEY FEATURE NOUVELLE GOULASH & CLASSIC COKE!

PHOOEY! WE'RE GOIN' OVER HERE TA DEAN'S FROSTY AN' GET A COUPLA CHILI-DOGS!!

THAT FEELS GOOD!

SMEK SMEK SMEK

1-2-3-4-5-

© 1985 A.& R. CRUMB

221

THE CRUMB FAMILY

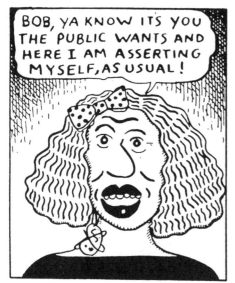

BOB, YA KNOW IT'S YOU THE PUBLIC WANTS AND HERE I AM ASSERTING MYSELF, AS USUAL!

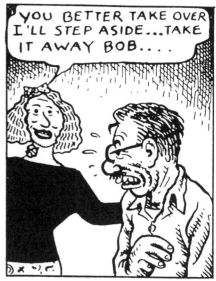

YOU BETTER TAKE OVER I'LL STEP ASIDE...TAKE IT AWAY BOB....

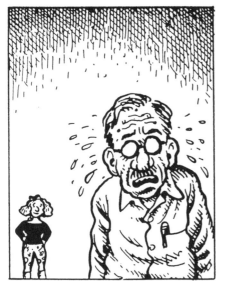

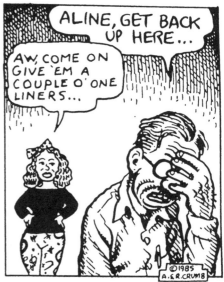

ALINE, GET BACK UP HERE...

AW, COME ON GIVE 'EM A COUPLE O' ONE LINERS...

©1985 A.&R.CRUMB

THE CRUMB FAMILY

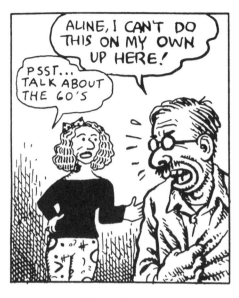

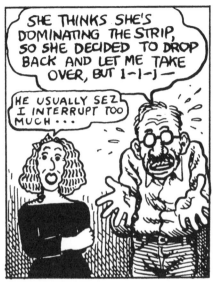

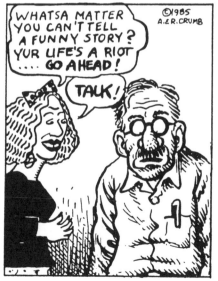

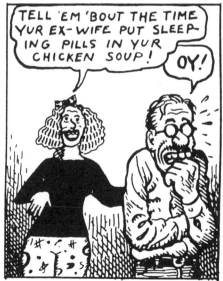

THE CRUMB FAMILY

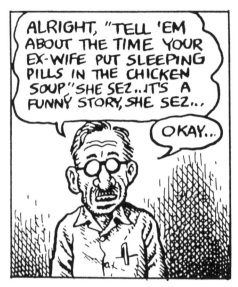

ALRIGHT, "TELL 'EM ABOUT THE TIME YOUR EX-WIFE PUT SLEEPING PILLS IN THE CHICKEN SOUP" SHE SEZ...IT'S A FUNNY STORY, SHE SEZ...

OKAY...

WHAT HAPPENED WAS... WELL, FIRST, THIS WAS 20 YEARS AGO.....YEP, 20 YEARS...JEEZIZ...ME AND MY FIRST WIFE WERE LIVING IN NEW YORK...

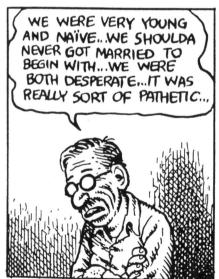

WE WERE VERY YOUNG AND NAÏVE...WE SHOULDA NEVER GOT MARRIED TO BEGIN WITH...WE WERE BOTH DESPERATE...IT WAS REALLY SORT OF PATHETIC...

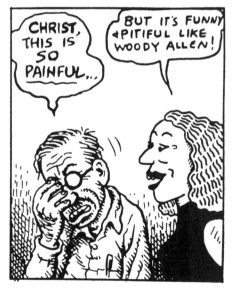

CHRIST, THIS IS SO PAINFUL...

BUT IT'S FUNNY & PITIFUL LIKE WOODY ALLEN!

THE CRUMB FAMILY

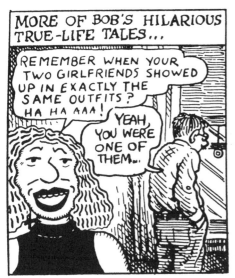

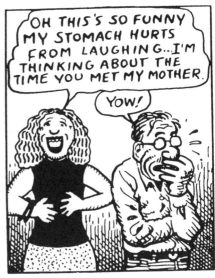

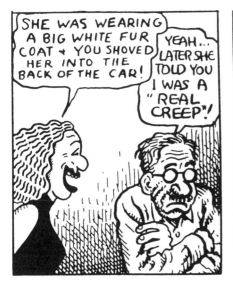

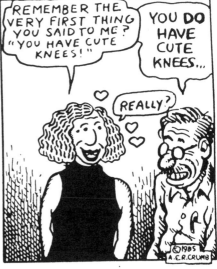

THE CRUMB FAMILY

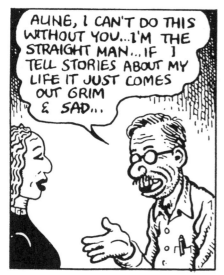

ALINE, I CAN'T DO THIS WITHOUT YOU...I'M THE STRAIGHT MAN...IF I TELL STORIES ABOUT MY LIFE IT JUST COMES OUT GRIM & SAD...

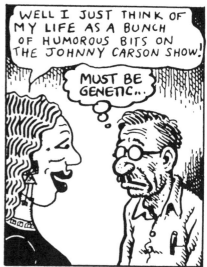

WELL I JUST THINK OF MY LIFE AS A BUNCH OF HUMOROUS BITS ON THE JOHNNY CARSON SHOW!

MUST BE GENETIC...

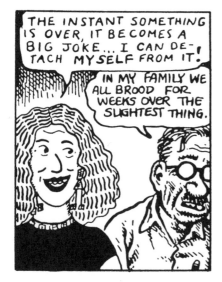

THE INSTANT SOMETHING IS OVER, IT BECOMES A BIG JOKE... I CAN DETACH MYSELF FROM IT!

IN MY FAMILY WE ALL BROOD FOR WEEKS OVER THE SLIGHTEST THING.

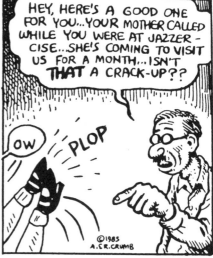

HEY, HERE'S A GOOD ONE FOR YOU...YOUR MOTHER CALLED WHILE YOU WERE AT JAZZER-CISE...SHE'S COMING TO VISIT US FOR A MONTH...ISN'T **THAT** A CRACK-UP??

OW

PLOP

©1985
A.&R.CRUMB

THE CRUMB FAMILY

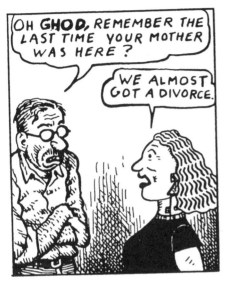

OH **GHOD,** REMEMBER THE LAST TIME YOUR MOTHER WAS HERE?

WE ALMOST GOT A DIVORCE.

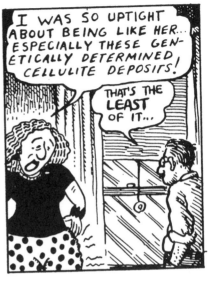

I WAS SO UPTIGHT ABOUT BEING LIKE HER... ESPECIALLY THESE GEN- ETICALLY DETERMINED CELLULITE DEPOSITS!

THAT'S THE **LEAST** OF IT...

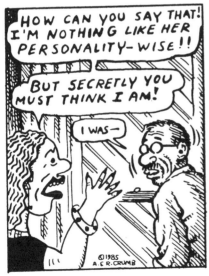

HOW CAN YOU SAY THAT! I'M NOTHING LIKE HER PERSONALITY-WISE!!

BUT SECRETLY YOU MUST THINK I AM!

I WAS—

©1985 A.F.R.CRUMB

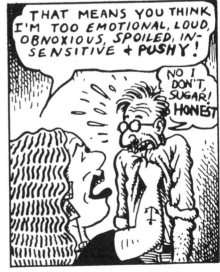

THAT MEANS YOU THINK I'M TOO EMOTIONAL, LOUD, OBNOXIOUS, SPOILED, IN- SENSITIVE & PUSHY!

NO I DON'T, SUGAR! HONEST

THE CRUMB FAMILY

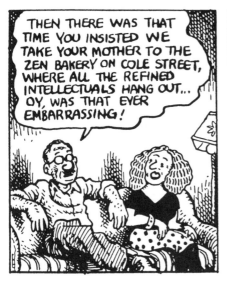

THEN THERE WAS THAT TIME YOU INSISTED WE TAKE YOUR MOTHER TO THE ZEN BAKERY ON COLE STREET, WHERE ALL THE REFINED INTELLECTUALS HANG OUT... OY, WAS THAT EVER EMBARRASSING!

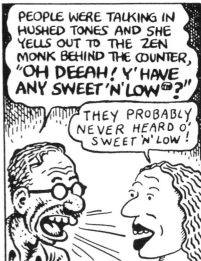

PEOPLE WERE TALKING IN HUSHED TONES AND SHE YELLS OUT TO THE ZEN MONK BEHIND THE COUNTER, "OH DEEAH! Y'HAVE ANY SWEET 'N'LOW®?"

THEY PROBABLY NEVER HEARD O' SWEET 'N' LOW!

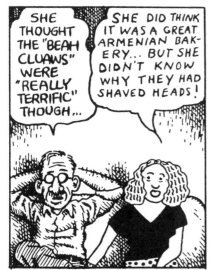

SHE THOUGHT THE "BEAH CLUANS" WERE "REALLY TERRIFIC" THOUGH...

SHE DID THINK IT WAS A GREAT ARMENIAN BAKERY... BUT SHE DIDN'T KNOW WHY THEY HAD SHAVED HEADS!

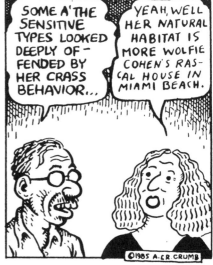

SOME A' THE SENSITIVE TYPES LOOKED DEEPLY OFFENDED BY HER CRASS BEHAVIOR...

YEAH, WELL HER NATURAL HABITAT IS MORE WOLFIE COHEN'S RASCAL HOUSE IN MIAMI BEACH.

©1985 A.CR CRUMB

228

THE CRUMB FAMILY

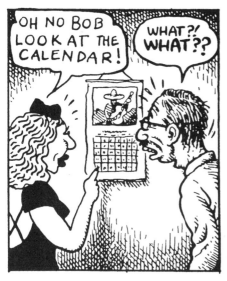

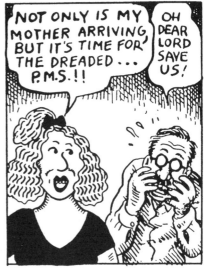

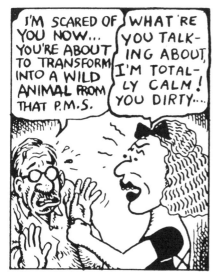

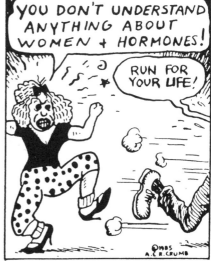

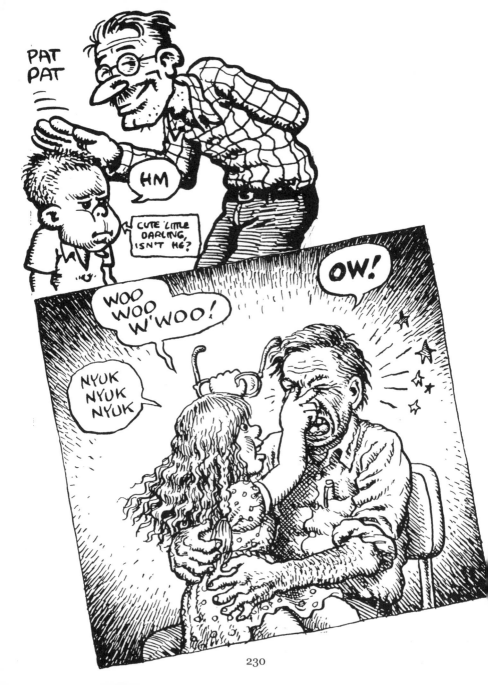

230

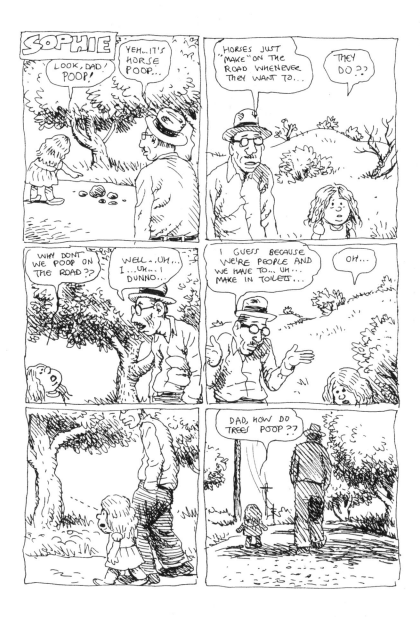

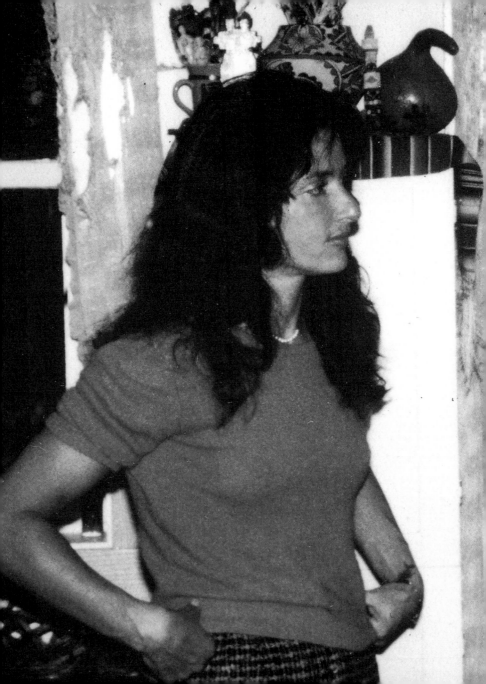

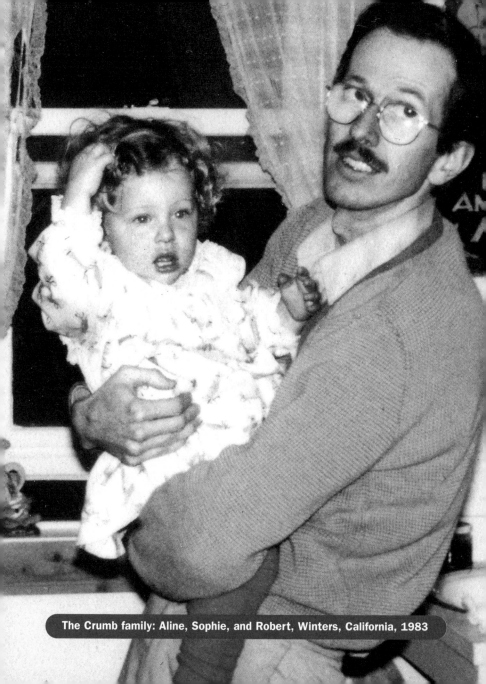

The Crumb family: Aline, Sophie, and Robert, Winters, California, 1983

HARVEY KURTZMAN
MAD MAGAZINE CREATOR

I often think of truth like the skin of an onion—you peel it back and what do you find? Another skin. And beneath that, another and another. Truth always has behind it, a more fundamental truth. A prime measure of an artist's work is how "true" it is. A dumb cartoon is empty, without originality. It offers clichés—surface without content. Crumb speaks reality and truth. If you are a discerning Crumb reader, if your interest goes beyond "the dirty parts," then you know him intimately. You know Crumb's life—his happiness, his disasters. You've gone deep inside his brain, into his sex, hate, love, dreams. He lays it all bare. He probes, he delves, he peels back the layers.

from the introduction to *R. Crumb's Carload of Comics*, 1976

Caught in the grips of
DESPAIR!?

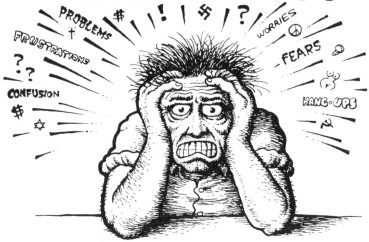

PROBLEMS · FRUSTRATIONS · CONFUSION · WORRIES · FEARS · HANG-UPS

IS THIS YOU?

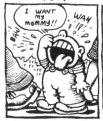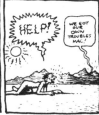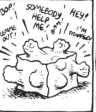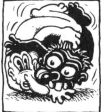

DO YOU SOMETIMES FEEL LIKE A MOTHERLESS CHILD? ...LOST IN THE DESERT? ..... BOXED IN? .... ARE YOU ALWAYS GRAPPLING WITH THE DUALITIES OF LIFE?

TIMES ARE TOUGH, HUH, BUD?

NOBODY EVER SAID IT WAS GOING TO BE A BED OF ROSES!! SO NOW YOU'VE MADE YOUR BED, SO NOW **EAT** IT!! OR, YOU MIGHT SAY, YOU'VE BUTTERED YOUR BREAD, NOW SLEEP IN IT! WHO DO YOU THINK **YOU** ARE? **GOD?** WHAT GIVES **YOU** THE RIGHT TO THINK YOU SHOULD HAVE IT ANY BETTER THAN THE **NEXT** GUY? **FORGET IT!!** THERE'S **NO HOPE!!** THAT'S RIGHT, KIDS! **NO HOPE!** FACE FACTS!! LOOK AT THE WORLD SITUATION!! HOW LONG CAN YOU GO ON DELUDING YOURSELF THAT THINGS WILL GET BETTER?? THE ONLY THING TO DO IS RESIGN YOURSELF TO THE FATAL INEVITABILITY OF IT ALL! WHILE WAITING FOR DEATH, READ "DESPAIR!" IT'S YOUR KIND OF COMIC!!

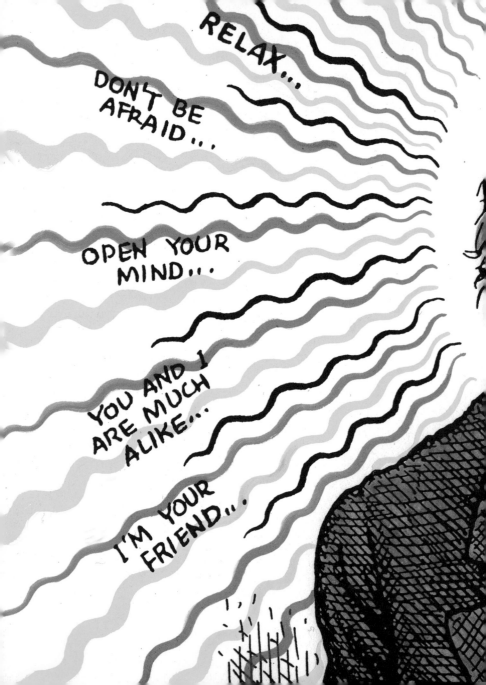

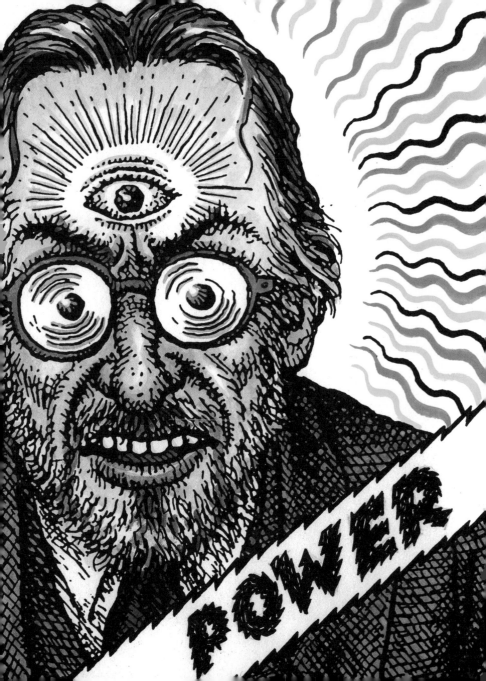

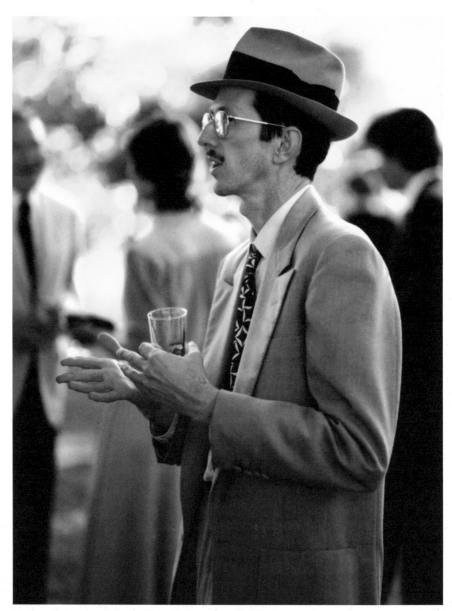

R. Crumb at an outdoor affair, California, mid-1980s

Chapter 5

Image-Maker versus Storyteller

In the media dominated world we live in, the artist is under constant pressure to do something new, something innovative. If an artist derives his style from older sources, his work runs the risk of being considered old fashioned, or anachronistic. Any use of a drawing style that looks as if it comes from the 1920s may seem archaic to some people. Still, in earlier times artisans invariably worked in traditional styles that had been established over generations through a system of apprenticeships and guilds. Artistic change for it's own sake, or for the sake of selling new product, was simply not part of the common culture.

Fashion was an exclusively aristocratic concern until the industrial era. But these days we're locked into a process of compulsory innovation where every artist must be a rebel to get any sort of recognition. To be merely at the top of your craft just isn't enough.

Pictures with words: William Hogarth was an eighteenth-century painter and printmaker who caricatured British society. An earlier series starring the picaresque hero Hudibras contains all the clichés found in the adventure genre today.

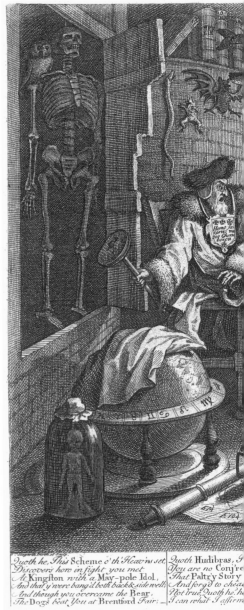

Quoth he, This Scheme o'th'Heav'ns set,
Discovers how in fight, you met
At Kingston with a May-pole Idol,
And that y'were bang'd both back& side well;
And though you overcame the Bear,
The Dogs beat you at Brentford Fair;

Quoth Hudibras, I
You are no Conj're
That Paltry Story
And forg'd to chea
Not true, Quoth he, h
I can what I affirm

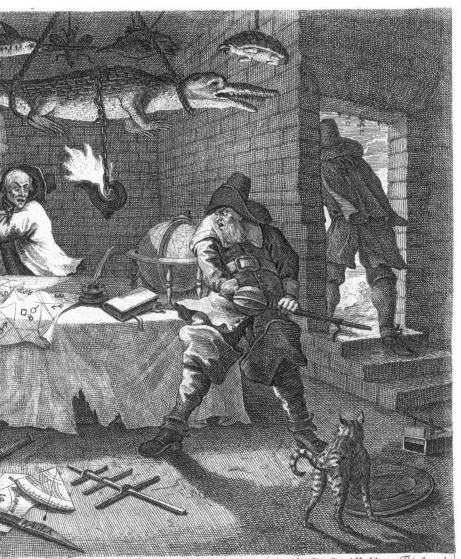

Hudibras beats SIDROPHEL and his man WHACUM.	*Whacum shall justifie't your face,* *And prove he was upon the Place.* *Nor have I hazarded my Art,* *And Neck, so long on the State's part,* *To be expos'd i'th End to suffer,* *By such a Braggadocio Huffer.*	*Huffer! Quoth* Hudibras, *This Sword* *Shall down thy false throat cram that word.* Ralpho, *make haste, and call an Officer,* *To apprehend this Stygian Sophister;* *Mean while I'll hold 'em at a Bay,* *Lest he and* Whacum *run away &c.*

I'LL BET THIS HAP-PENED TO YOU WHEN YOU WERE A KID!

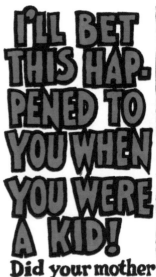

I WANT YOU SHOULD STOP WASTING YOUR TIME READING THESE CHEAP COMIC BOOKS!

Did your mother ever tear up **YOUR** comic books? Did you ever recieve warnings about how comic books were going to RUIN your MIND? Were you given lectures about how comics were CHEAP TRASH put out by evil men? Do you feel a spark of GUILT every time you pick up a comic book? Do you feel like you ought to be reading a good book instead? Let ZAP comics wisk away all such foolish notions! Takes only 15 minutes! Read ZAP comics!

THIS AD IS NOT INTENDED FOR THOSE FORTUNATES A-MONG US WHOSE PARENTS DIDN'T GIVE A SHIT IF THEY READ COMIC BOOKS.

— A MESSAGE FROM YOUR EDITOR, R. CRUMB

242

Because I'm an acutely visual person, storytelling is secondary to me. It's been my observation that most people aren't all that visually attuned. What they respond to more than anything else are stories. Strong, simple narratives.

It was through Charles' relentless criticism that I learned how to be a coherent storyteller. Charles was a highly narrative conscious cartoonist, whereas I was more pictorial. As a kid, drawing the cover was always the part of doing a comic book that I enjoyed most.

I constantly marveled at Charles' devotion to the comics medium. His own comics, *Funny Friends* and other titles, were always tightly, patiently drawn, with carefully devised stories. He was much more prolific than I was. He was totally dedicated. He made hundreds and hundreds of well executed comic books as a kid and adolescent. He had no other interests.

It all started because I understood the idea of PERSPECTIVE when I was five years old, and adults were impressed that I drew a picture of a ship cutting through the water, coming towards the observer and tapering towards the horizon, which meant I had artistic talent. Drawing became a way to win admiring oohs and ahhs from adults—mostly women, come to think of it—my mother, various female teachers, etc. My father's praise was always qualified, tempered with little criticisms or suggestions.

And then, too, I always and ever had a big ego. Where does THAT come from? Damned if I know,.., I think I was born with it... and I was a DREAMER, shy, socially awkward, always,... an oddball, even in early childhood... then I was drawn into the COMICBOOK thing by my older brother....

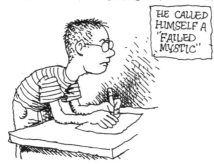

HE CALLED HIMSELF A "FAILED MYSTIC"

It was very intimidating for me. I always felt like such a second-rate artist compared to him.

The best comics combine both powerful images and strong narrative. Most cartoonists are stronger in one or the other. Many artists with technical ability are good image makers, basically illustrators. Other artists have minimal art skills, but are good storytellers, with an understanding of plot structure, character development and dialogue. It's rare to find in one artist both of these elements combined with equal strength.

If you look at a comic page drawn by Jack Davis or at Wally Wood's science fiction stuff, who cares about the narrative? But the artwork is wonderful, a true pleasure to the eye. What technique! With Charles Schulz or Jules Feiffer, it's quite the opposite. The story's great, but the artwork's not much to look at. In comics there's always this dichotomy.

In his late teens, my brother Charles eventually gave up drawing completely, and just became a writer. He was always a story guy first. As young boys, Charles and I were already connoisseurs of comics. We were deeply into Carl Barks, one of the rare cartoonists to combine great art with great storytelling. We didn't know his name since he wasn't allowed to sign the work he did for *Walt Disney's Comics and Stories*. We spoke of him as "the good artist." Barks drew *Donald Duck* and *Uncle Scrooge* comics.

John Stanley, creator of the *Little Lulu* comic books, was another great storyteller of those days, and though he wasn't a particularly outstanding image maker, the artwork was entirely appropriate to the narrative. *Donald Duck* and *Little Lulu* are outstanding as humanistic storytelling in the comic book medium. Most old funny animal comics fell into a whole other category from the work of Barks and Stanley, but even the second- and third-rate comics had other qualities that we liked.

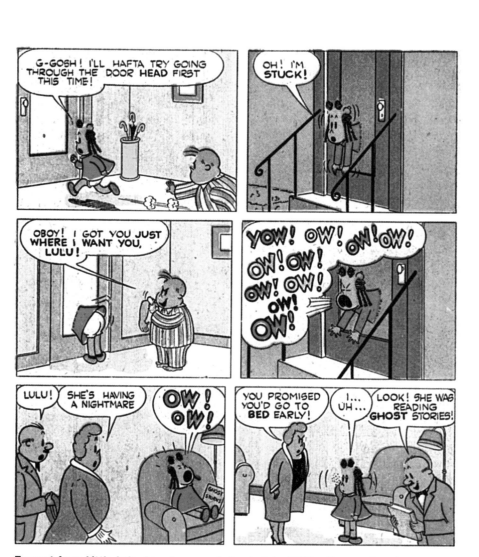

Excerpt from *Little Lulu,* American comic book, late 1940s. Unconscious inspiration? this Little Lulu sequence from the late 1940s bears an uncanny resemblance to the adolescent sex fantasies of young Crumb. The same idea is found in his sketchbook drawings and on the back cover of *Snatch* comics like the one on the next page.

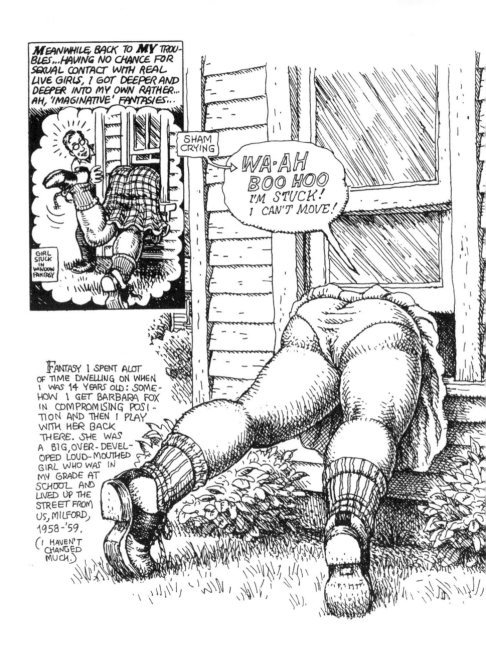

MEANWHILE, BACK TO **MY** TROUBLES... HAVING NO CHANCE FOR SEXUAL CONTACT WITH REAL LIVE GIRLS, I GOT DEEPER AND DEEPER INTO MY OWN RATHER... AH, 'IMAGINATIVE' FANTASIES...

GIRL STUCK IN WINDOW FANTASY

SHAM CRYING

WA·AH BOO HOO I'M STUCK! I CAN'T MOVE!

FANTASY I SPENT A LOT OF TIME DWELLING ON WHEN I WAS 14 YEARS OLD: SOMEHOW I GET BARBARA FOX IN COMPROMISING POSITION AND THEN I PLAY WITH HER BACK THERE. SHE WAS A BIG, OVER-DEVELOPED LOUD-MOUTHED GIRL WHO WAS IN MY GRADE AT SCHOOL AND LIVED UP THE STREET FROM US, MILFORD, 1958-'59.

(I HAVEN'T CHANGED MUCH.)

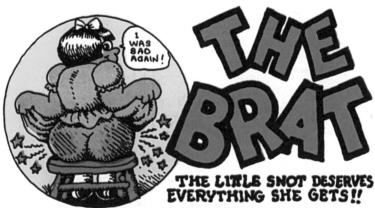

THE BRAT

THE LITTLE SNOT DESERVES EVERYTHING SHE GETS!!

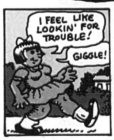

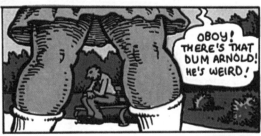

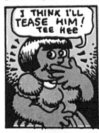

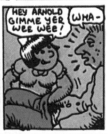

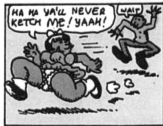

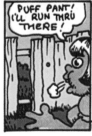

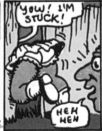

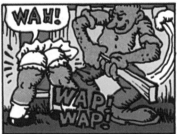

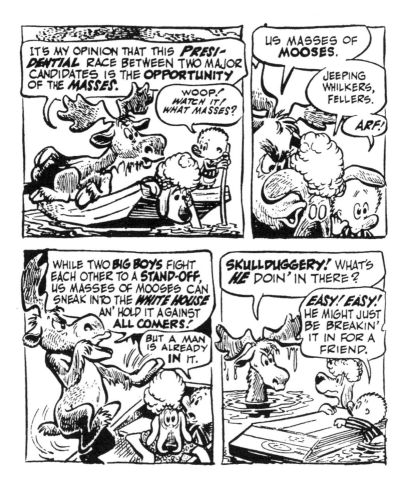

For instance, *Felix the Cat,* by Otto Mesmer, had a light, breezy, fast moving story line that was easy to read, and Mesmer had a hell of a charming visual style. *Pogo Possum,* by Walt Kelly, was another great 1950s comic strip. It was much more adult, more intellectual and not really a kid's comic, although it gave the appearance of being one. It was all talk, word play, but there was also sophisticated, left liberal political satire in it.

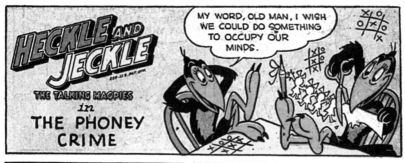

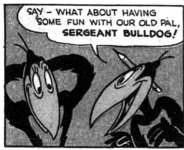

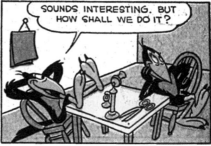

Some of the other comics that Charles and I liked, *Heckle and Jeckle, Super Duck*, things of that ilk, featured very primitive stories on the crudest proletarian level. They were basically simple fables of tricksters and how they got themselves into trouble, or how they outwitted their enemies. These comics were all crude, slapstick violence.

The super-hero comics of the 1940s also had this rough, working class quality. A cartoonist like Jack Kirby is a perfect example. His characters—Captain America, for instance—were an extension of himself. Kirby was a tough little guy from the streets of New York's lower East side, and he saw the world in terms of harsh, elemental, forces. How do you deal with these forces? You fight back! This was the message of all the comic strips created during the Great Depression of the 1930s, from *Popeye* to *Dick Tracy* to *Superman*.

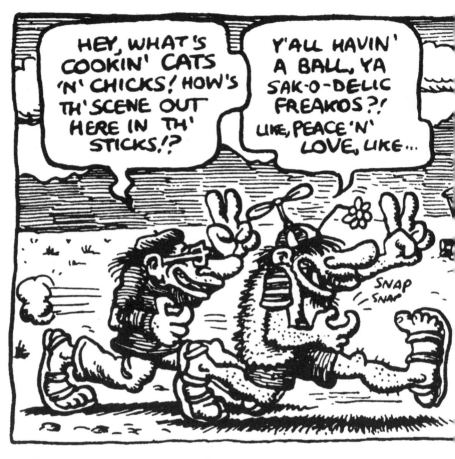

These were extremely basic, hell-raising comics. No wonder all those nice middle class people—teachers, doctors, sociologists —were scared of comic books in the 1950s! *What are these so-called "funny books" doing to our children?"* They wanted to shut it all down. Those 1940s to early 1950s comic books were on the same level as 16th and 17th century penny prints sold in the streets, showing the torture and dismemberment of saints, armies invading cities, lurid scenes of massacre and pillaging.

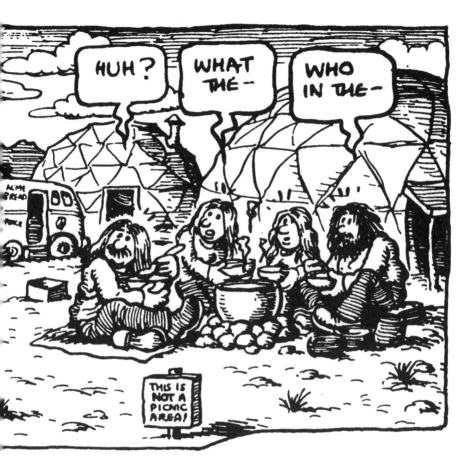

Low, popular stuff. The result of this uproar in 1955 was The Comics Code Authority approval stamp on all comic book covers. This let the public know that the comic they held in their hands had been reviewed and met supposedly high standards of morality and good taste. For Charles and me, this change didn't matter much. It was already obvious to us that comics had been in decline since the early 1950s. In any case, most cartoonists have about a ten year run of inspiration or creativity.

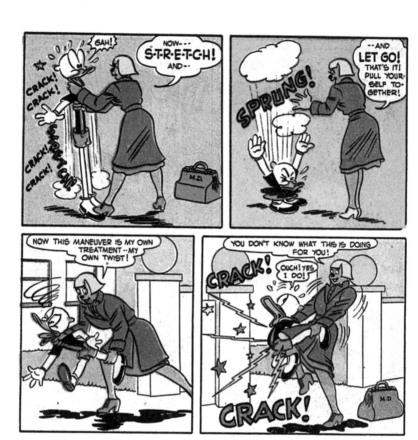

Excerpt from American comic book *Superduck*, late 1940s

After that they begin to burn out from the relentlessness of churning out comics on a regular basis. They are totally locked into their contract, their standard of living, their family responsibilities. They're forced to keep producing, like it or not. Carl Barks' best work was from 1947 to 1957. John Stanley had ten good years on *Little Lulu,* 1944 to 1954.

Two exceptions to this rule were George Herriman's *Krazy Kat,* which was highly personal and surrealistic, and Chester Gould's *Dick Tracy*, because Gould was just plain crazy. Their

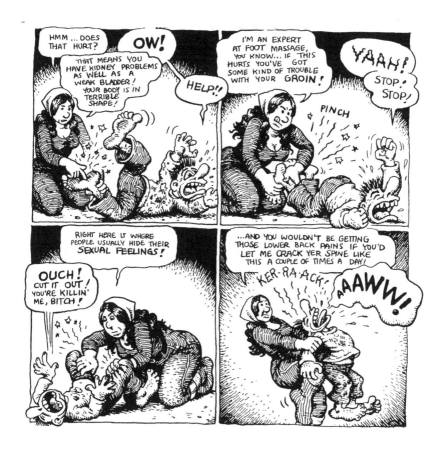

work stayed interesting over a thirty or forty year span.

I was fifteen years old when I became obsessed over Harvey Kurtzman and his crew of artists in *Mad* magazine and then *Humbug* in 1958. I was deeply influenced by these artists' work—Kurtzman, Will Elder, Jack Davis and Wallace Wood. I still aspire to emulate what they did in the late 1950s. After *Humbug* proved to be an utter commercial failure, Kurtzman ended up under the wing of Hugh M. Hefner, publisher and editor of the phenomenally successful *Playboy* magazine.

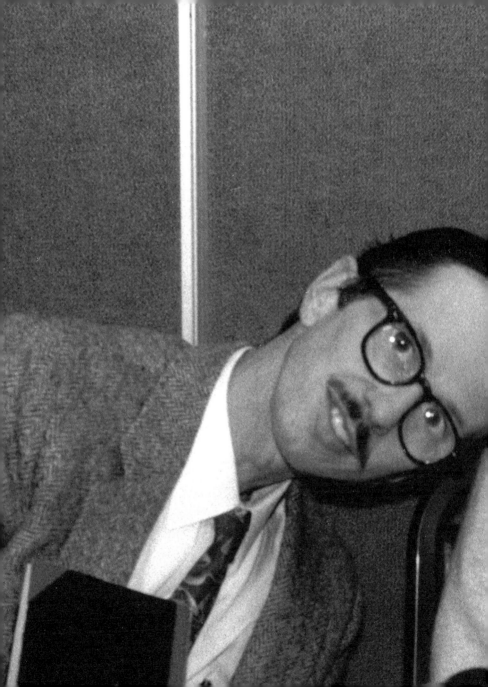

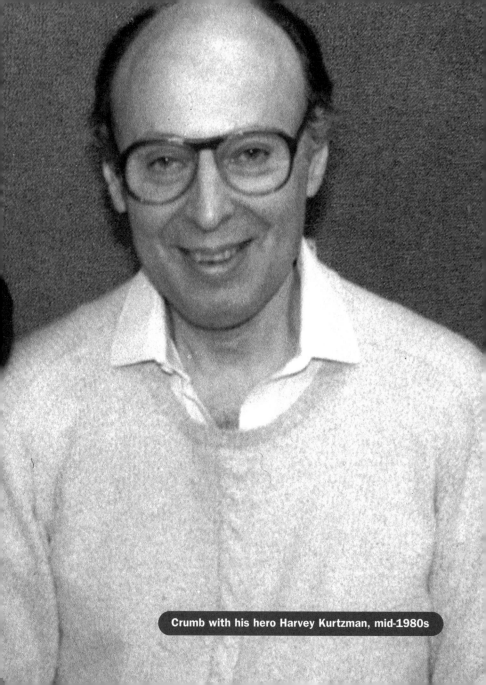

Crumb with his hero Harvey Kurtzman, mid-1980s

Kurtzman was caught, trapped. I saw him break down and weep once, describing the way Hefner was always blue penciling his roughs for *Little Annie Fanny*. It was terrible to witness.

I was lucky to be part of the "underground comix" thing in which cartoonists were completely free to express themselves. To function on those terms means putting everything out in the open—no need to hold anything back—total liberation from censorship, including the inner censor! A lot of my satire is considered by some to be "too hard." My "negro" characters are not about black people, but are more about pushing these "uncool" stereotypes in readers' faces, so suddenly they have to deal with a very tacky part of our human nature. Yeah, it's tough.

Maybe it's too much for them, I dunno. Even Kurtzman was shocked. Who did I think I was appealing to? I don't know. I was just being a punk, putting down on paper all these messy parts of the culture we internalize and keep quiet about. I admit I'm occasionally embarrassed when I look at some of that work now.

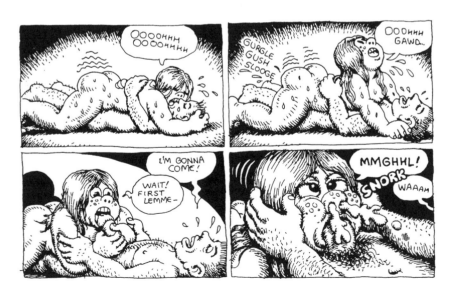

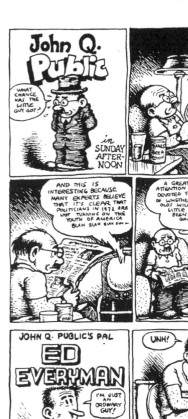

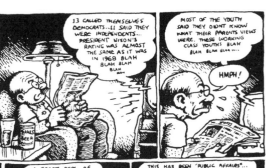

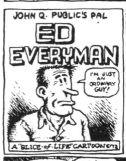

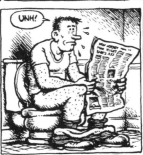

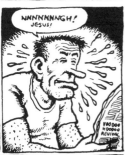

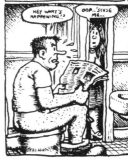

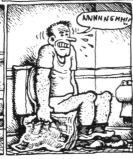

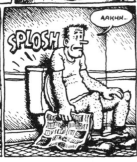

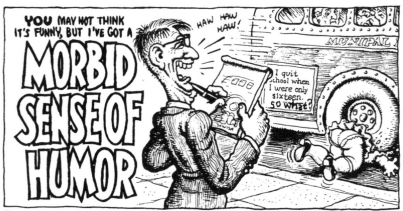

YOU MAY NOT THINK IT'S FUNNY, BUT I'VE GOT A

MORBID SENSE OF HUMOR

HAW HAW HAW!

I quit school when I were only sixteen. SO WHAT!

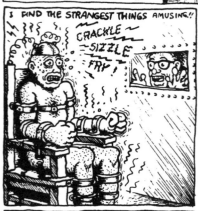

I FIND THE STRANGEST THINGS AMUSING!!

CRACKLE SIZZLE FRY!

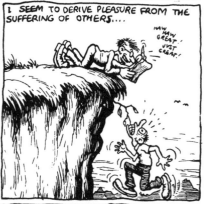

I SEEM TO DERIVE PLEASURE FROM THE SUFFERING OF OTHERS....

HAW HAW GREAT JUST GREAT!

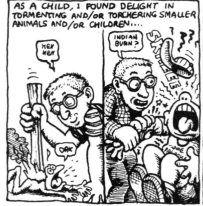

AS A CHILD, I FOUND DELIGHT IN TORMENTING AND/OR TORCHERING SMALLER ANIMALS AND/OR CHILDREN....

HEH HEH

INDIAN BURN?

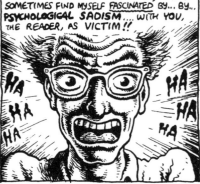

EVEN NOW, AS AN ADULT AND AN EMINENTLY RESPECTED AMERICAN CARTOONIST, I STILL SOMETIMES FIND MYSELF FASCINATED BY... BY.. **PSYCHOLOGICAL SADISM**.... WITH YOU, THE READER, AS VICTIM!!

HA HA HA HA HA HA

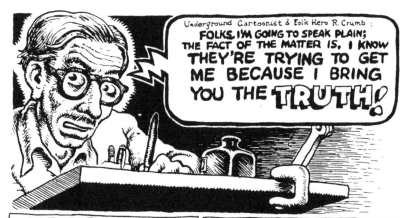

Underground Cartoonist & Folk Hero R. Crumb :

FOLKS, I'M GOING TO SPEAK PLAIN; THE FACT OF THE MATTER IS, I KNOW THEY'RE TRYING TO GET ME BECAUSE I BRING YOU THE TRUTH!

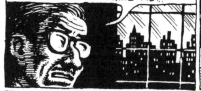

...AND THE **TRUTH** IS THE ONE THING THESE BASTARDS CAN'T TOLERATE!! I ONLY HOPE TO GOD I AM ABLE TO COMPLETE MY MISSION ON THIS PLANET BEFORE THEY SUCCEED IN EXTERMINATING ME!!!

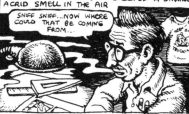

WHY, THIS VERY EVENING, AS I SET ABOUT TO DRAW A CARTOON, I DETECTED A STRANGE ACRID SMELL IN THE AIR

SNIFF SNIFF...NOW WHERE COULD THAT BE COMING FROM...

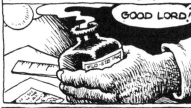

A LITTLE INVESTIGATING ON MY PART AND I REALIZED THE PUNGEANT ODOR WAS COMING FROM MY **INK BOTTLE**!!

GOOD LORD!

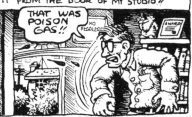

I GRABBED THE INK BOTTLE AND FLUNG IT FROM THE DOOR OF MY STUDIO!!

THAT WAS POISON GAS!!

NO PEDDLERS!

AWARD

AFTERWARD, I TRIED TO THINK BACK...WHO HAD BEEN IN MY STUDIO THIS MORNING? AND THEN, IN A FLASH, I KNEW WHO IT WAS THAT WAS TRYING TO KILL ME!!!

OF COURSE!! I SHOULD HAVE KNOWN ALL ALONG! HE'S A GOVERNMENT AGENT!! IT'S SO OBVIOUS TO ME NOW... I'VE GOT TO BE MORE CAUTIOUS IN THE FUTURE...

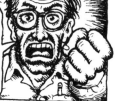

I WON'T NAME NAMES HERE, FOR THAT WOULD ONLY GET ME IN DEEPER TROUBLE WITH **THEM**, BUT LET ME JUST SAY THIS TO THOSE ROTTEN MOTHERFUCKERS!!

IT DOESN'T MATTER WHAT YOU DO TO ME, YOU SWINE! YOU'VE ALREADY SEALED YOUR OWN DOOM!! FREEDOM LIVES ON!!

PETER POPLASKI
ARTIST, WRITER AND EDITOR

COMMENT ON R. CRUMB'S HARD SATIRE
FAIR WARNING: FOR ADULT INTELLECTUALS ONLY!

Joseph Campbell, the scholar of mythology, once complained that people don't know what a metaphor is so, for these people, a myth is a lie. Many of Robert Crumb' s readers and their police departments don't understand what a metaphor is either. As a result, Crumb's hard satire comic stories are treated as obscenities. "Angelfood McSpade" becomes blatant racism. "Joe Blow," a satire on family values and parental influence, becomes an incest story. "Mr Natural and the Big Baby" is child molestation, whereas actually, the big baby is a caricature of one of Crumb's girl friends from his hippy days. Drawing a cartoon character urinating for the cover of YOUR HYTONE COMIC, Crumb asks, "is this obscene?" These matters were debatable until 1973, when the United States Supreme Court voted that local communities could determine their own definition of obscenity. After that, many comic and head shops were busted for selling these comics, earning Crumb his "bad boy" reputation. Crumb himself told the press in 1976: "people have no idea of the sources for my work. I didn't invent anything; it's all there in the culture; it's not a big mystery. I just combine my personal experience with classic cartoon stereotypes."

FREAK OUT FUNNIES

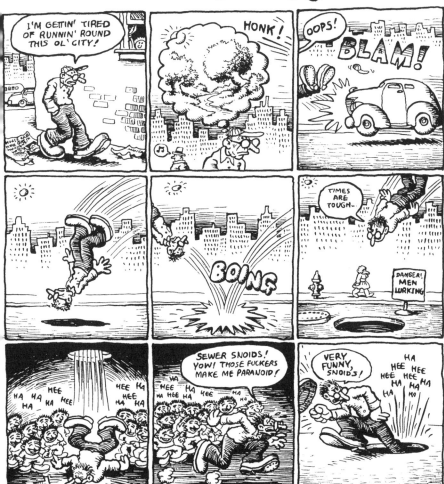

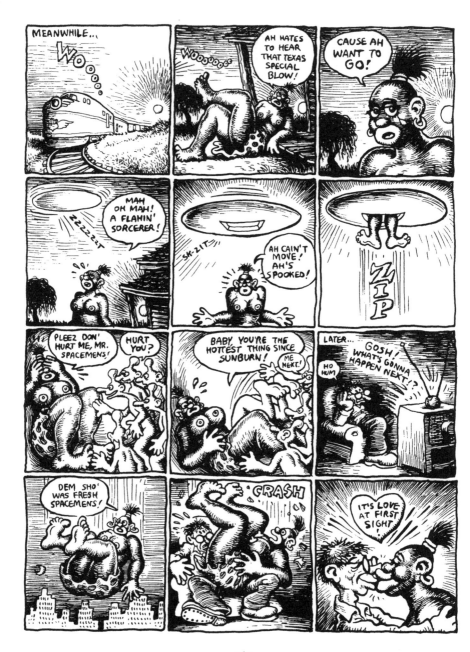

262

ANGELFOOD McSPADE

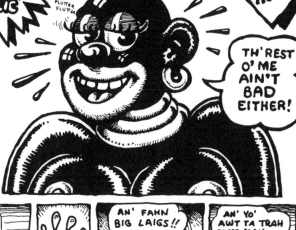

SHE'S "SOCK-A-DELIC"

FLUTTER FLUTTER

"She's All Heart"

TH'REST O' ME AIN'T BAD EITHER!

"ZAP" COMIX **DREAM GIRL** OF THE MONTH

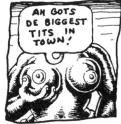

AH GOTS DE BIGGEST TITS IN TOWN!

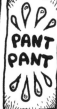

PANT PANT

AN' FAHN BIG LAIGS!!

AN' YO' AWT TA TRAH SOME MAH SWEET JELLYROLL!

MM M!

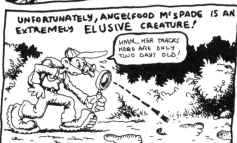

UNFORTUNATELY, ANGELFOOD McSPADE IS AN EXTREMELY ELUSIVE CREATURE!

HMM... HER TRACKS HERE ARE ONLY TWO DAYS OLD!

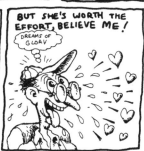

BUT SHE'S WORTH THE EFFORT, BELIEVE ME!

DREAMS OF GLOAV

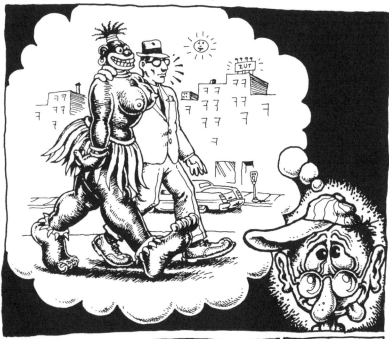

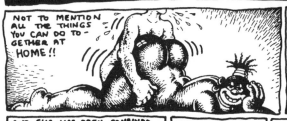

NOT TO MENTION ALL THE THINGS YOU CAN DO TOGETHER AT HOME!!

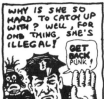

WHY IS SHE SO HARD TO CATCH UP WITH? WELL, FOR ONE THING, SHE'S ILLEGAL!

GET BACK PUNK!

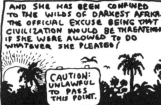

AND SHE HAS BEEN CONFINED TO THE WILDS OF DARKEST AFRICA. THE OFFICIAL EXCUSE BEING THAT CIVILIZATION WOULD BE THREATENED IF SHE WERE ALLOWED TO DO WHATEVER SHE PLEASES!

CAUTION: UNLAWFUL TO PASS THIS POINT.

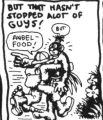

BUT THAT HASN'T STOPPED A LOT OF GUYS!

BUT

ANGEL-FOOD!

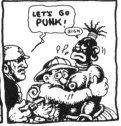

LET'S GO PUNK!

SIGH

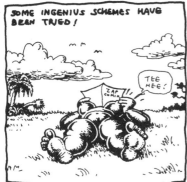

SOME INGENIUS SCHEMES HAVE BEEN TRIED!

ZAP COMIN'

TEE HEE!

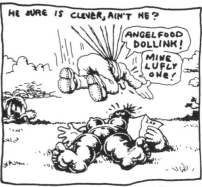

HE SURE IS CLEVER, AIN'T HE?

ANGELFOOD DOLLINK!

MINE LUFLY ONE!

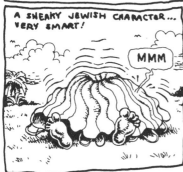

A SNEAKY JEWISH CHARACTER... VERY SMART!

MMM

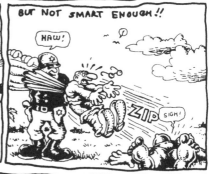

BUT NOT SMART ENOUGH!!

HAW!

ZIP

SIGH!

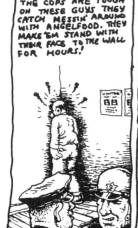

THE COPS ARE TOUGH ON THESE GUYS THEY CATCH MESSIN' AROUND WITH ANGELFOOD. THEY MAKE 'EM STAND WITH THEIR FACE TO THE WALL FOR HOURS!

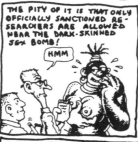

THE PITY OF IT IS THAT ONLY OFFICIALLY SANCTIONED RE-SEARCHERS ARE ALLOWED NEAR THE DARK-SKINNED SEX BOMB!

HMM

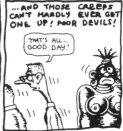

...AND THOSE CREEPS CAN'T HARDLY EVER GET ONE UP! POOR DEVILS!

THAT'S ALL... GOOD DAY!

I MEAN, THERE SHE IS, ALL READY, WILLING, AND ABLE, WITH PLENTY OF WHAT IT TAKES, DYING JUST TO GIVE IT AWAY, BUT NO! THEY INSIST SHE'S TOO HOT TO HANDLE! SHE'S TOO RISKY! SOMETHING MIGHT...UH... HAPPEN!

AH DON'T MAHND A BIT, SO GO AHAID!

265

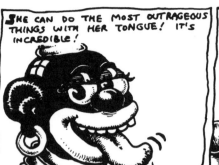

SHE CAN DO THE MOST OUTRAGEOUS THINGS WITH HER TONGUE! IT'S INCREDIBLE!

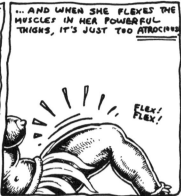

...AND WHEN SHE FLEXES THE MUSCLES IN HER POWERFUL THIGHS, IT'S JUST TOO <u>ATROCIOUS</u>!

FLEX! FLEX!

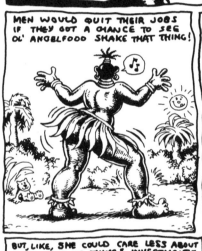

MEN WOULD QUIT THEIR JOBS IF THEY GOT A CHANCE TO SEE OL' ANGELFOOD SHAKE THAT THING!

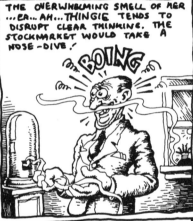

THE OVERWHELMING SMELL OF HER ...ER...AH...THINGIE TENDS TO DISRUPT CLEAR THINKING. THE STOCKMARKET WOULD TAKE A NOSE-DIVE!

BOING

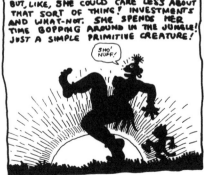

BUT, LIKE, SHE COULD CARE LESS ABOUT THAT SORT OF THING! INVESTMENTS AND WHAT-NOT. SHE SPENDS HER TIME BOPPING AROUND IN THE JUNGLE! JUST A SIMPLE PRIMITIVE CREATURE!

SHO' NUFF!

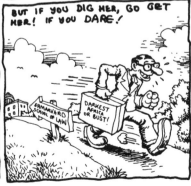

BUT IF YOU DIG HER, GO GET HER! IF YOU DARE!

DARKEST AFRICA OR BUST!

SHMAVARD SCHOOL OF LAW

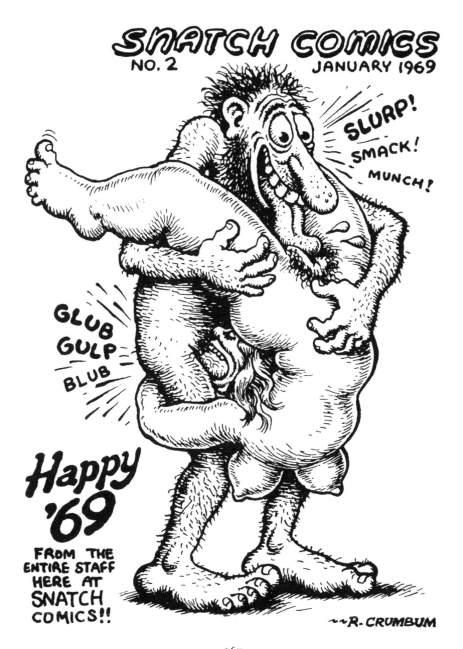

267

The family that LAYS

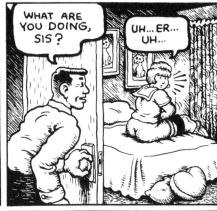

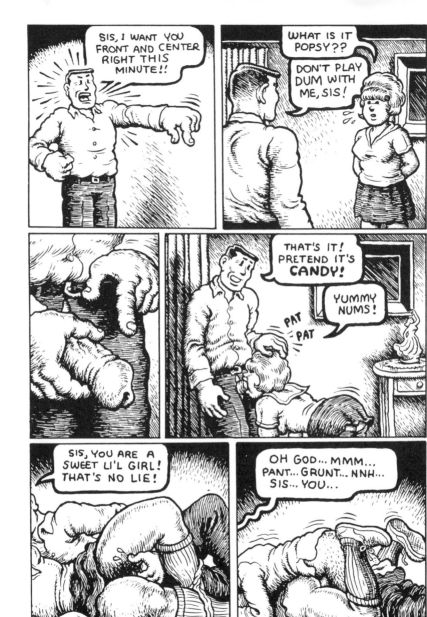

273

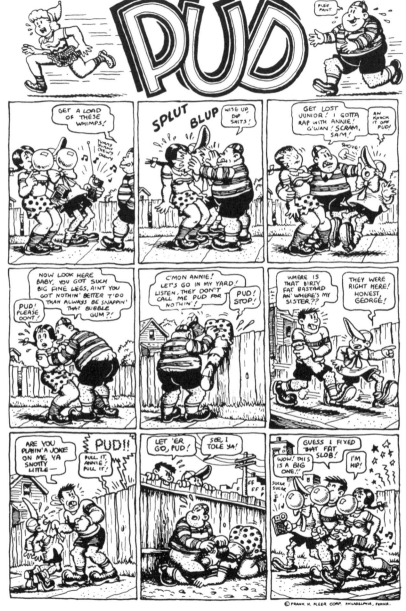

276

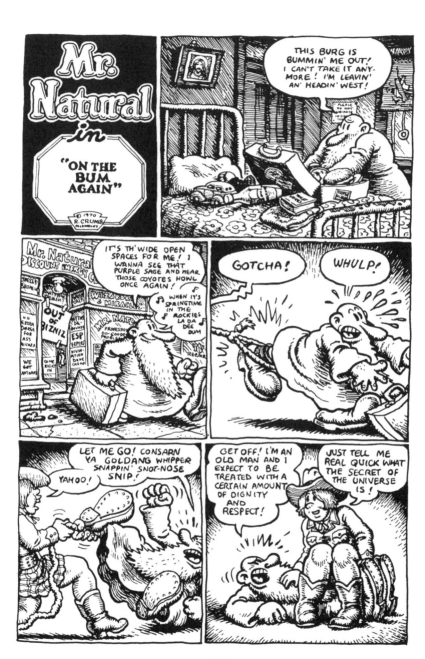

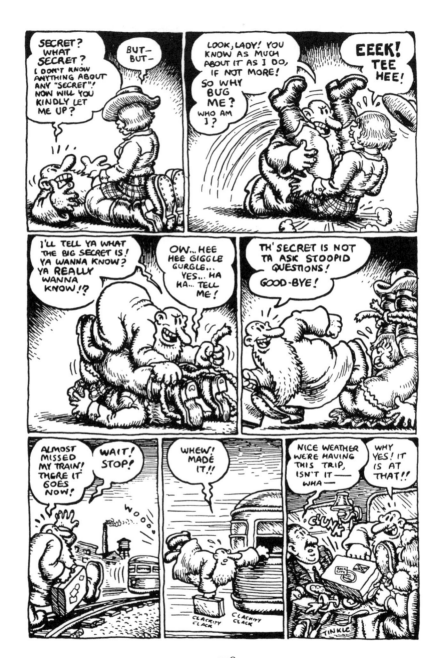

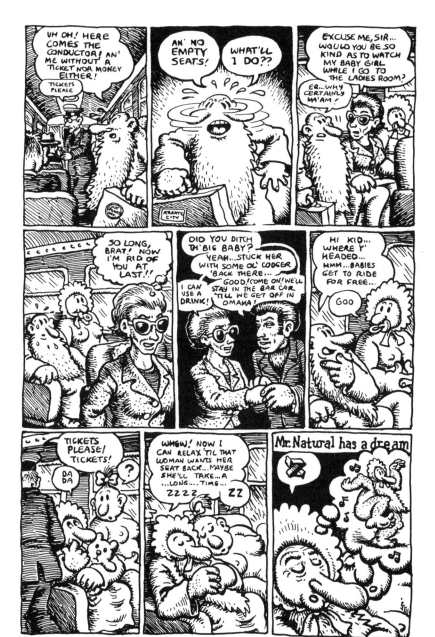

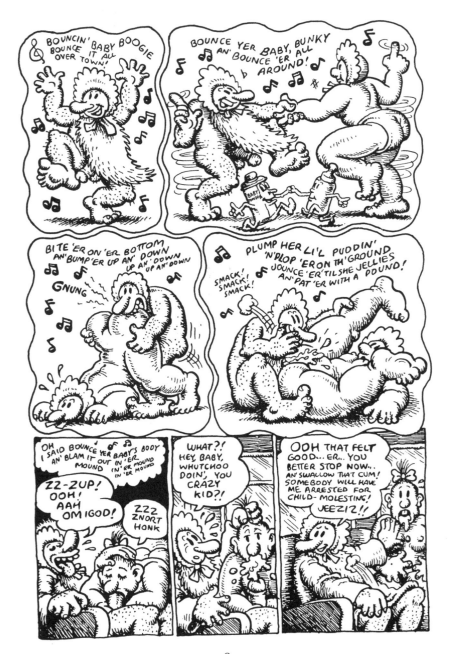

280

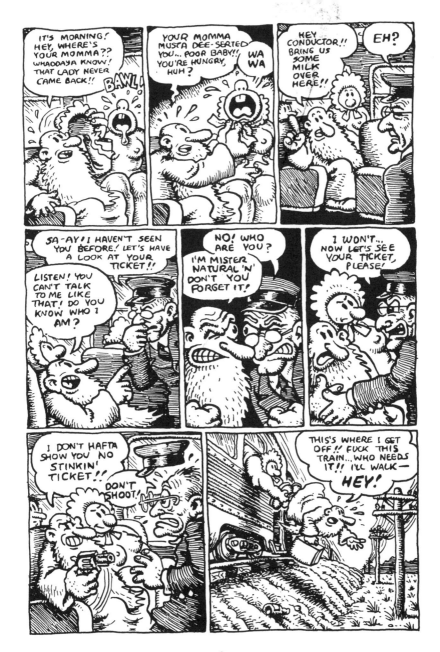

281

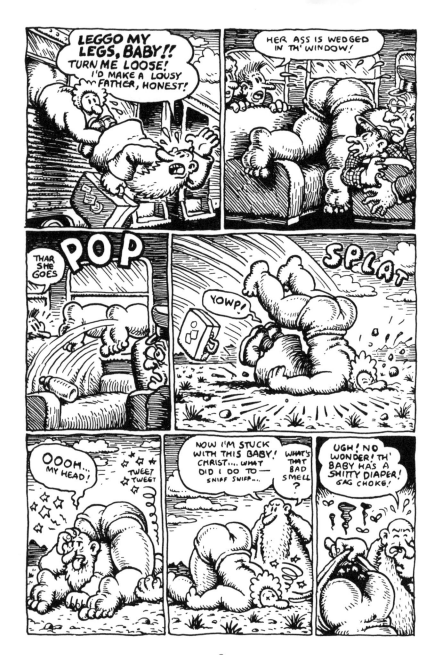

282

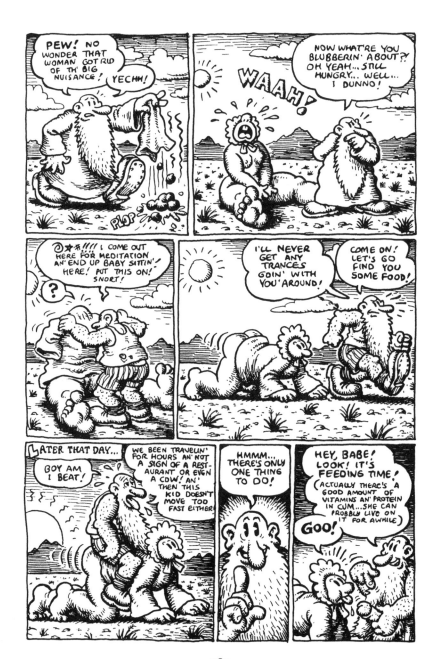

283

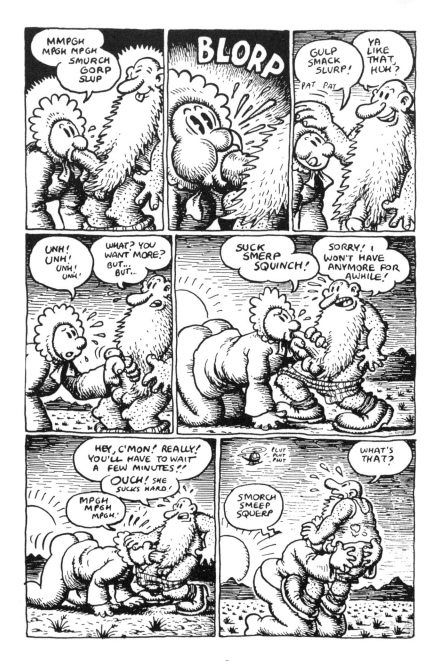

284

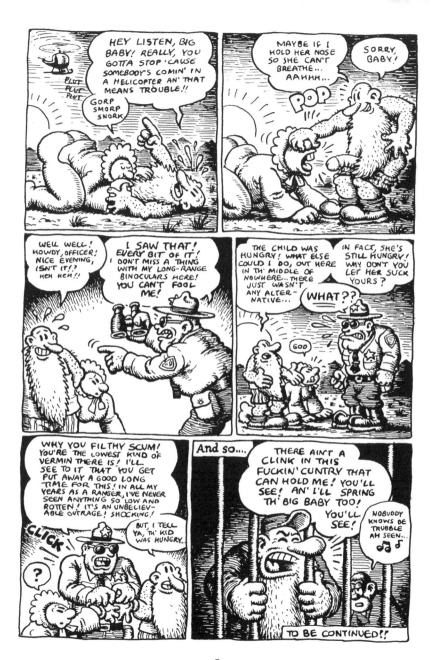

285

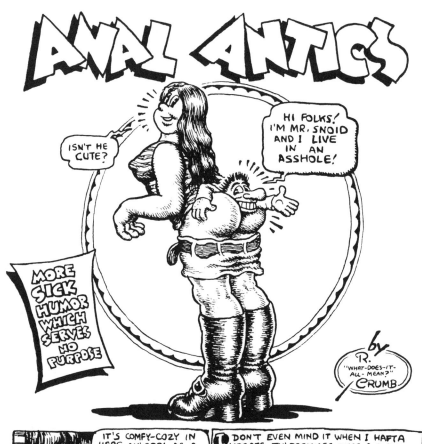

ANAL ANTICS

ISN'T HE CUTE?

HI FOLKS! I'M MR. SNOID AND I LIVE IN AN ASSHOLE!

MORE SICK HUMOR WHICH SERVES NO PURPOSE

by R. "WHAT-DOES-IT-ALL-MEAN?" CRUMB

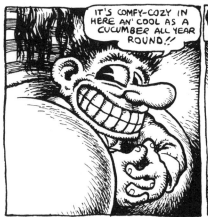

IT'S COMFY-COZY IN HERE AN' COOL AS A CUCUMBER ALL YEAR ROUND!!

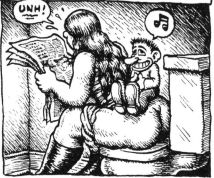

I DON'T EVEN MIND IT WHEN I HAFTA VACATE TH' PREMISES ONCE A DAY WHILE TH' LANDLADY DOES HER BIZNIZ!

UNH!

♪

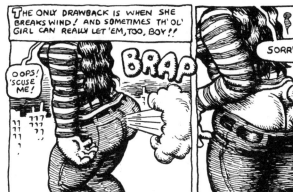

THE ONLY DRAWBACK IS WHEN SHE BREAKS WIND! AND SOMETIMES TH' OL' GIRL CAN REALLY LET 'EM, TOO, BOY!!

OOPS! 'SCUSE ME!

BRAP

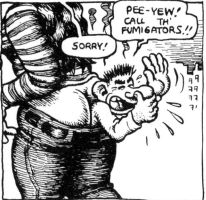

PEE-YEW! CALL TH' FUMIGATORS!!

SORRY!

MOST OF THE TIME LIFE IN AN ASSHOLE IS TH' GOOD LIFE... THERE'S ALWAYS SOMETHING DOING... LIKE WHEN SHE GOES SKINNY-DIPPING!!

OH TH' SAILOR'S LIFE IS TH' LIFE FOR ME!

HA HA HA

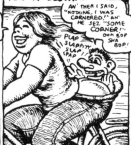

OR WHEN SHE'S RIDING HER BYCICLE, I AMUSE HER WITH OLD JOKES AND GENERALLY PLAY TH' CLOWN...

AN' THEN I SAID, "NOTHING, I WAS CORNERED!" AN' HE SEZ "SOME CORNER!" OOM BOP SHA BOP!

PLAP SLAPPITY SLAP! SPAP!

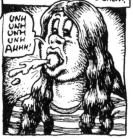

WHEN I GET TO ITCHIN' FOR A LITTLE NOOKY, I JUS' CRAWL ON UP RIGHT THROUGH HER INTESTINAL TRACK, THROUGH HER STOMACH AND UP HER THROAT, THEN SHE PUCKERS UP AN' I FUCK HER MOUTH FROM TH' INSIDE! IT'S GREAT!

UNH UNH UNH UNH AHHH!

AH YES! IT MIGHT BE JUST ANOTHER BUNG-HOLE TO YOU, BUT IT'S HOME-SWEET-HOME FOR ME!!

ZZ ZZ

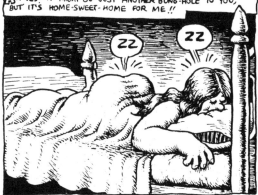

THE SAD PART OF THIS STORY IS THAT THIS VERY NIGHT THERE ARE SNOIDS OUT WALKING THE STREETS, COLD AND LONELY!

BRRR! WISH I HAD A NICE SWEET LI'L ASSHOLE TO SNUGGLE UP INSIDE OF!

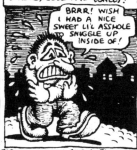

WHY DON'T YOU GIVE A SNOID A HOME IN YOUR ASSHOLE TODAY!!

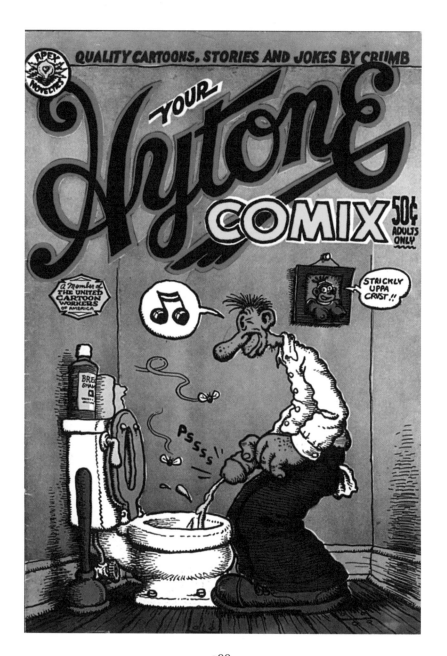

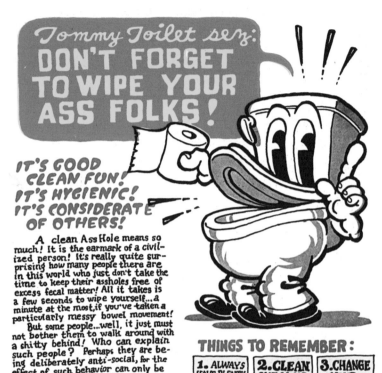

Tommy Toilet sez:

DON'T FORGET TO WIPE YOUR ASS FOLKS!

IT'S GOOD CLEAN FUN! IT'S HYGIENIC! IT'S CONSIDERATE OF OTHERS!

A clean Ass Hole means so much! It is the earmark of a civilized person! It's really quite surprising how many people there are in this world who just don't take the time to keep their assholes free of excess fecal matter! All it takes is a few seconds to wipe yourself...a minute at the most, if you've taken a particularly messy bowel movement!

But some people...well, it just must not bother them to walk around with a shitty behind! Who can explain such people? Perhaps they are being deliberately anti-social, for the effect of such behavior can only be to make a person friendless and a social outcast. You might not mind the smell of your own shit (in fact, many people like it!), but let's face it, nobody but a pervert likes to smell other people's excrement! So take Tommy's advice... keep it wiped!!

THINGS TO REMEMBER:

1. ALWAYS HAVE PLENTY OF YOUR FAVORITE BRAND OF **TOILET TISSUE** ON HAND!

2. CLEAN OUT YOUR TOILET BOWL EVERY ONCE IN AWHILE!

3. CHANGE YOUR UNDERPANTS AT LEAST TWICE A WEEK!

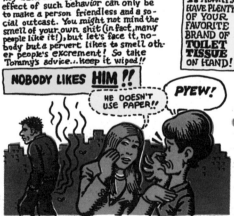

NOBODY LIKES HIM!!

HE DOESN'T USE PAPER!!

PYEW!

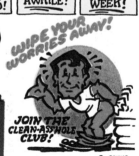

WIPE YOUR WORRIES AWAY!

JOIN THE CLEAN-ASSHOLE CLUB!

R. CRUMB

CARL BARKS
DONALD DUCK CARTOONIST

A thought came to me the other day ... about my influence on the underground comics. The thing that is most important about my comics is this: I told it like it is. I told the kids that the bad guys have a little good in them, and the good guys have a lot of bad in them, and that you just couldn't depend on anything much, that nothing was going to always turn out roses. In fact I laid it right on the line that there was no difference between my comic characters and the life these kids—the readers—were going to have to face. So when Donald had some adventures, and he got buffeted around, I tried to put it over in a way that the kids—the readers—could see, well, that could happen to them. It was the way life goes. I just didn't disguise anything or make things rosy.

... As for "Superman" and all those type of stories, they were quite an artificial thing. They did have a little bit of the human element in them, where Superman was trying to keep his identity secret from Lois Lane. In most of the fighting and menaces and all, it was just complete fabrication. It didn't seem to me to have much depth. It certainly had no parallel in human experience. My own stories—they had parallels in human experience.

from *"Carl Barks, Telling It Like It Is,"* 1973 interview by Donald Ault,
reprinted in *Carl Barks: Conversations,* 2003

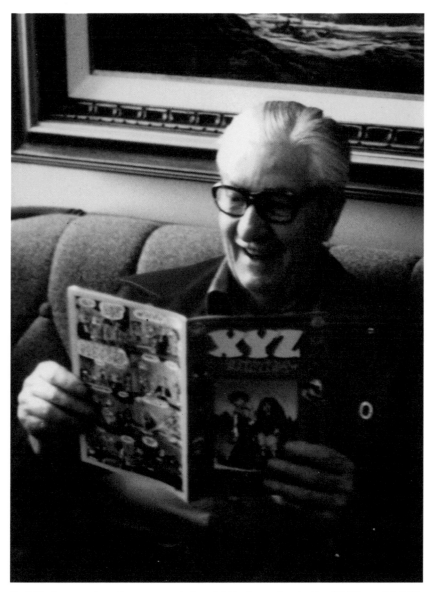

Carl Barks, creator of many great *Donald Duck* comics in the 1940s and 1950s, reading a R. Crumb comic, 1980s

WE INTERRUPT THIS STORY NOW BECAUSE...

MR. NATURAL WANTS TO *TALK* TO YOU!

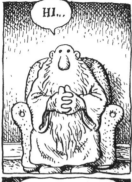

HI...

GOSH, WHAT'S GONNA HAPPEN TO POOR LI'L MO-RON?! WE'LL FIND OUT IN A MINUTE OR TWO, BUT FIRST, THERE'S SOMETHING I THINK YOU SHOULD BE AWARE OF...

Y'KNOW, IT'S FUNNY, ISN'T IT? EVEN THOUGH THIS IS ONLY *LINES* ON *PAPER* I'M ACTUALLY *TALKING* TO YOU... SORTA *MIRACULOUS,* WHEN YOU STOP TO THINK ABOUT IT...

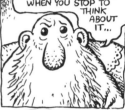

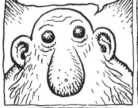

FOR THIS MOMENT IN TIME, I HAVE YOUR ATTENTION... *I* HAVE *YOUR ATTENTION!*

DID YOU KNOW THAT *ATTENTION* IS *POWER*?!

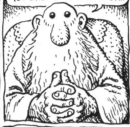

DID THAT EVER OCCUR TO YOU BEFORE? PROBABLY NOT, BECAUSE, LET'S BE HONEST, YOU'RE ACTUALLY NOT TOO BRIGHT— KIND OF A DIM BULB, REALLY... YOU KNOW IN YOUR HEART IT'S TRUE, PAINFUL AS IT IS TO ADMIT...

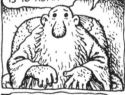

YOUR IDEAS ARE A LOT OF HALF-BAKED, WARMED-OVER BANALITIES, ISN'T THAT SO?? EVERYBODY KNOWS IT! BE-HIND YOUR BACK ALL YOUR SO-CALLED FRIENDS JOKE ABOUT WHAT A LONG-WIND-ED *BORE* YOU ARE! NO, REALLY!

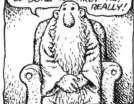

OF COURSE, NO ONE WOULD *DARE* TELL YOU THE *TRUTH,* BECAUSE YOU'RE OH-SO-SENS-*ITIVE!* BUT THE TRULY EM-BARRASSING PART IS HOW *HIP* AND *COOL* YOU THINK YOU ARE! OH MAN, WHAT A TRAVESTY! IF I WERE YOU I'D HIDE MY FACE IN *SHAME.!!*

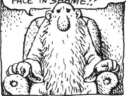

NAH! JUST KIDDING! YOU KNOW THAT COULDN'T *POSSIBLY* BE TRUE! COME ON, ONLY A PERSON OF EX-CEPTIONAL DISCERNMENT WOULD EVEN BE READING THIS ESOTERIC, HARD-TO-FIND COMIC-BOOK IN THE FIRST PLACE! THAT'S OBVIOUS, ISN'T IT? SURE IT IS! AW COME ON, *LAFF IT OFF.!!*

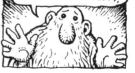

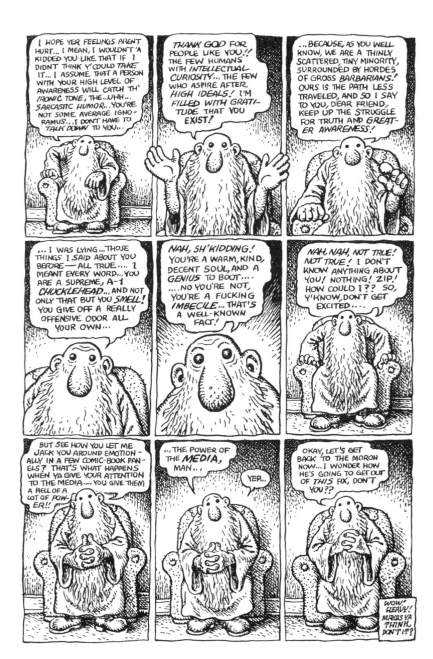

ROBERT HUGHES
Time Magazine ART CRITIC

I think that Crumb, basically, he is the Brueghel of the last half of the 20th century. I mean, there was no Brueghel of the first half, but there is one of the last half and that is Robert Crumb because he gives you that tremendous kind of impaction of lusting, suffering, crazed humanity in all sorts of desired gargoyle like allegorical forms. He's just got this very powerful imagination which goes right over the top a lot of the time, but it very seldom lies.

I think he is a very remarkable artist indeed. The tradition I see him belonging to is essentially the one of say, graphic art as social protest, social criticism, which, of course, has extremely long roots, and goes way back. I see elements of Goya in Crumb ... Goya's sense of monstrosity comes out in those menacing bird-headed women of Crumb's, for instance.

Crumb's material comes out of a deep sense of the absurdity of human life. At a certain kind of psychological level there aren't any heroes, there aren't any villains, there aren't any heroines and even the victims are comic. And I think it is this which people in America find rather hard to take because it conflicts with their basic feelings of a mixture of utopianism on one hand and puritanism on the other (which is just another form of utopianism) which has given us the kind of messy discourse which we have today. So naturally, Crumb, like all great satirists, is somewhat an outsider in his own country today.

interviewed in Terry Zwigoff's film Crumb, 1994

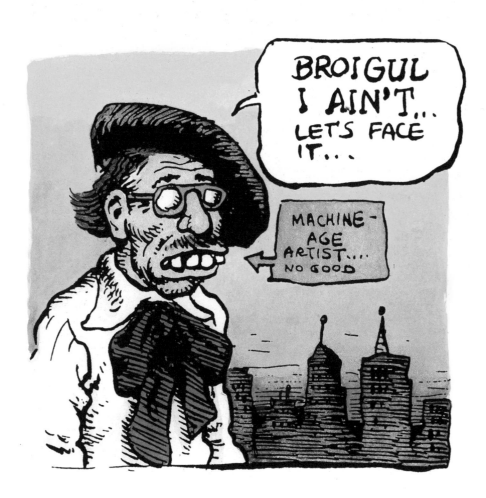

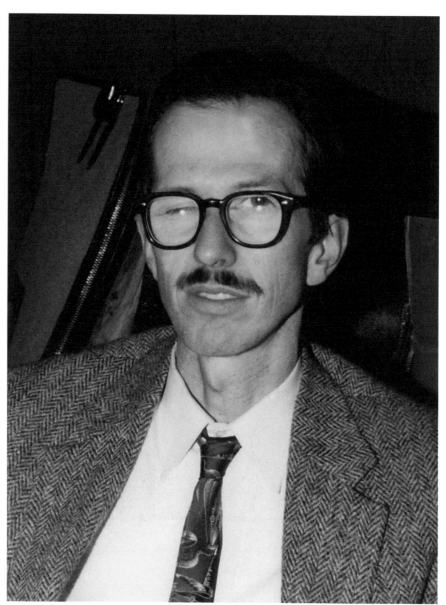

R. Crumb, 1980s

Chapter 6

Kicked Upstairs!

The fine art world and the commercial art industry are both all about money. It's hard to say which is more contemptible: the fine art world with its double talk and pretensions to the cultural high ground, or the world of commercial art trying to sell to the largest mass market it can reach. A serious artist really shouldn't be too deeply involved in either of these worlds. It's best to be on the fringe of them.

In general, if you want to be a success and make the big money, you have to play the game. It's no different in the fine art world, it's just a slightly different game. Essentially, you're marketing an illusion. It's much easier to lie to humans and trick them than to tell them the truth. They'd much rather be bamboozled than be told the truth, because the way to trick them is to flatter them and tell them what they want to hear, to reinforce their existing illusions. They don't *want* to know the truth. Truth is a bring-down, a bummer, or it's just too complicated, too much mental work to grasp.

Curators and gallery people are not oriented toward cartoons, comics, or commercial art. That world is quite alien to them.

Now, through complex circumstances, they have decided that I am somebody worth promoting and displaying in galleries and museums. My work has some value economically, and then, too, I've been around a long time. I'm sixty years old. There has been a successful movie made about me. Reputable critics have praised my work, all of which has validated me to some degree to the museum and gallery people.

Otherwise, I'm not sure that they really appreciate what my work is all about. I'm not sure that they really know what they're looking at. I've talked with them about it and we just don't have the same background. They come from an entirely different school. Whatever they see in my work and praise about it comes from this other mentality.

I think for the most part they are buying into my work because of this critical acclaim. They'll turn around and say the very same things about Gerhard Richter or Cy Twombly ... Geez, what that guy can do with a few scribbles! I don't understand how they can fit me into the same mental space along with Cy Twombly. It's a mystery to me.

I love the work of Norman Rockwell, Reginald Marsh, Thomas Hart Benton, and Edward Hopper. They all did illustrative work. Hopper, for years, split his week between doing commercial work and personal work. I like the social realists, surrealists, and expressionists of the 1920s and 1930s, but you lose me with post-war abstract expressionism.

The "fine" art after World War II doesn't do it for me. It just seems lifeless, a posture, a pose. Jackson Pollock, Willem DeKooning, on down to pop art, performance art, minimalism, whatever ... I don't get what it's about. You're supposed to express yourself, but you're not supposed to say anything?—or, certainly, nothing that's too obvious? If your statement is too straightforward, easily grasped, then it's not "fine art," or what?

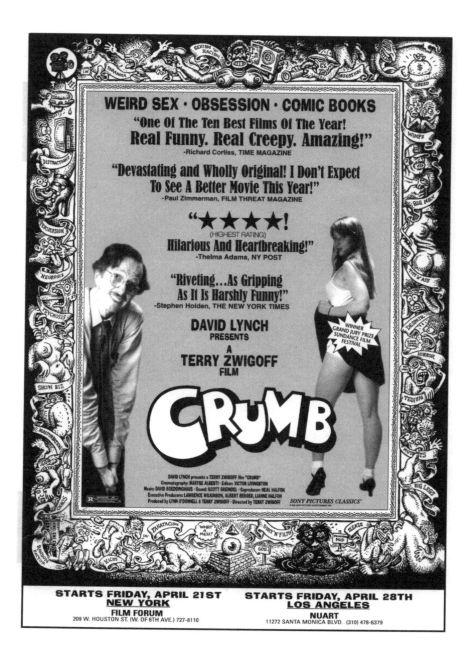

WEIRD SEX · OBSESSION · COMIC BOOKS

"One Of The Ten Best Films Of The Year!
Real Funny. Real Creepy. Amazing!"
-Richard Corliss, TIME MAGAZINE

"Devastating and Wholly Original! I Don't Expect
To See A Better Movie This Year!"
-Paul Zimmerman, FILM THREAT MAGAZINE

"★★★★!
(HIGHEST RATING)
Hilarious And Heartbreaking!"
-Thelma Adams, NY POST

"Riveting...As Gripping
As It Is Harshly Funny!"
-Stephen Holden, THE NEW YORK TIMES

DAVID LYNCH
PRESENTS
A
TERRY ZWIGOFF
FILM

CRUMB

WINNER
GRAND JURY PRIZE
SUNDANCE FILM
FESTIVAL

DAVID LYNCH presents a TERRY ZWIGOFF film "CRUMB"
Cinematography: MARYSE ALBERTI · Editor: VICTOR LIVINGSTON
Music: DAVID BOEDDINGHAUS · Sound: SCOTT BRENDEL · Coproducer: NEAL HALFON
Executive Producers: LAWRENCE WILKINSON, ALBERT BERGER, LIANNE HALFON
Produced by LYNN O'DONNELL & TERRY ZWIGOFF · Directed by TERRY ZWIGOFF

SONY PICTURES CLASSICS™

Many people have congratulated me just because my work has appeared on the covers of *Art Forum* and *Art News,* and because the various shows I've had were seriously reviewed in them. What are they saying in these art magazines? Beats the hell out of me! You read it, I can't!

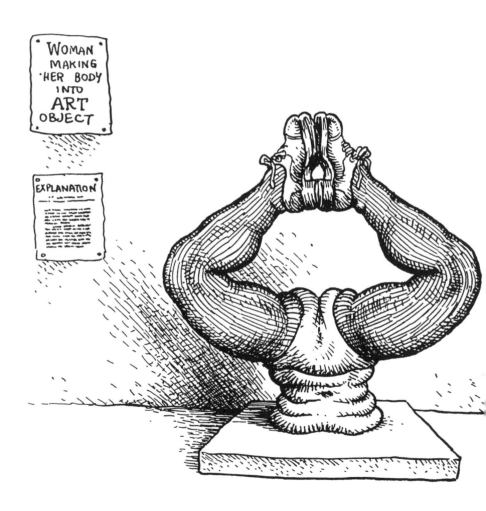

WOMAN MAKING HER BODY INTO ART OBJECT

EXPLANATION

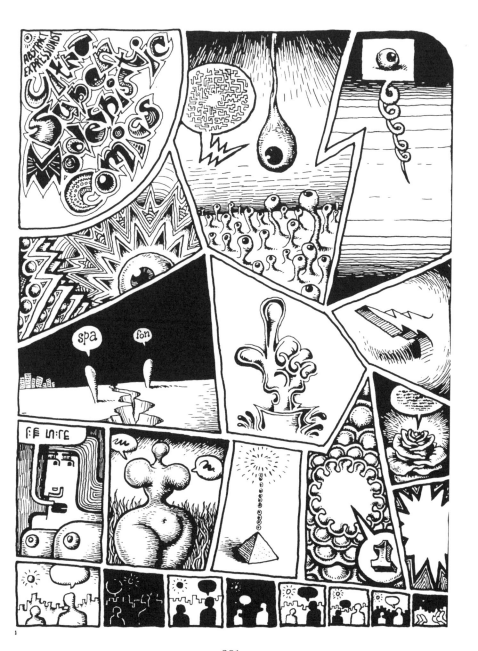

301

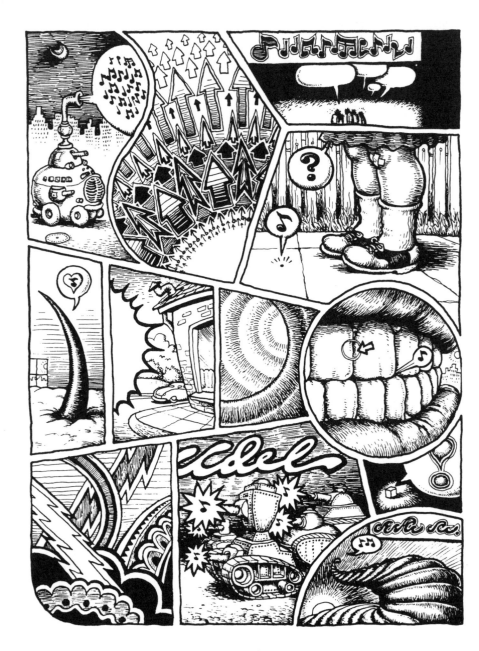

302

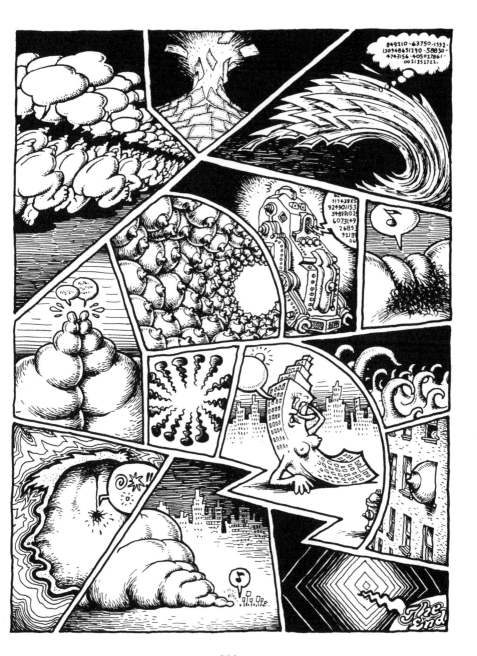

303

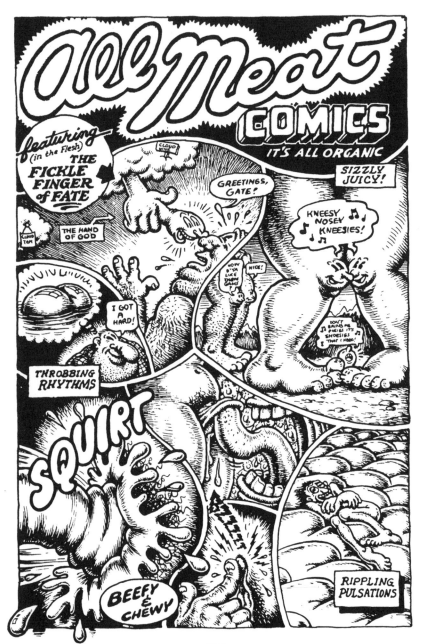

304

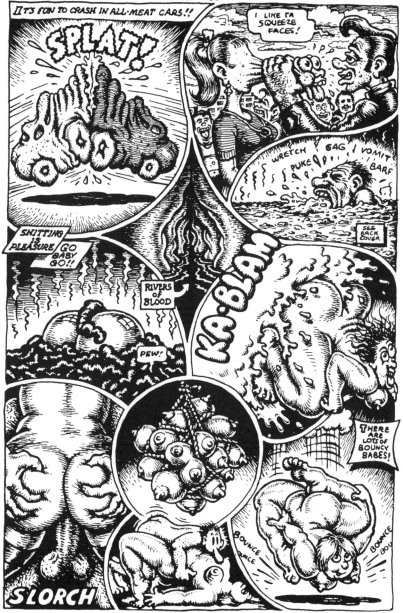

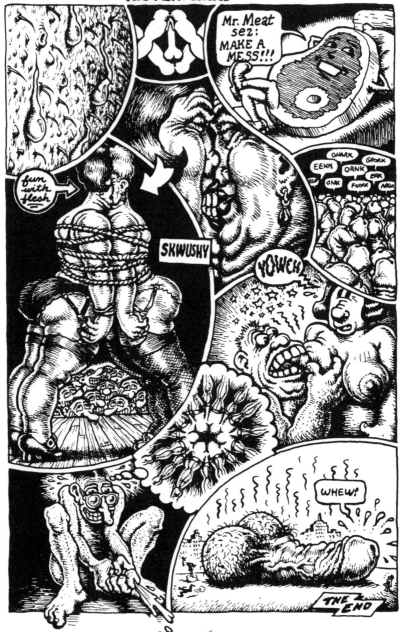

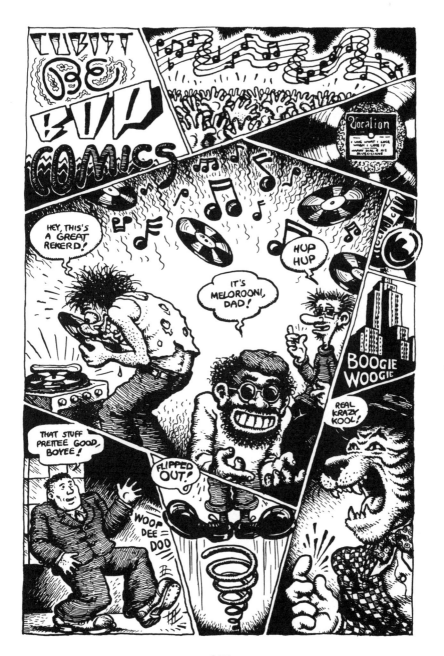

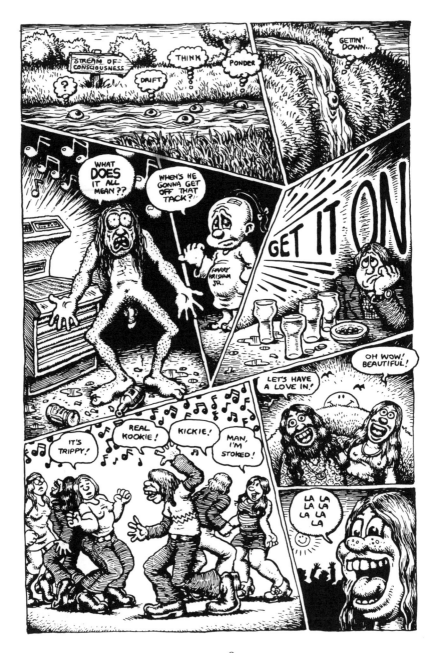

308

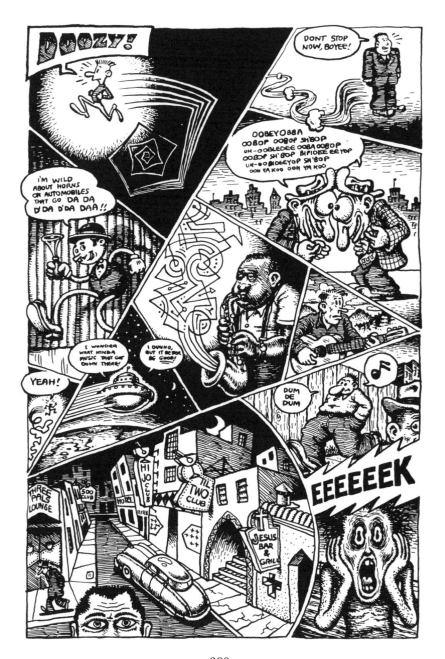

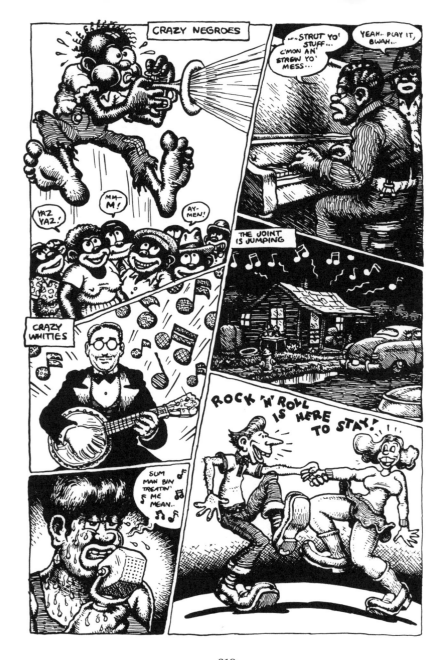

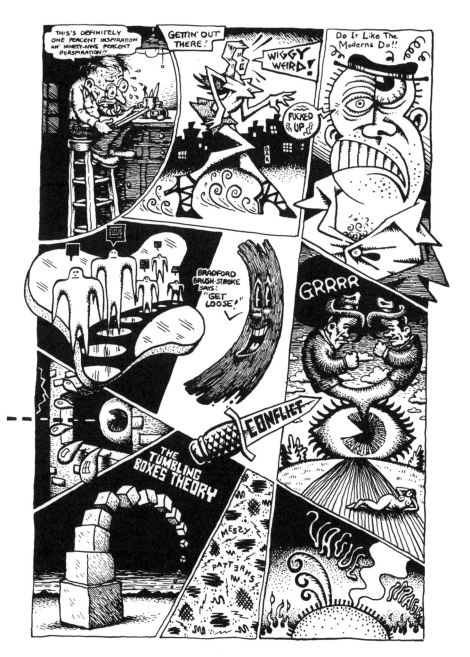

311

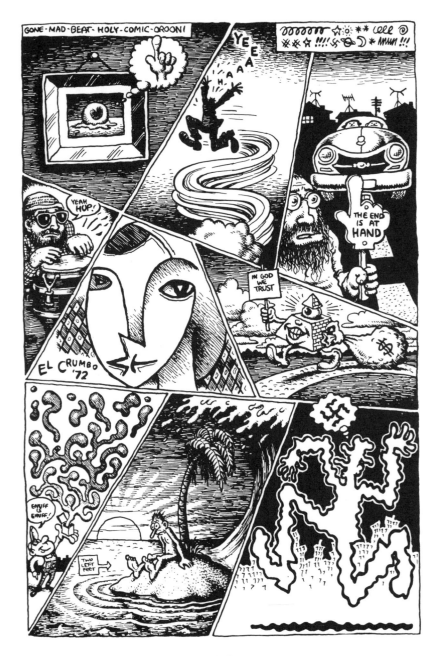

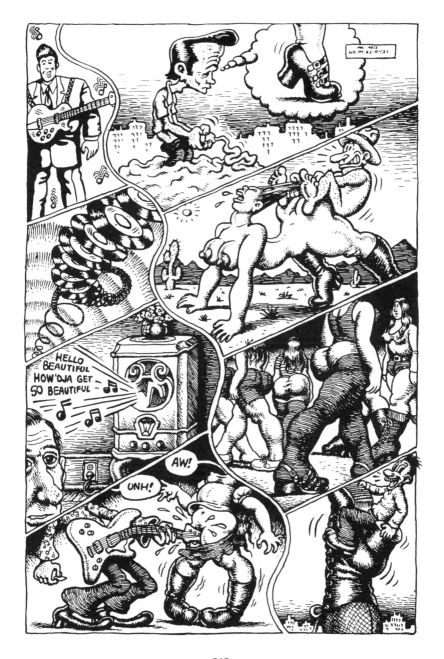

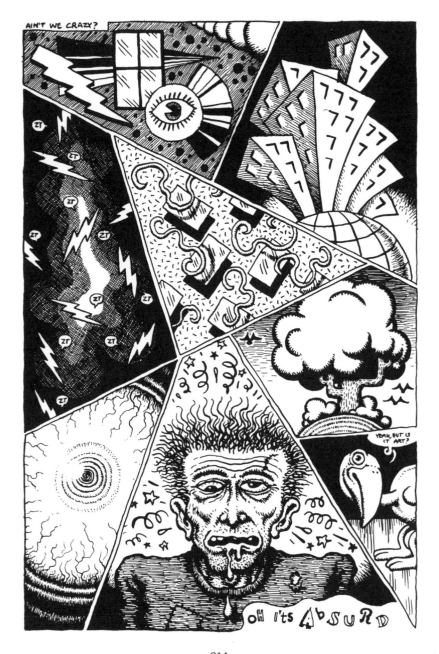

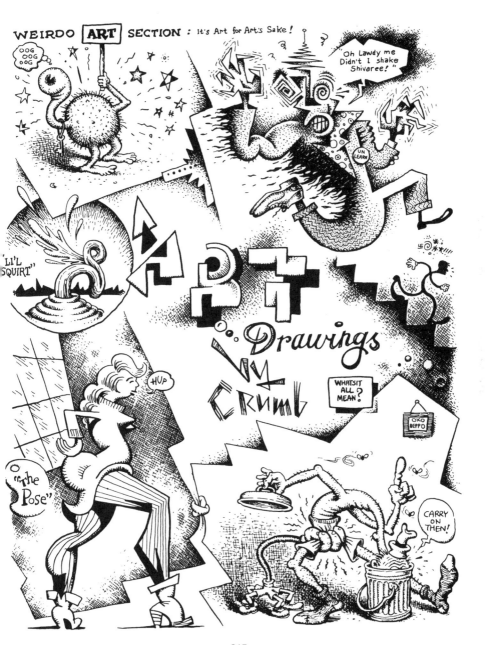

315

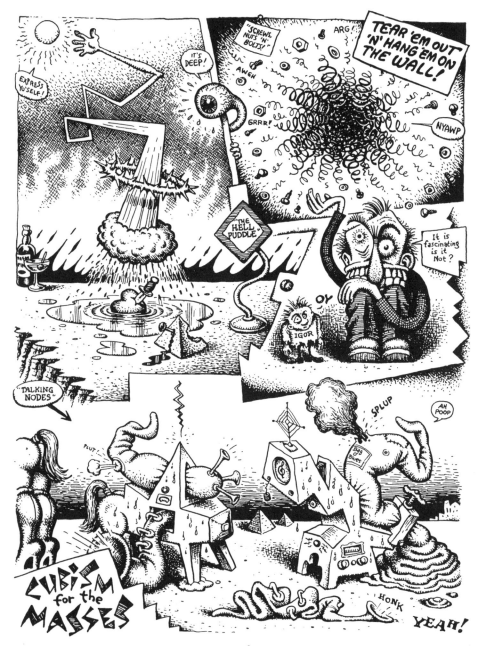

316

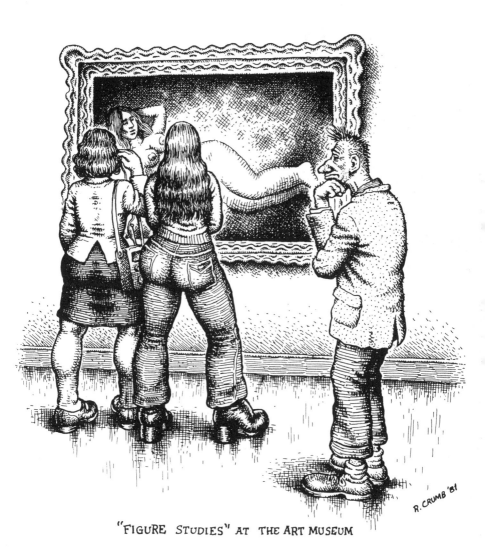

"FIGURE STUDIES" AT THE ART MUSEUM

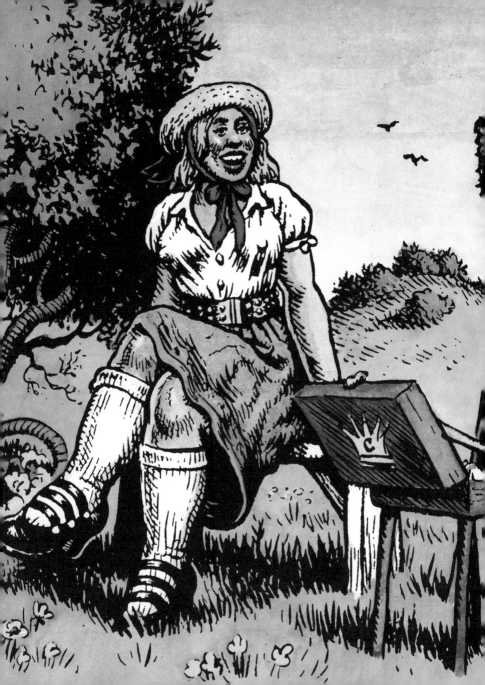

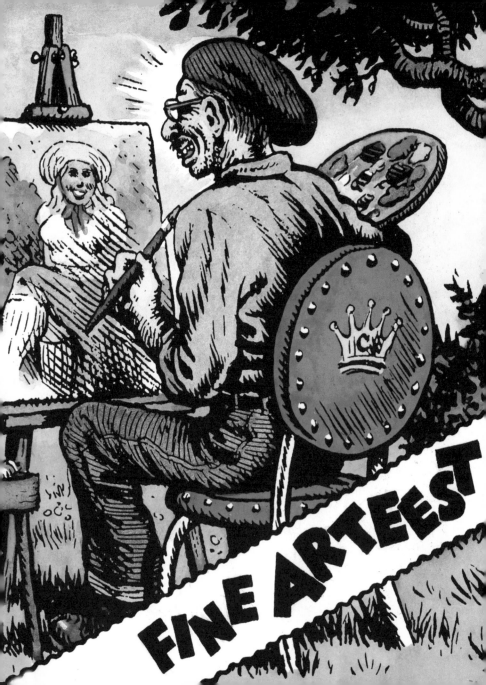

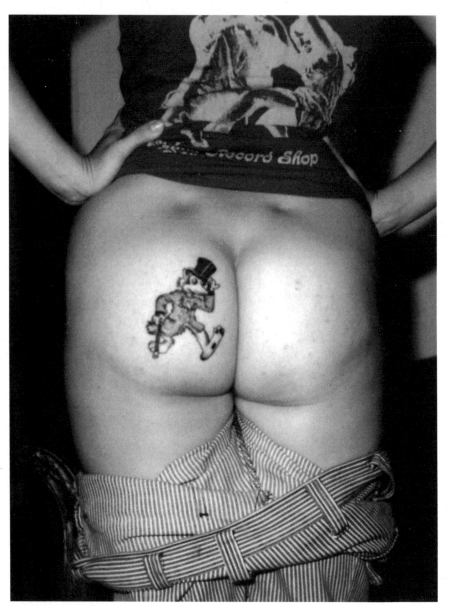

Tattoos designed by R. Crumb

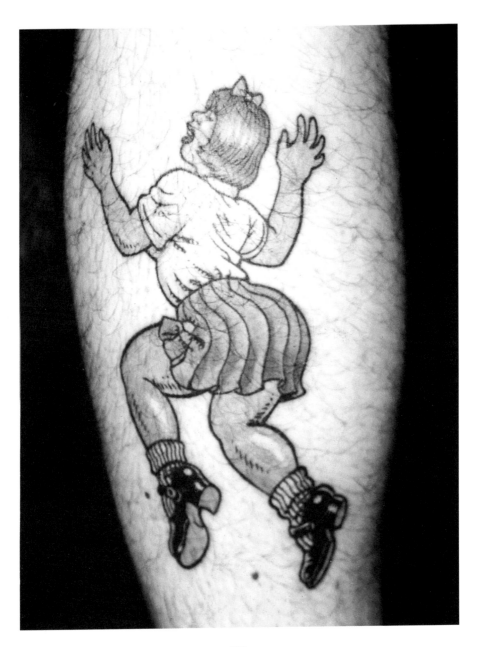

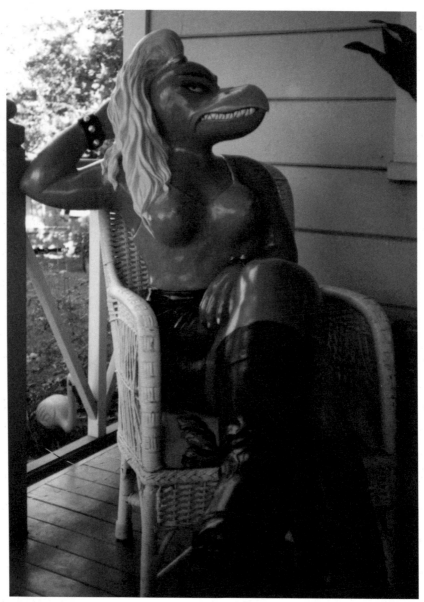

Life-size statue of *Vulture Goddess* made by R. Crumb, 1990

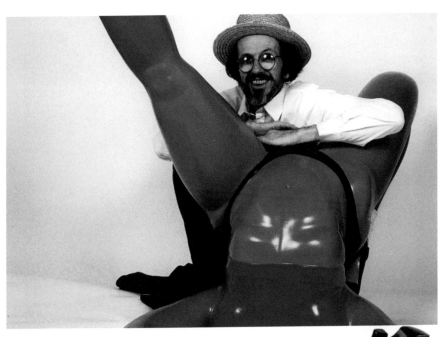

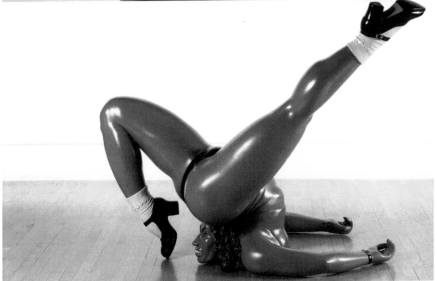

Crumb with *Devil Girl* statue, made in 1996

323

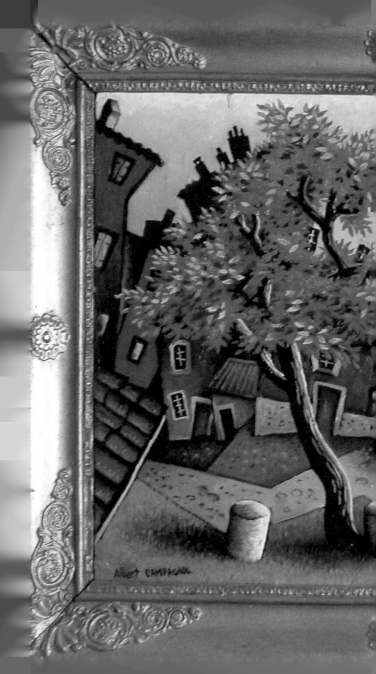

Albert CAMPAGNA

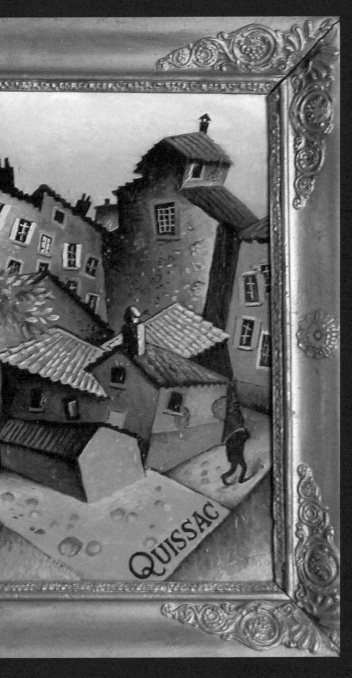

Old oil painting from the flea market reworked by Crumb, late 1990s

Next page: Another old oil painting reworked by Crumb, *circa* 2000

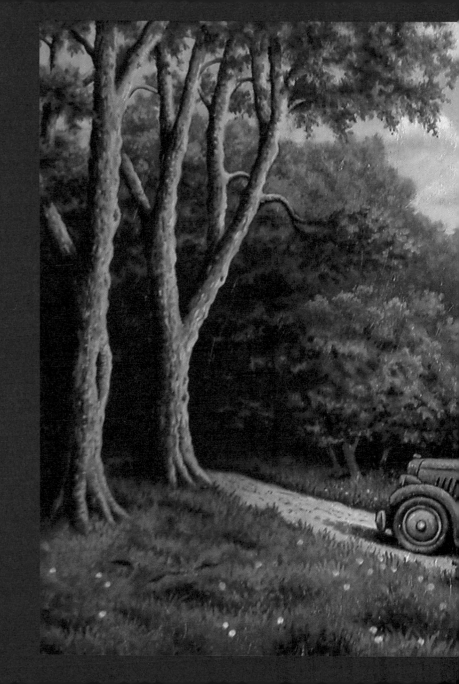

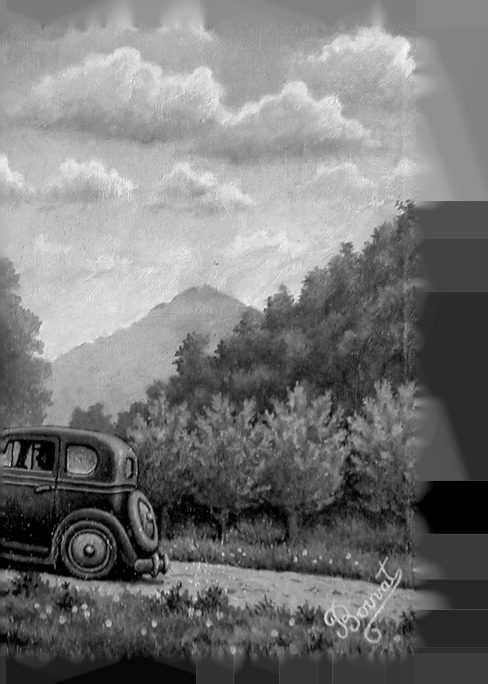

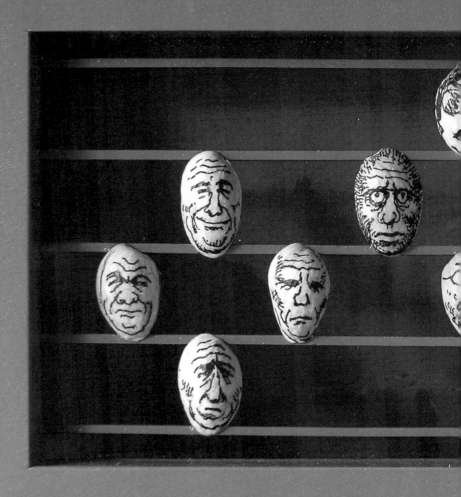

Faces drawn on pistachio nut shells by R. Crumb,
mounted by Raoul Philip, 2004

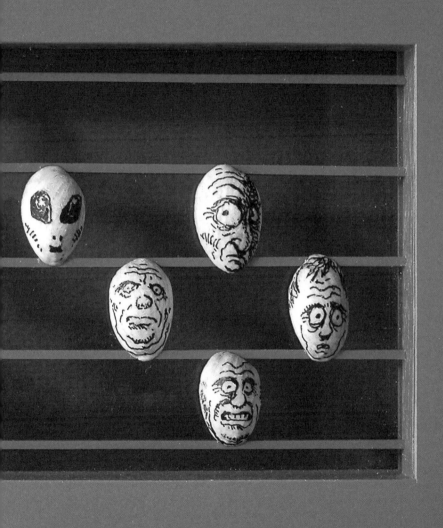

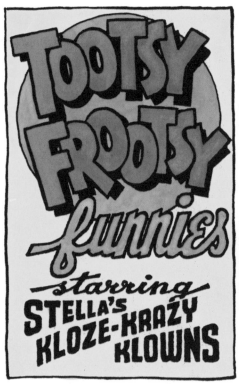

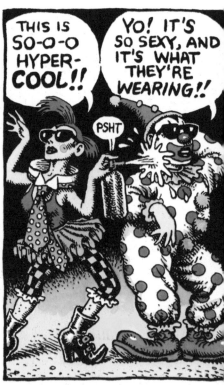

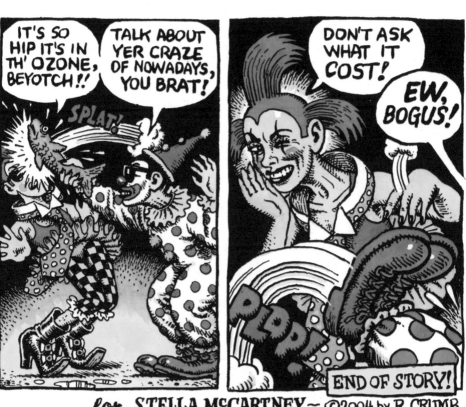

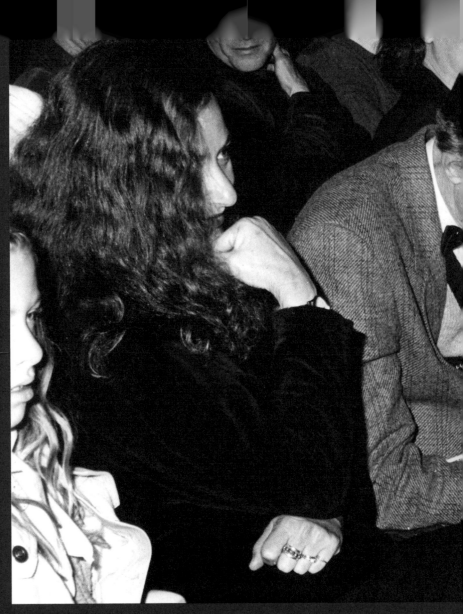

Sophie, Aline, and R. Crumb at the Teylers Museum, Haarlem, Holland.

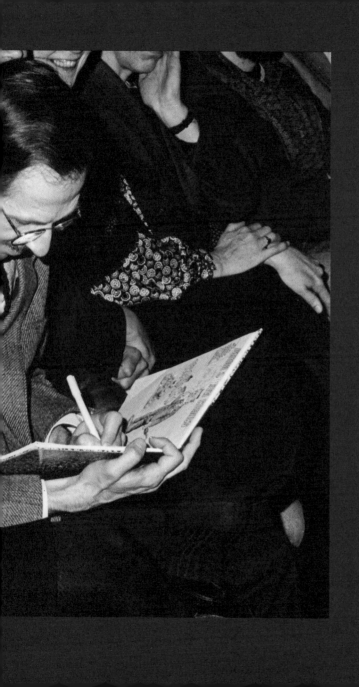
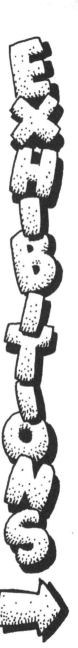

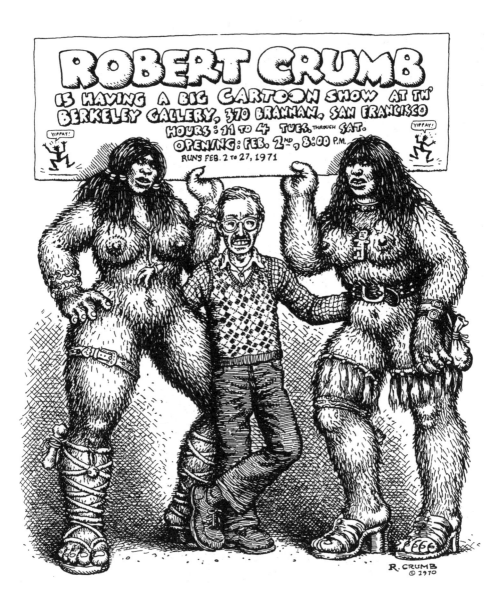

334

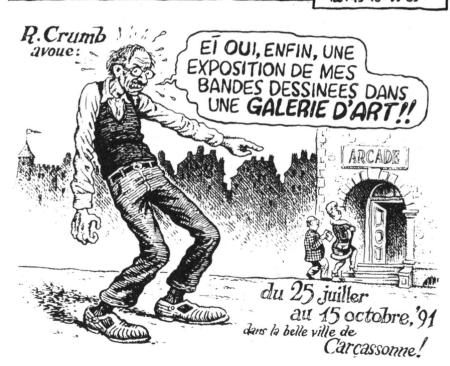

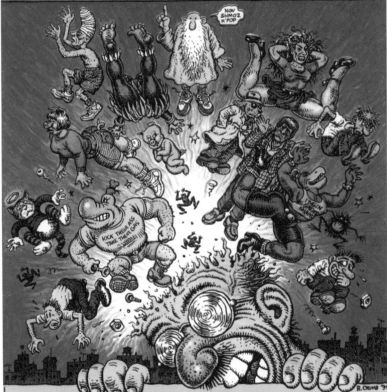

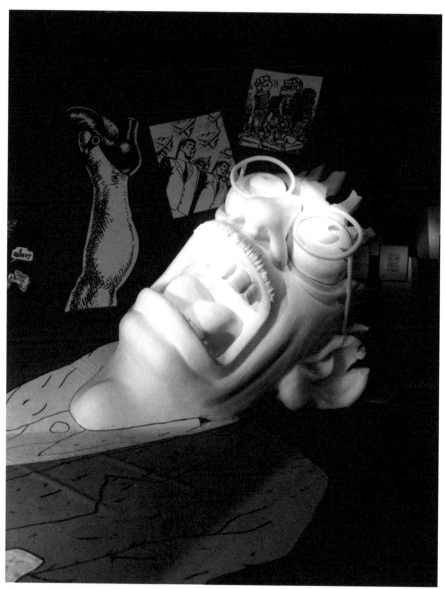

Huge walk-in head built for R. Crumb exhibit at Angoulême Comics Festival, France, 1992, organized by Jean-Pierre Mercier

JEAN-PIERRE MERCIER
C.N.B.D.I. (NATIONAL CENTER FOR COMICS AND IMAGE) ANGOULÊME, FRANCE

When I was a small comics publisher in the 1970s, there was a joke we would play on the comics fans every year. We had a small booth set up at the Angoulême Comics Festival and we'd get a beautiful girl to go on the loud speaker and announce to everyone that Robert Crumb would be signing books at our table. One hundred people would immediately come over to our booth to see him. Robert, of course, was not there. We pulled this joke year after year and it always worked. French people knew Robert's work from ACTUEL an alternative culture magazine, and they were desperate to meet him.

I met Robert in 1985, when he was on tour and visited the festival. One by one, all the comics artists came up and asked, "Is that really Robert Crumb?" This time it wasn't a joke.

When the Crumbs moved permanently to the south of France in 1990, I was now working for the Comics Center. I went to the director and told him we should do a Crumb exhibition. He said, "Why not?" It took a couple of years to convince everyone else. We decided to make the theme of the 1992 festival, the trends that were developing in the American comics scene. Robert's exhibition "Le Monde Selon Crumb" ("The World According to Crumb") would be part of this American theme. We had a really good budget and I worked with a designer named Corbex who created the exhibition sets, environments you could also call them, which reflected the various themes in Robert's work.

An exhibition is a tricky thing to create. You have to tell a story. It's made to be enjoyed like that. We wanted to sum up Robert's career to 1992. Some people thought he was dead. We wanted to prove he was still active. I read all of Robert's work several times, noting the themes he kept returning to over and over at different times in his career. Corbex kept demanding visual ideas. I had made files and there was a recurring image of an exploding head. When we had a meeting at Gilbert Shelton's apartment, Corbex came in with a shoe box containing a model of a sculpture of Robert's head exploding. Robert saw it and said, "Oh my God!"

The model was enlarged to fifteen feet high and became the first room of the exhibition: a giant Crumb head exploding into different rooms and themes. America, nostalgia, sex, music, and Robert and Aline's work together, were topics that had their own sets. The exhibition was like a circus. Robert played in concert with his musician friends, "Les Primitifs du Futur," at the opening. The Salle Nemo was totally packed. I thought there was going to be a riot. The exhibition received a very enthusiastic reaction. It toured to another part of France, Finland and Germany. People still talk about it. The catalog I put together is a good memory of the show.

In 1999 Robert was voted, by all the French comics artists, the winner of the Grand Prix of Angoulême, which meant he had to be President of the Comic Festival for 2000 and have another exhibition. "Qui a Peur de Robert Crumb?" ("Who's Afraid of Robert Crumb?") was the title of this show and I also did the catalog. Again, it was another memorable event.

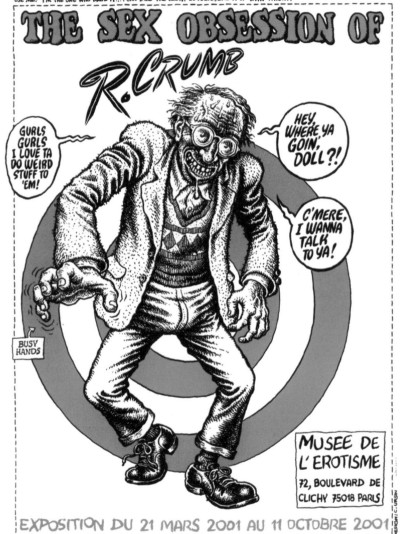

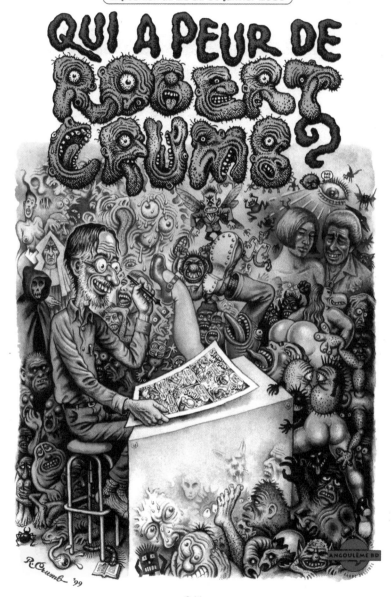

PAUL MORRIS
THE PAUL MORRIS GALLERY, NEW YORK

I show mostly drawings and photographs in my gallery in New York. I wanted to show Robert Crumb for years as he is an extraordinary draftsman. He brought up very charged subjects years before many younger artists who are celebrated for their approach to difficult material. There is not much of a filter between Robert's mind and pen. Robert anticipated a lot of work that gets a great deal of attention in museum and gallery shows. It was only a matter of time before the fine art world acknowledged Robert with the same attention as the publishing world.

My first show with Robert was a three person exhibition that included Barry McGee at the emerging end of the spectrum and Philip Guston as the established old guard, with Robert in the middle both in age and acclaim. Together they all looked very fresh in their approaches to a "down and out, sad sack" sort of figuration.

To one extent or another all three artists celebrated the alienated or marginalized figure. McGee's south of Market Street bums, and Guston's lumpish Klansmen seemed the perfect company for Robert's cast of eccentric figures that addressed everything from Robert's existential questioning with "Mr.Natural," to his sexual fantasies, articulated through the firmly packed "Devil Girl."

If I were to expand the list of artists that in one way or another have a relationship to Robert's work I would include Raymond Pettibone, Mike Kelly, Peter Saul, Louise Bourgeois, Tip Dunham, Barnaby Furnas, Dr. Lakra and Warhol. I think the next show I would like to do would be a Cocteau, Warhol from the 1950s and Crumb from the 1950s. I would like to compare the thin languid lines that each artist uses to celebrate their romantic desires.

Robert's exhibitions are a mix of students with skateboards, museum trustees, publishers, curators and everyone in between. Funnily enough only two artists in my career have warned me that their works would be stolen from their shows—Barry McGee and Robert—and in fact, in twenty-three years, the only works I have ever had stolen from my gallery are works by these two artists. When I told Robert about the theft he replied "Ahh the scum of the earth, those are my people." There is an obsession around Robert's work that I have never seen before. I think his characters and their lives hit very deep feelings in their audience. I would put Robert on the "Artist's Artist" list.

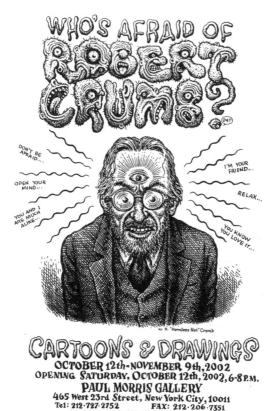

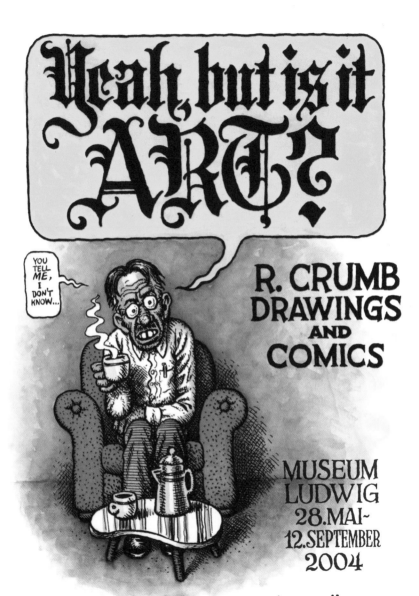

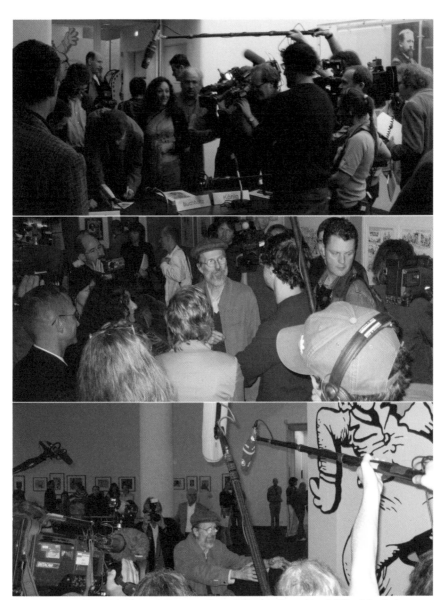

Too much media attention at the opening of the R. Crumb exhibit at Ludwig Museum, Cologne, Germany, May 2004

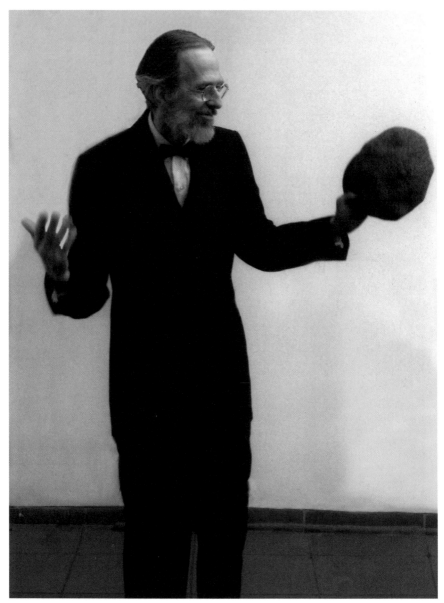

Crumb at the podium, Ludwig Museum, July 2004

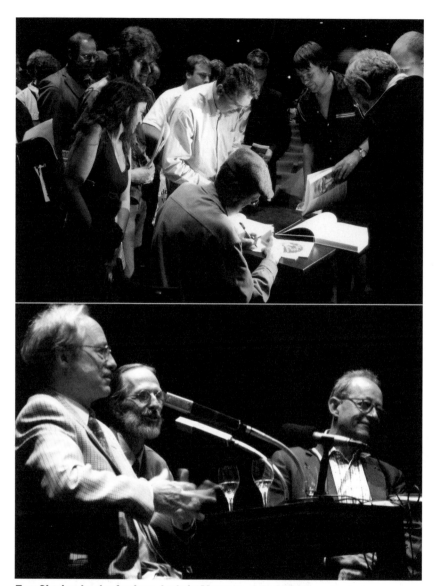

Top: Signing books for fans, Ludwig Museum, July 2004
Bottom: Crumb with Dr. Alfred Fischer, Curator, and Kasper König, Director, on stage at the Ludwig Museum, July 2004

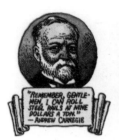

54th CARNEGIE INTERNATIONAL

CARNEGIE MUSEUM of ART
PITTSBURGH, PENNSYLVANIA

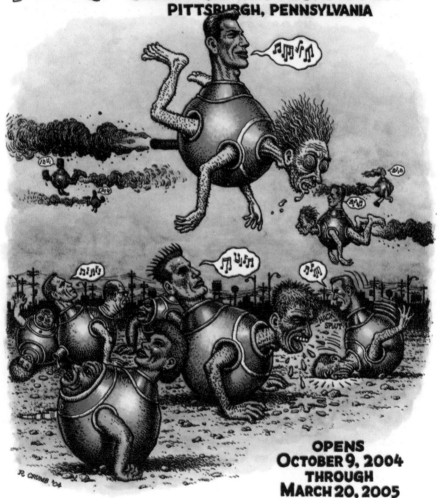

OPENS
OCTOBER 9, 2004
THROUGH
MARCH 20, 2005

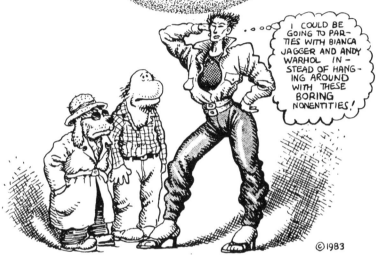

Mode O'Day
and her pals

I COULD BE GOING TO PARTIES WITH BIANCA JAGGER AND ANDY WARHOL INSTEAD OF HANGING AROUND WITH THESE BORING NONENTITIES!

© 1983

She's just a small-town gal who dreams of being a fashion model in New York City. Her problem is she's LAZY!

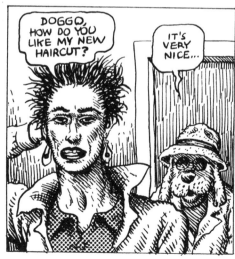

DOGGO, HOW DO YOU LIKE MY NEW HAIRCUT?

IT'S VERY NICE...

MODE O'DAY & HER PALS

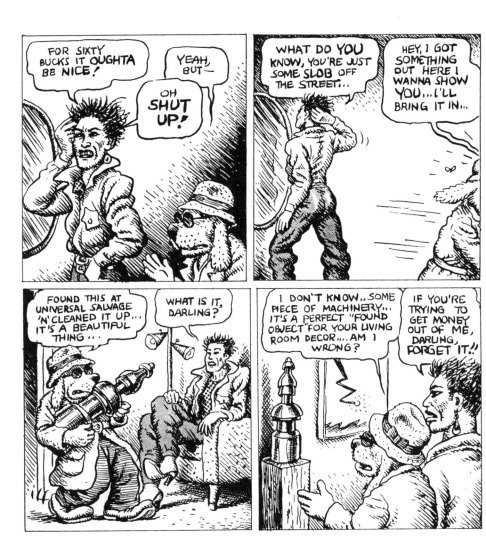

MODE O'DAY & HER PALS

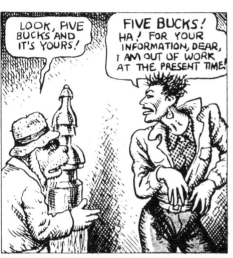

LOOK, FIVE BUCKS AND IT'S YOURS!

FIVE BUCKS! HA! FOR YOUR INFORMATION, DEAR, I AM OUT OF WORK AT THE PRESENT TIME!

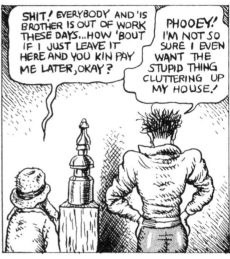

SHIT! EVERYBODY AND 'IS BROTHER IS OUT OF WORK THESE DAYS...HOW 'BOUT IF I JUST LEAVE IT HERE AND YOU KIN PAY ME LATER, OKAY?

PHOOEY! I'M NOT SO SURE I EVEN WANT THE STUPID THING CLUTTERING UP MY HOUSE!

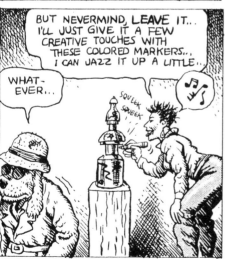

BUT NEVERMIND, LEAVE IT... I'LL JUST GIVE IT A FEW CREATIVE TOUCHES WITH THESE COLORED MARKERS... I CAN JAZZ IT UP A LITTLE...

WHAT- EVER...

SQUEEK SQUEEK

♪♫

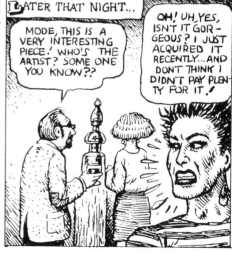

LATER THAT NIGHT...

MODE, THIS IS A VERY INTERESTING PIECE! WHO'S THE ARTIST? SOME ONE YOU KNOW??

OH! UH, YES, ISN'T IT GOR- GEOUS? I JUST ACQUIRED IT RECENTLY...AND DON'T THINK I DIDN'T PAY PLEN- TY FOR IT!

MODE O'DAY & HER PALS

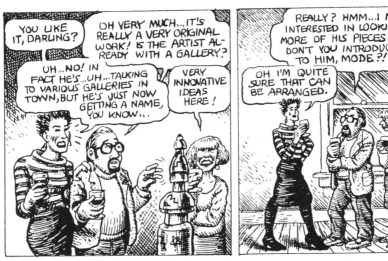

YOU LIKE IT, DARLING?

OH VERY MUCH...IT'S REALLY A VERY ORIGINAL WORK! IS THE ARTIST ALREADY WITH A GALLERY?

UH...NO! IN FACT HE'S...UH...TALKING TO VARIOUS GALLERIES IN TOWN, BUT HE'S JUST NOW GETTING A NAME, YOU KNOW...

VERY INNOVATIVE IDEAS HERE!

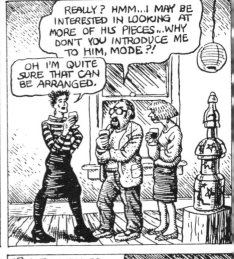

REALLY? HMM...I MAY BE INTERESTED IN LOOKING AT MORE OF HIS PIECES...WHY DON'T YOU INTRODUCE ME TO HIM, MODE?!

OH I'M QUITE SURE THAT CAN BE ARRANGED.

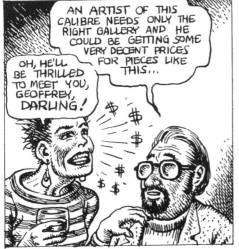

AN ARTIST OF THIS CALIBRE NEEDS ONLY THE RIGHT GALLERY AND HE COULD BE GETTING SOME VERY DECENT PRICES FOR PIECES LIKE THIS...

OH, HE'LL BE THRILLED TO MEET YOU, GEOFFREY, DARLING!

$ $ $ $ $ $

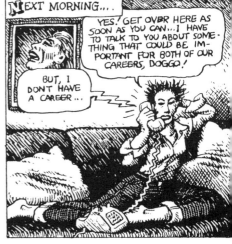

NEXT MORNING....

YES! GET OVER HERE AS SOON AS YOU CAN...I HAVE TO TALK TO YOU ABOUT SOMETHING THAT COULD BE IMPORTANT FOR BOTH OF OUR CAREERS, DOGGO!

BUT, I DON'T HAVE A CAREER...

MODE O'DAY & HER PALS

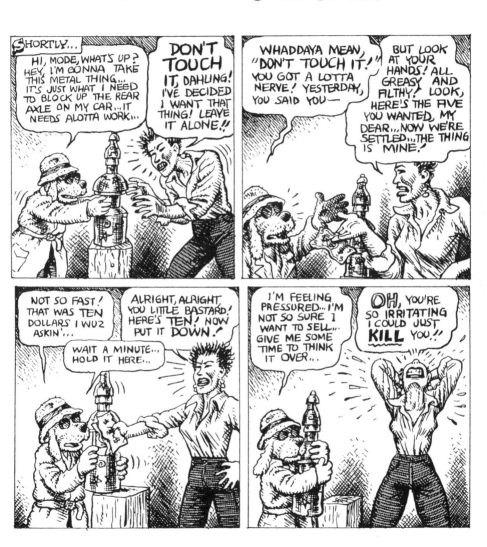

MODE O'DAY & HER PALS

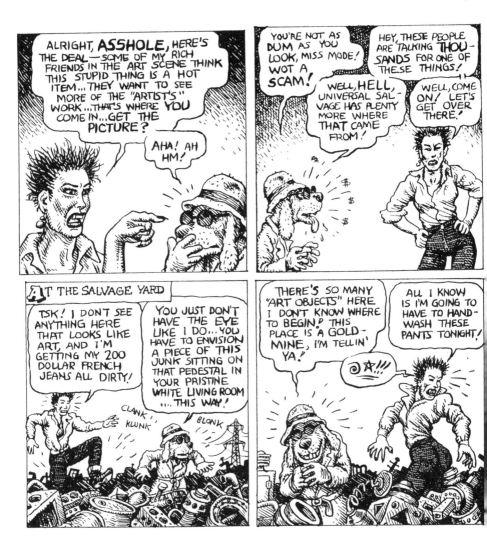

MODE O'DAY & HER PALS

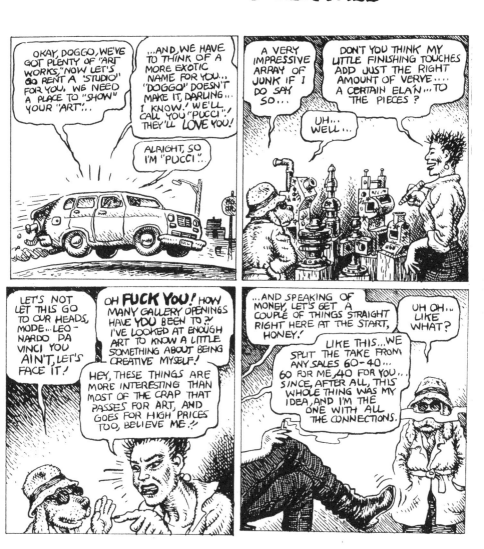

OKAY, DOGGO, WE'VE GOT PLENTY OF "ART WORKS." NOW LET'S GO RENT A "STUDIO" FOR YOU. WE NEED A PLACE TO "SHOW" YOUR "ART"...

...AND, WE HAVE TO THINK OF A MORE EXOTIC NAME FOR YOU... "DOGGO" DOESN'T MAKE IT, DARLING... I KNOW! WE'LL CALL YOU "PUCCI." THEY'LL LOVE YOU!

ALRIGHT, SO I'M "PUCCI"...

A VERY IMPRESSIVE ARRAY OF JUNK IF I DO SAY SO...

DON'T YOU THINK MY LITTLE FINISHING TOUCHES ADD JUST THE RIGHT AMOUNT OF VERVE... A CERTAIN ELAN... TO THE PIECES?

UH... WELL...

LET'S NOT LET THIS GO TO OUR HEADS, MODE... LEONARDO DA VINCI YOU AIN'T, LET'S FACE IT!

OH **FUCK YOU!** HOW MANY GALLERY OPENINGS HAVE YOU BEEN TO?! I'VE LOOKED AT ENOUGH ART TO KNOW A LITTLE SOMETHING ABOUT BEING CREATIVE MYSELF!

HEY, THESE THINGS ARE MORE INTERESTING THAN MOST OF THE CRAP THAT PASSES FOR ART, AND GOES FOR HIGH PRICES TOO, BELIEVE ME!!

...AND SPEAKING OF MONEY, LET'S GET A COUPLE OF THINGS STRAIGHT RIGHT HERE AT THE START, HONEY!

UH OH... LIKE WHAT?

LIKE THIS... WE SPLIT THE TAKE FROM ANY SALES 60-40... 60 FOR ME, 40 FOR YOU... SINCE, AFTER ALL, THIS WHOLE THING WAS MY IDEA, AND I'M THE ONE WITH ALL THE CONNECTIONS.

MODE O'DAY & HER PALS

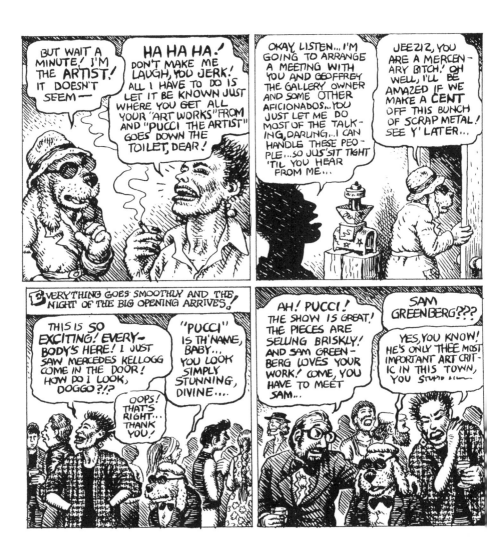

MODE O'DAY & HER PALS

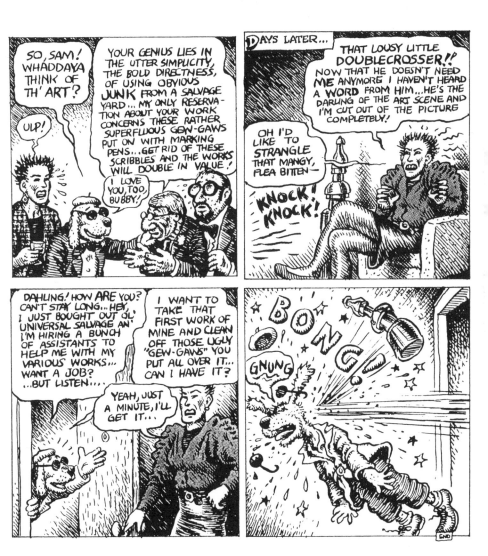

357

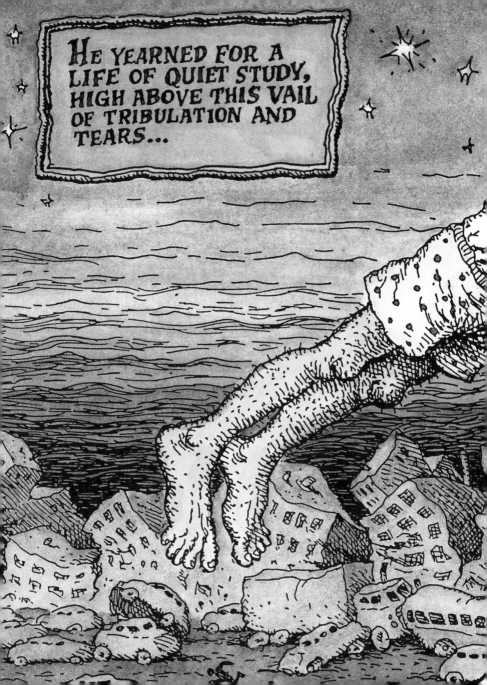

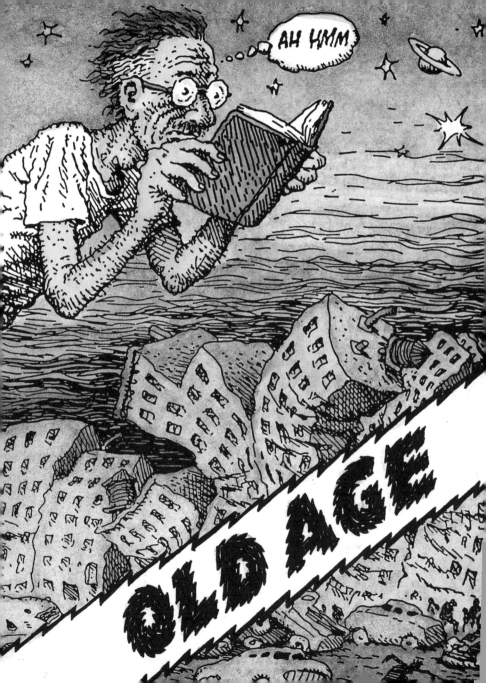

ROD SERLING
TWILIGHT ZONE CREATOR AND SCRIPT WRITER INTRODUCES AN EPISODE IN THE SERIES

The prostrate form of Mr. David Ellington, scholar, seeker of truth and, regrettably, the finder of truth. A man who will shortly arise from his exhaustion to confront a problem that has tormented mankind since the beginning of time. A man who knocked on a door seeking sanctuary and found instead the outer edges of ... the Twilight Zone.

Introduction to *The Howling Man,* Charles Beaumont, 1960

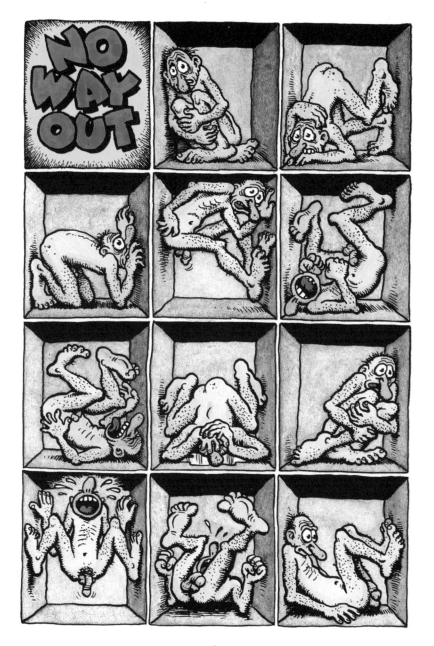

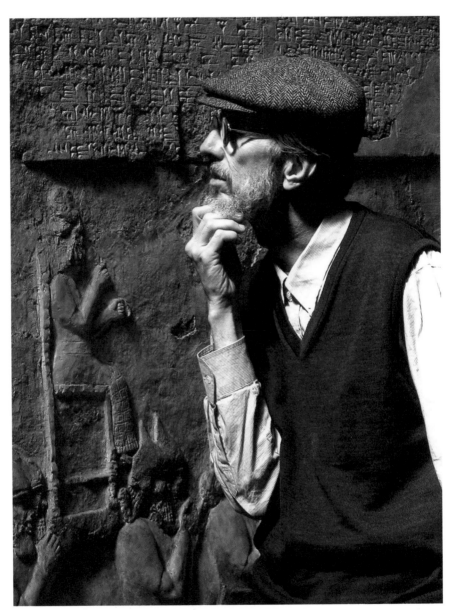

Crumb examining Assyrian bas-reliefs, British Museum, 2004

Chapter 7

Chopped Liver

Recently, I had a chance to look at the Assyrian and Babylonian reliefs in the British Museum. There are large, powerful figures with predatory bird heads, creatures that are truly brutal and scary looking. Here is a warrior holding a sword over a group of prisoners. Here there are defeated warriors being run over by a chariot. In another room there's a relief of a giant mill wheel grinding up the dead enemies of the king after a battle.

It's incredible. They're bragging about all the people they've captured and killed. The king wants everyone to remember how many peoples he conquered and enslaved! It's all a homage to the king's glory. I was very inspired by the lurid, harsh, visual narratives depicted in these early Mesopotamian reliefs. I like them much better than the more refined, stylized Egyptian stuff from the same period. It's more rough and ready, a bit more individualistic, perhaps, than the Egyptian art.

My generation comes from a world that has been molded by crass TV programs, movies, comic books, popular music, advertisements and commercials. My brain is a huge garbage dump of all this stuff and it is this, mainly, that my work comes out of, for better or for worse.

I hope that whatever synthesis I make of all this crap contains something worthwhile, that it's something other than just more smarmy entertainment—or at least, that it's genuinely high quality entertainment. I also hope that perhaps it's revealing of something, maybe. On the other hand, I want to avoid becoming pretentious in the eagerness to give my work deep meanings!

I have an enormous ego and must resist the urge to come on like a know-it-all. Some of the imagery in my work is sorta scary because I'm basically a fearful, pessimistic person. I'm always seeing the predatory nature of the universe, which can harm you or kill you very easily and very quickly, no matter how well you watch your step.

The way I see it, we are all just so much chopped liver. We have this great gift of human intelligence to help us pick our way through this treacherous tangle, but unfortunately we don't seem to value it very much.

Most of us are not brought up in environments that encourage us to appreciate and cultivate our intelligence. To me, human society appears mostly to be a living nightmare of ignorant, depraved behavior. We're all depraved, me included. I can't help it if my work reflects this sordid view of the world. Also, I feel that I have to counteract all the lame, hero-worshipping crap that is dished out by the mass-media in a never-ending deluge.

*The guy was still alive but
not in very good shape when I
found him....*

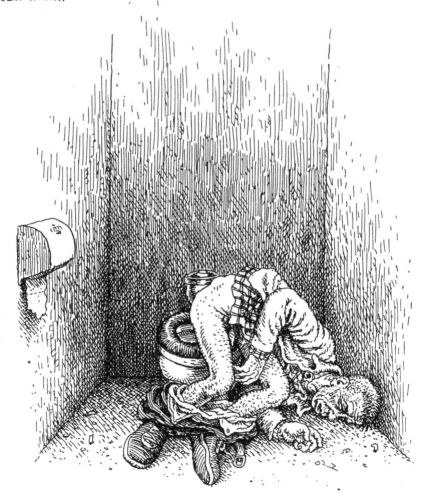

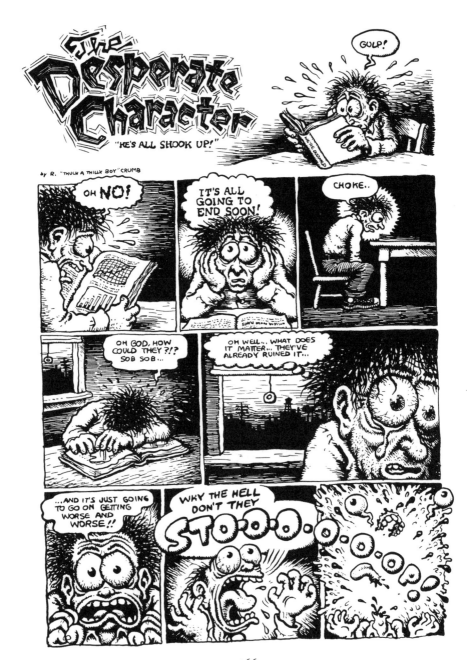

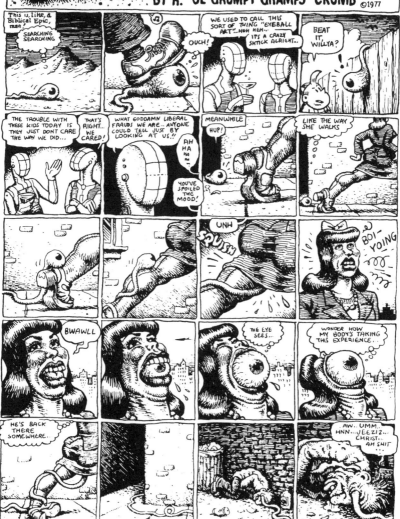

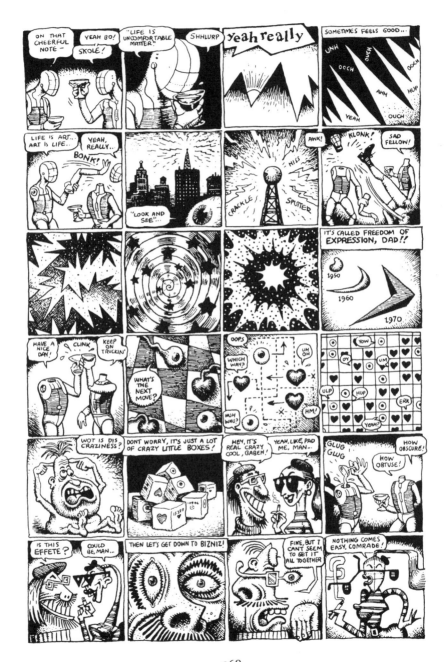

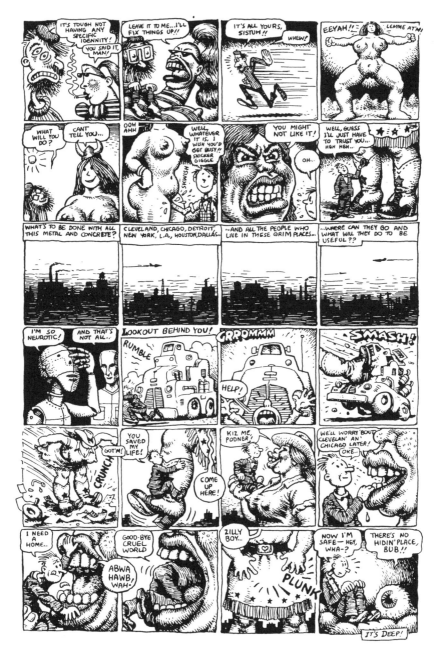

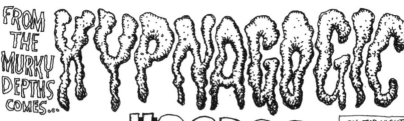

FROM THE MURKY DEPTHS COMES... HYPNAGOGIC HOODOO

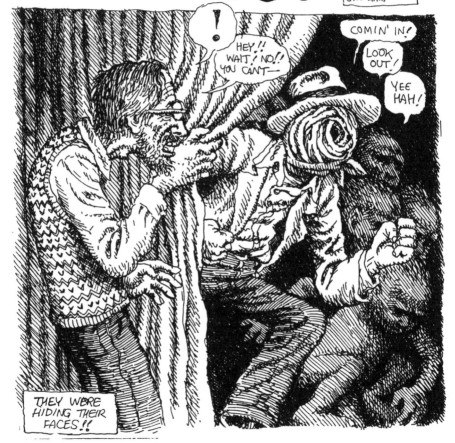

ON THE NIGHT OF MARCH 4TH, 2001, APPROX. 3:00 A.M.

!

HEY!! WAIT! NO!! YOU CAN'T—

COMIN' IN!

LOOK OUT!

YEE HAH!

THEY WERE HIDING THEIR FACES!!

370

EVERY SECOND COUNTS!

EVERY THOUGHT, EVERY ACTION... NOW IS THE TIME TO REACH OUT AND CONNECT WITH

NON-HUMAN INTELLIGENCE! OOH SCARY

WE ARE NOT THE *ONLY* "INTELLIGENT" BEINGS OR "ENTITIES" IN THE UNIVERSE, NOR EVEN ON THIS EARTH... WE'RE NOT AS SMART AS WE THINK... OUR KNOWLEDGE, UNDERSTANDING, AWARENESS IS NARROW AND LIMITED...

IS THERE ANY LIMIT TO WHAT CAN BE KNOWN BY US, ANY LIMIT TO WHAT CAN BE *DISCOVERED* BY US?? OR IS THERE A VAST *INFINITY* THAT, FOR US IN OUR HUMAN FORM, IS...

UNKNOWABLE?!

MAN, THAT'S HUMBLING...

WHAT HAPPENS TO US WHEN WE DIE? WE DON'T KNOW. IT'S ALL CONJECTURE...

THE MIND CAN'T KNOW IT...

So is it alright to go ahead and, you know, enjoy life while you're still, you know, "in the pink"??

ANSWER: YEAH, SURE, IF YOU CAN TAKE THE *PAIN* ALONG WITH THE *PLEASURE*... MAYBE THERE'S *NO CHOICE* IN THESE MATTERS...

THE MIND CAN'T KNOW IT... THE MIND CAN'T KNOW IT—

WHAT THE HELL *IS THIS*??
WHO CAN TELL ME??
DOES ANYBODY KNOW???
HOW CAN I FIND OUT MORE ABOUT IT??

ONE THING'S SURE :

    THE HUMAN MIND CAN'T "KNOW" IT....

WHY DOES ONE WANT TO "KNOW"?? IS IT A QUEST FOR "FREEDOM"? ONE NO LONGER WISHES TO BE A PUPPET, DANGLING ON THE STRINGS OF... OF WHAT? ANIMAL IN-STINCTS?? LEARNED REFLEXES? PROGRAMMED BEHAVIOR?? INGRAINED HABITS OF PERCEPTION ??

    HOW LIMITED ARE WE BY THE EXPERIENCE OF OUR SEN-CES, BY OUR PHYSICAL NATURE??

    TO BE FULLY ALIVE IS A *STUPENDOUS STRUGGLE!* WE WANT THE REWARDS WITHOUT THE STRUGGLE---

            --- *A FATAL ERROR!*

... NO SUCH THING AS *AN EASY LIFE!* EVERYBODY HAS A HARD TIME... STRUGGLE OR *DIE!*

    TO FIND OUT WHAT'S REALLY GOING ON IT'S NECESSARY TO GET AROUND THE *EGO*...AN ART REQUIRING PER-SISTENT AND DETERMINED EFFORT...

    ME, ME, ME... MYSELF & I...

OH NO!!

    TRAPPED IN MY STUPID SELF! MARCH 28TH, '98

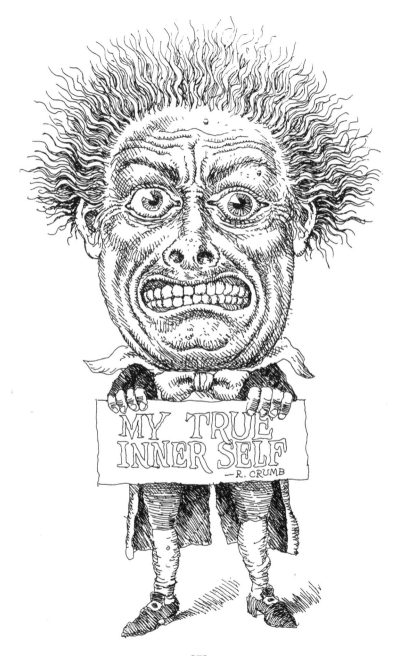

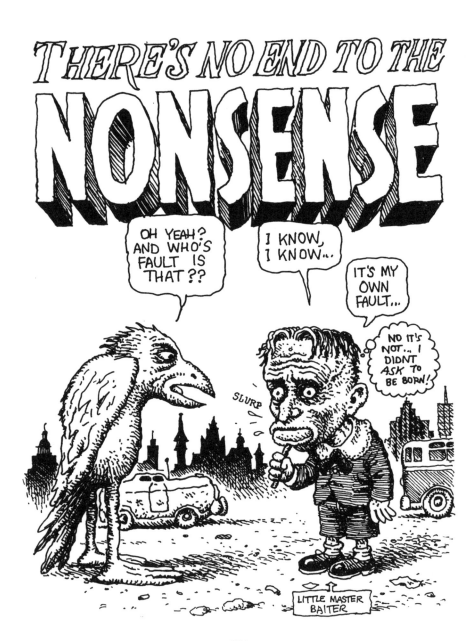

DETAILS... THOUSANDS AND MIL-
LIONS AND TRILLIONS OF DETAILS!
EVERY DAY! EVERY WAKING MOM-
ENT! INFINITE IN NUMBER, AND NO
TWO EXACTLY ALIKE! AND EACH
AND EVERY ONE OF THEM IS A... A
CLUE, A HINT, A... A METAPHOR!

PAY ATTENTION!

Oh The Wonder Of It All...

OH FOR ONE OF THOSE NEGROES OF GLADNESS..

"THE PURPOSE OF HUMAN LIFE IS TO INCREASE
AWARENESS" — CARLOS CASTANEDA

THERE ARE APPROXIMATELY *SIX BILLION* HUMAN
BEINGS ON THIS PLANET! SIX BILLION OF US! A HUND-
DRED PEOPLE IS ALOT! A THOUSAND IS A CROWD! TEN
THOUSAND IS A HUGE CROWD! A HUNDRED-THOUSAND IS A HORDE!
TRY TO GRASP FIVE-HUNDRED-THOUSAND PEOPLE. THAT'S HALF A
MILLION... DOUBLE THAT IS A MILLION... DOUBLE THAT IS TWO
MILLION... FIVE TIMES THAT IS TEN-MILLION... THE POPULATION OF
A LARGE CITY... DOUBLE THAT IS TWENTY-MILLION: MEXICO CITY...
TEN TIMES THAT IS TWO-HUNDRED-MILLION HUMAN-BEINGS! CAN
YOU COMPREHEND TWO-HUNDRED-MILLION HUMAN BEINGS?? ONE
BILLION IS A *THOUSAND-MILLION!*...TIMES *SIX* IS THE
POPULATION OF THE EARTH!! CONSIDER, IF YOU WILL, HOW MUCH
TROUBLE ONE HUMAN-BEING CAN CAUSE, THEN CONSIDER *SIX*
BILLION OF THEM! GASP! GAG! I'M GOING TO BE SICK!!!

STOP CHASING ILLUSIONS,

YOU DOPE, YOU SAP, YOU FOOL!

YEAH, BUT WHAT ELSE *IS* THERE?!? IT'S *ALL* ILLUSION...

YES, IT IS, BUT STOP *RUNNING AFTER* IT.

OH...

DON'T *LOOK FOREWARD* TO THINGS... LOOK AT *THIS MOMENT*... DO NOT *LAMENT* IF YOU CAN HELP IT.

SURE YOUR STRUGGLE IS UNIQUE, BUT SO IS THE NEXT FELLOW'S...

YEAH, WORDS TO LIVE BY, EXCEPT THAT WHEN I'M NOT CHASING ILLUSIONS I'M LAMENTING MY FATE... ONE OR THE OTHER, EVERY SECOND... YEP... I'VE SPENT A LARGE PORTION OF MY LIFE WALLOWING IN FEELINGS OF PERSECUTION AND MARTYRDOM... VICTIMHOOD....

TAKE A DEEP BREATH... CALM DOWN... SIT STILL... DON'T "DO" ANYTHING....

THURSDAY, SEPT. 3RD 1998

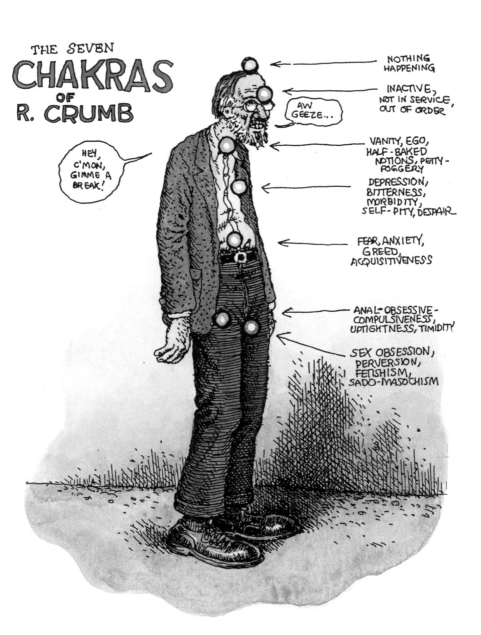

377

EVERYTHING WE DO HAS SIGNIFICANCE.

EVERY ACTION, EVERY THOUGHT LEAVES AN *IMPRINT* — NOT ONLY ON THE *SELF*, BUT ON THE *WORLD*, ON THE *OTHERS*, AND EVEN ON *TIME*, ON *ALL* WHO COME AFTER US!

THIS IMPLIES A RESPONSIBILITY FOR ONE'S THOUGHTS & ACTIONS THAT SHOULD BE TAKEN MOST *SERIOUSLY!*

AND YET ONE FEELS *HELPLESS*, A HAPLESS VICTIM OF CIRCUMSTANCES BEYOND ONE'S CONTROL, AS IF ONE'S BEHAVIOR AND THOUGHTS DID NOT OR-IGINATE IN THE *SELF*, BUT WERE A *PRODUCT*, AN AC-CUMULATION OF *IMPRINTS* FROM THE WORLD, FROM OUR *ANCESTORS*, FROM THE PEOPLE AROUND US.

IT BEHOOVES ONE TO *TAKE RESPONSIBILITY*, TO TAKE THE *POWER TO DECIDE* HOW ONE WILL *ACT*, AND EVEN HOW ONE WILL *THINK!* NOT ONLY FOR THE BETTER-MENT OF ONE'S SELF, BUT FOR THE BETTERMENT OF THE *WORLD*, ALL THE OTHERS, AND ALL WHO WILL COME AFTER US!

IT'S TOUGH..

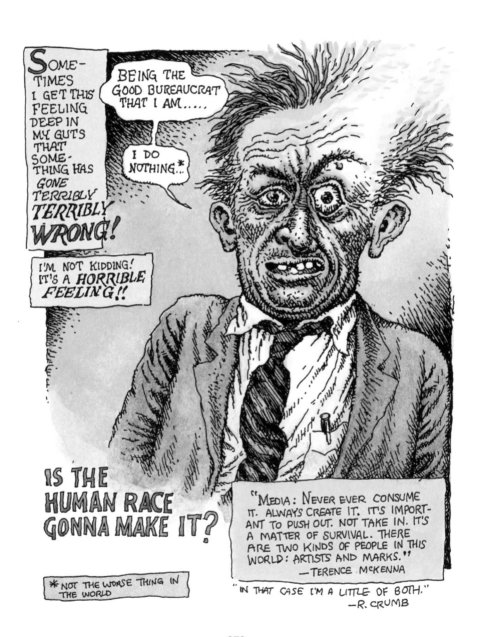

THIS MORNING I HAD THE APPALLING
REALIZATION THAT...

I NEVER HAD A STRATEGY
IN MY DEALINGS WITH OTHER
HUMANS! I'VE ALWAYS BEEN VERY
PASSIVE SOCIALLY. I WENT ALONG
WITH THEIR AGENDA. I HAD NONE
OF MY OWN! LEFT TO MY OWN DE-
VICES I STAYED IN MY ROOM OR WAN-
DERED AIMLESSLY IN THE STREETS,
FANTASIZING ABOUT BIZARRE THINGS I
YEARNED TO DO TO BIG LADIES, OR FILLED
WITH SELF-PITY AND RESENTMENT. I WAS
HELPLESS IN THE PRESENCE OF OTHER
PEOPLE! MY MAIN CONCERN WAS TO MAKE
THEM LIKE ME BY BEING AS AGREEABLE AS POS-
SIBLE, AND SECONDLY TO IMPRESS THEM WITH MY
BRILLIANCE, MY SHARP WIT, MY ORIGINALITY, AND
MY FUNDAMENTAL SAINTLINESS. OVER TIME,
AND AFTER YEARS-DECADES- OF DILIGENT PRAC-
TICE, I BECAME VERY GOOD AT THIS CUTE LITTLE
PERFORMANCE OF MINE.
　　　BUT THIS PERFORMANCE WAS IMPROVISED IN THE MOM-
ENT, CATERED TO SUIT WHOEVER I HAPPENED TO BE WITH. THERE
WAS NO STRATEGY. IT WAS ALWAYS AN EFFORT. ONLY IN SOLI-
TUDE WAS I COMPLETELY RELAXED. FUNNY THING...

HOW I USED TO WANDER UP AND DOWN THE STREETS FEELING LONELY, DEJECTED AND DISCONNECTED...

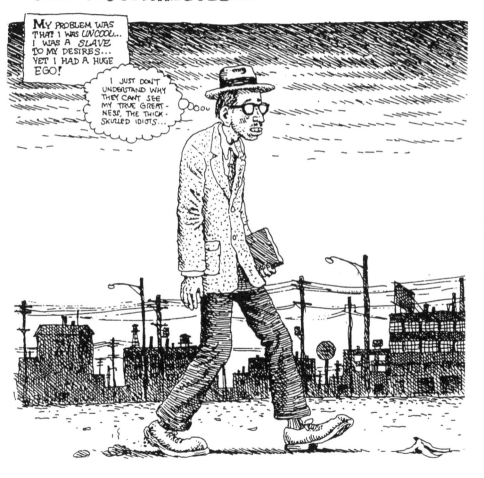

WHENEVER I AM ABLE TO WORK UP THE COURAGE TO TAKE A GOOD LOOK AT THE HUMAN WORLD, OR AT ONE OF MY FELLOW HUMANS, OR EVEN AT *MYSELF*, I AM....

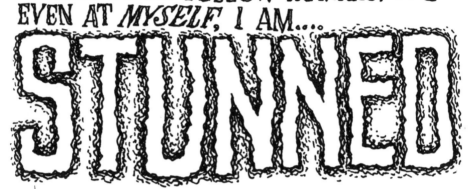

STUNNED

IT'S NOT OFTEN THAT I HAVE THAT LEVEL OF COURAGE...MOST OF THE TIME I HIDE FROM IT, INSULATE MYSELF WITH...*DISTRACTIONS... FANTASIES... AMUSEMENTS...EVEN THE "SERIOUS STUDY"* OF THOUGHTS AND OB-SERVATIONS OF "DEEP THINKERS" IN BOOKS IS JUST A RESPECTABLE FORM OF *ESCAPE* INTO *WORDS, IDEAS, CONCEPTS* ABOUT THE WORLD... WE ALL HAVE MANY THICK LAYERS SHIELDING US FROM *DIRECT EXPERIENCE* OF THE WORLD...EVEN THE *HUMAN* WORLD THAT WE *OURSELVES* HAVE CREATED... AND OUR MANY FORMS OF *MASS MEDIA MAKE ESCAPE EASIER, MORE ATTRACTIVE THAN EVER BEFORE....*

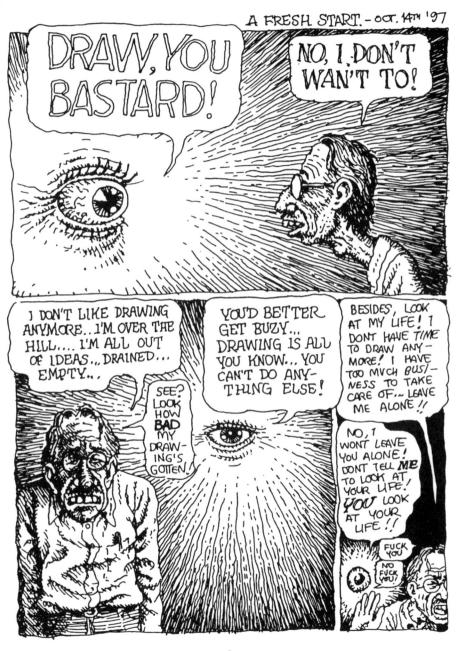

I WONDER... I WONDER....

WHERE IS MY PATH LEADING ME??
WHO CAN I TALK TO ABOUT THIS??
WHO CAN TELL ME ANYTHING??
WHAT REALITY LIES BEYOND THE...
"NEURO-LINGUISTIC PROGRAM"?

.... S-SOMETHING ABOUT ENERGY... DIFFERENT
LEVEL OF ENERGY... INVOLVED WITH....
W-W--WITH ELECTRO-MAGNETIC
ENERGY... SUBTLE BUT POWERFUL...MUST
BE READY FOR IT...NOT OVERCOME WITH
FEAR OF THIS FORCE, THIS GREAT
POWER~~ NOT EVIL, NOT ALIEN...
EMBRACE IT... "WRESTLE" WITH IT...MAKE
IT "ALLY".... GOT IT...WOW... WORDS
USELESS... HASNOTHING⌐⌐⌐⌐⌐⌐
⌐⌐⌐⌐⌐⌐⌐⌐⌐⌐⌐⌐⌐....

JAN. 5TH, '98

384

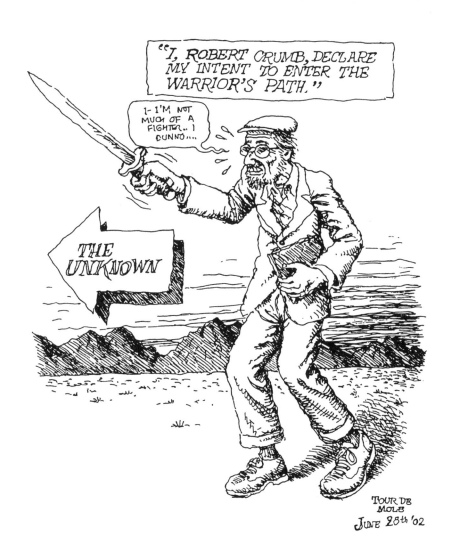

ROBERT CRUMB

THE LITANY OF HATE

I'm such a negative person, and always have been. Was I born that way?
I don't know. I am constantly disgusted by reality, horrified and afraid.
I cling desperately to the few things that give me some solace, that
make me feel good.

I hate most of humanity. Though I might be very fond of particular
individuals, humanity in general fills me with contempt and despair. I hate
most of what passes for civilization. I hate the modern world. For one thing
there are just too goddamn many people. I hate the hordes, the crowds in
their vast cities, with all their hateful vehicles, their noise, their constant
meaningless comings and goings. I hate cars. I hate modern architecture.
Every building built after 1955 should be torn down!

I despise modern popular music. Words cannot express how much it gets
on my nerves—the false, pretentious, smug assertiveness of it. I hate
business, having to deal with money. Money is one of the most hateful
inventions of the human race. I hate the commodity culture, in which
everything is bought and sold. No stone is left unturned. I hate the mass
media, and how passively people suck up to it.

I hate having to get up in the morning and face another day of this
insanity. I hate having to eat, shit, maintain the body—I hate my body. The
thought of my internal functions, the organs, digestion, the brain, the nervous
system, horrify me.

Nature is horrible. It's not cute and lovable. It's kill or be killed. It's very
dangerous out there. The natural world is filled with scary, murderous
creatures and forces. I hate the whole way that nature functions. Sex is
especially hateful and horrifying, the male penetrating the female, his dick
goes into her hole, she's impregnated, another being grows inside her, and then
she must go through a painful ordeal as the new being pushes out of her, only
to repeat the whole process in its time. Reproduction—what could be more
existentially repulsive?!

How I hate the courting ritual! I was always repelled by my own sex drive, which in my youth, never left me alone. I was constantly driven by frustrated desires to do bizarre and unacceptable things with and to women. My soul was in constant conflict about it. I never was able to resolve it. Old age is the only relief.

I hate the way the human psyche works, the way we are traumatized and stupidly imprinted in early childhood and have to spend the rest of our lives trying to overcome these infantile mental fixations. And we never ever fully succeed in this endeavor.

I hate organized religions. I hate governments. It's all a lot of power games played out by ambition-driven people, and foisted on the weak, the poor, and on children. Most humans are bullies. Adults pick on children. Older children pick on younger children. Men bully women. The rich bully the poor. People love to dominate.

I hate the way humans worship power—one of the most disgusting of all human traits. I hate the human tendency toward revenge and vindictiveness. I hate the way humans are constantly trying to trick and deceive one another, to swindle, cheat, and take unfair advantage of the innocent, the naïve and the ignorant.

I hate all the vacuous, false, banal conversation that goes on among people. Sometimes I feel suffocated. I want to flee from it.

For me, to be human is, for the most part, to hate what I am. When I suddenly realize that I am one of them, I want to scream in horror.

"Hell is other people"— Jean-Paul Sartre.
"Hell is also yourself"—R. Crumb.

Eternity

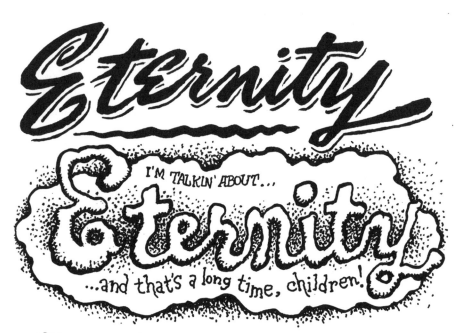

I'M TALKIN' ABOUT...

Eternity!

...and that's a long time, children!

ONE LIFETIME AIN'T NOTHIN'....

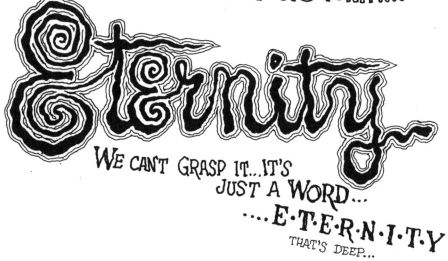

Eternity

WE CAN'T GRASP IT...IT'S JUST A WORD... ....E·T·E·R·N·I·T·Y THAT'S DEEP...

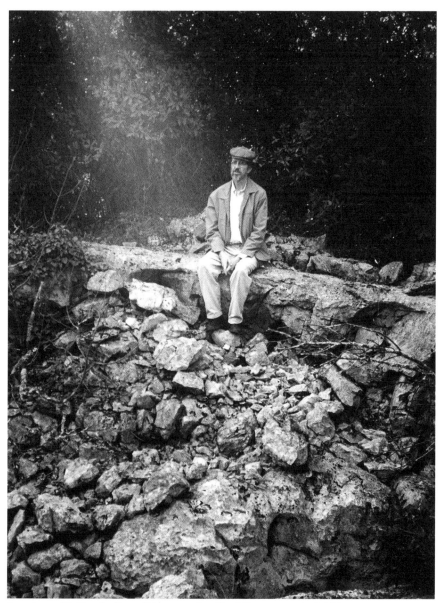

Crumb meditating in the wilderness, South of France, early 2000

DR. CARL G. JUNG
PSYCHOLOGIST

... But it is a fact that, in addition to memories from a long-distant conscious past, completely new thoughts and creative ideas can also present themselves from the unconscious—thoughts and ideas that have never been conscious before. They grow up from the dark depths of the mind like a lotus and form a most important part of the subliminal psyche.

We find this in everyday life, where dilemmas are sometimes solved by the most surprising new propositions; many artists, philosophers, and even scientists owe some of their best ideas to inspirations that appear suddenly from the unconscious. The ability to reach a rich vein of such material and translate it effectively into philosophy, literature, music, or scientific discovery is one of the hallmarks of what is commonly called genius.

from *Man And His Symbols,* edited by Carl G. Jung (posthumously published in 1964)

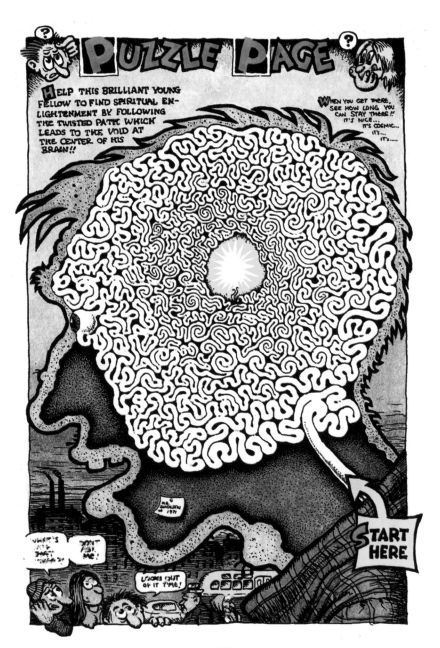

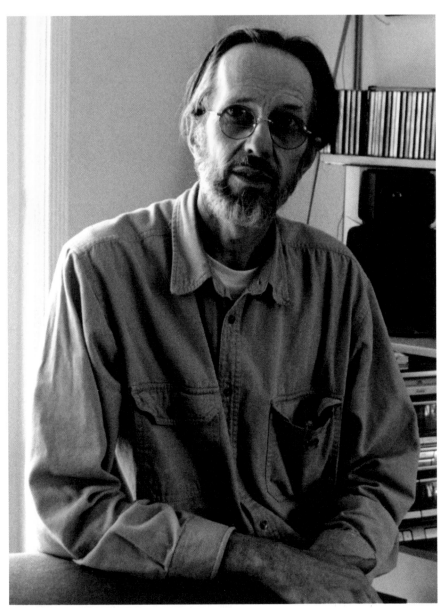

Robert Crumb, 2001

Chapter 8

The Artist and the Grim Reaper

As a matter of survival I've created this anti-hero alter-ego, a guy in an ill-fitting suit—part humunculus and part clown. Yep, that's me alright ... I could never relate to heroes. I have no interest in drawing heroic characters. It's not my thing, man. I'm more inclined toward the sordid underbelly of life. I find it more interesting to draw grotesque, lurid, or absurd pictures, and I especially enjoy depicting my fevered sexual obsessions. Some people don't like to see this perverse sexual stuff; ugly, weird little guys doing bizarre, twisted things to beautiful buxom women. This part of my work repels a lot of people. But as fate would have it, I became famous anyway. It's a curious thing. And then I got to live out my fantasies in real life! I was "lucky." As my fellow underground cartoonist, Jay Lynch, once put it, *"You get what you draw!"*, and it is true. I've gotten everything I've ever drawn. The good and the bad. It's a kind of concentrated focus, I guess, that makes it work that way.

But, the clock is ticking. At this point in my life it's a race against time. It is possible to incorporate Death into your life in some harmonious way, or, you can go on letting it be a scary, terrible, horrible thing. My father joined the Marine Corps when he was young and was sent to China in 1937 when the Japanese were bombing Shanghai. He saw death and starvation in the streets. He survived World War II and was sent in to Hiroshima ten days after the Americans dropped the atomic bomb. I can't even imagine the things he witnessed. He never talked about it.

For me, the most profound confrontation with death I ever experienced took place in 1966 after ingesting a powerful dose of LSD. I don't remember precisely what it was that terrified me, because at that moment I told myself that if I ever wanted to be sane again, I had to forget what I saw. I forced amnesia on myself so that I could return to the normal world. Bummer, man ... With LSD, you don't have to kill or be killed ... it all happens on some other plane of existence.

My work has a strong negative element. I have my own inner demons to deal with. Drawing is a way for me to articulate things inside myself that I can't otherwise grasp. What I don't want to do, what I dread more than anything, is to leave a legacy of crap. I don't want my work to be tossed in the dustbin of history, and become more of the second rate, mediocre junk that future connoisseurs will have to move out of the way so they can get at the good stuff.

Lately though, I've become more interested in "the journey within," the great adventure into the unknown inside one's self. Isn't it strange that we are such a mystery to ourselves? What a crazy paradox! I think one of the greatest powers we humans possess is "singular focus." In my youth all my power was focused down into my left hand, through the pen and on to the paper. Because I lived on paper, my work was strong.

DON'T BE AFRAID!
BE BRAVE, TAKE A CHANCE!

WHAT HAVE YOU GOT TO LOSE??

LOOK DEATH IN THE

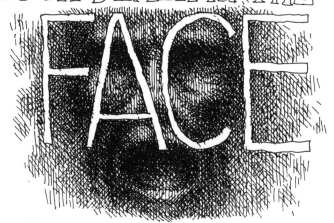

FACE

IT'S NOT DEATH I FEAR SO MUCH AS IT IS THE DENTIST...

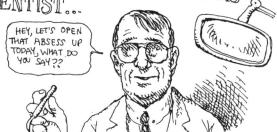

HEY, LET'S OPEN THAT ABSESS UP TODAY, WHAT DO YOU SAY??

As a person, I was weak and helpless in the real world. To be so narrowly focused is dangerous to one's mental health and can kill you. If you have no ability to "take care of business" you might find that you'll have trouble surviving in this world. It's a jungle out there! But, since I'd rather be dead than mediocre, my motto is: *Every Drawing a Masterpiece!*

Recently, after I saw the movie, *Gladiator*, I decided I had to leave the "arena." I didn't want to be there any more for the spectators to see if I was going to win or fall. I want to bow out, abdicate, renounce ... I like the *"Rocky"* metaphor. This world is always going to be bigger and more powerful than you are, but you've got to deal with it. Life is active struggle. As Rocky says, *"I know I can't beat this guy, I just wanna go the distance with him. I just wanna still be standing at the end of the fight, that's all ..."* That's the only victory you can hope for. You've got to figure out a way to stay in shape, and stay alert, to keep standing. *Rocky* may be a dumb movie but it contained this great metaphor.

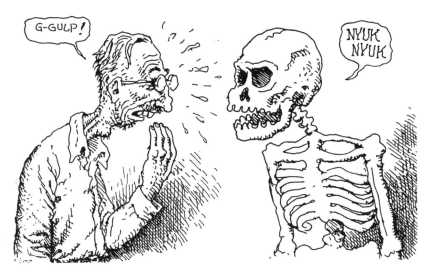

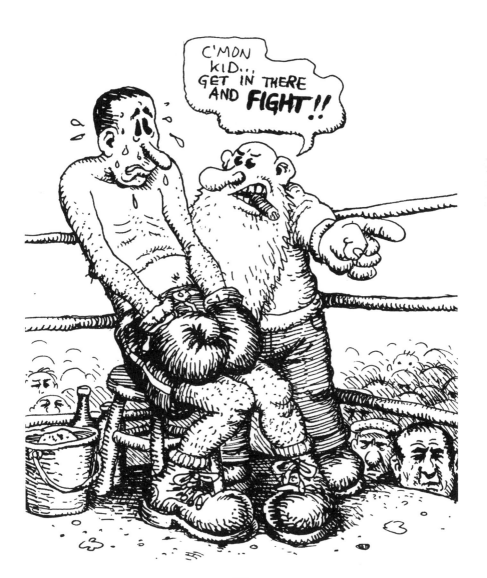

ROBERT CRUMB

THE SEARCH FOR OLD MUSIC

"Happy Days and Lonely Nights" by Charlie Fry and His Million Dollar Orchestra—it was a moment of revelation the first time I played that record. I was fifteen-years old; the year was 1959. I was an eccentric kid, woefully out of step with my own time. I liked old things. I went around wearing an old Abe Lincoln frock coat. I kind of liked some of the early rock and roll records, but I loved the background music in the old 1930s Laurel and Hardy and "Little Rascals" comedies that I watched on TV kiddie shows. I bought a few LPs and 45s of current Dixieland jazz and recreations of twenties music, but they didn't have it—some quality I couldn't define. I'm still trying to figure it all out. I was always snooping around in second hand stores, looking for old comic books. One day I noticed some old 78 records with very intriguing labels. They radiated some kind of power—a magical aura, even though the names of the tunes and the bands were unknown to me. At ten cents apiece, I bought a few of them. Ten seconds after putting the needle on that Charlie Fry record I knew—This is it! I was thrilled to the core, overjoyed! This was the music I'd been searching for! It existed on old records! In that moment I became a record collector for life! Four decades have passed and I'm still at it, still searching, and even yet discovering old shellac discs with obscure, forgotten byways of incredible music hidden in the grooves, silently waiting for the turntable to move, the needle to drop. There's a wealth of great music recorded in the 78 era, before the onslaught of mass media profoundly changed everything … forever!

R. Crumb, August, 1998

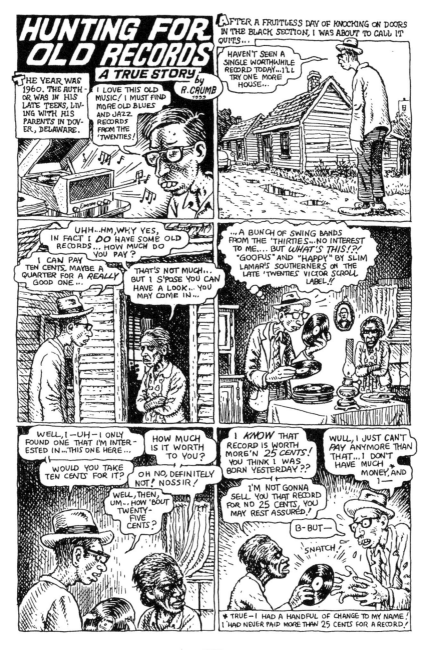

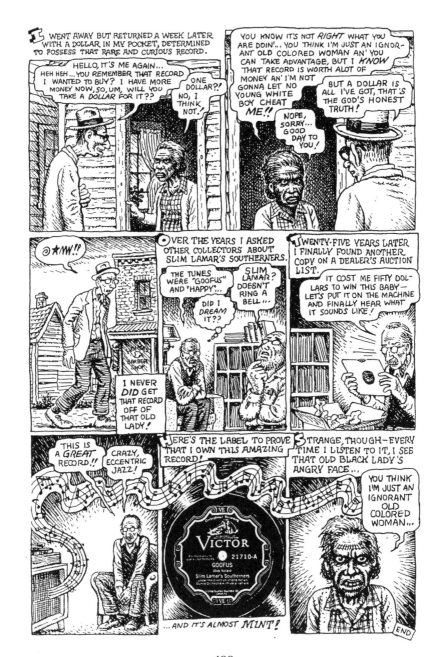

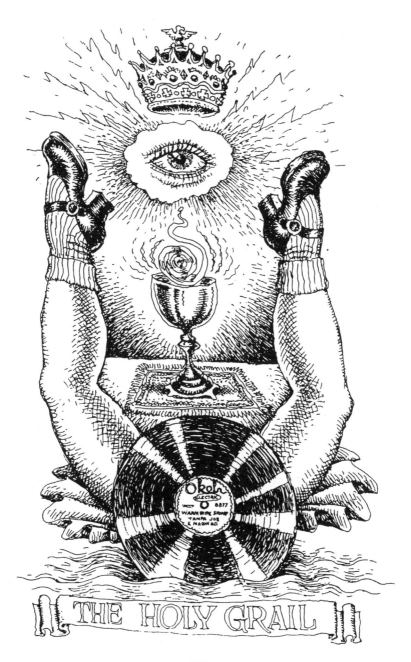

THE HOLY GRAIL

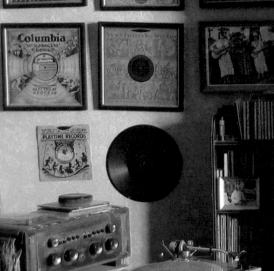
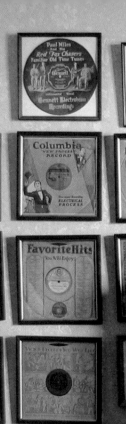
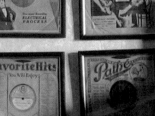
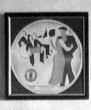
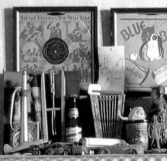
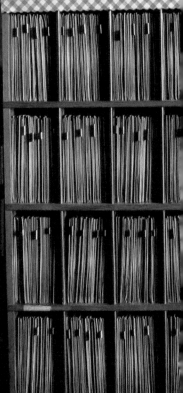

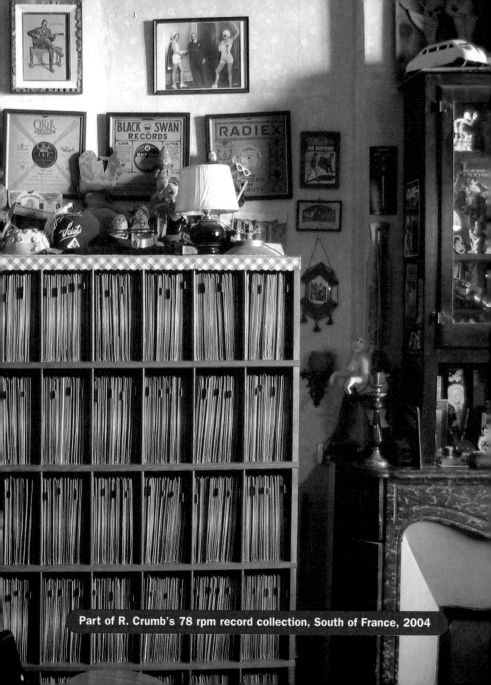

Part of R. Crumb's 78 rpm record collection, South of France, 2004

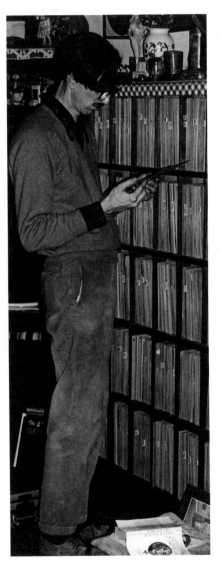

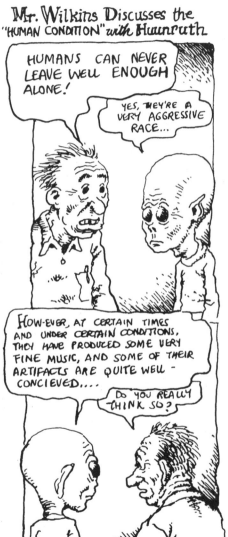

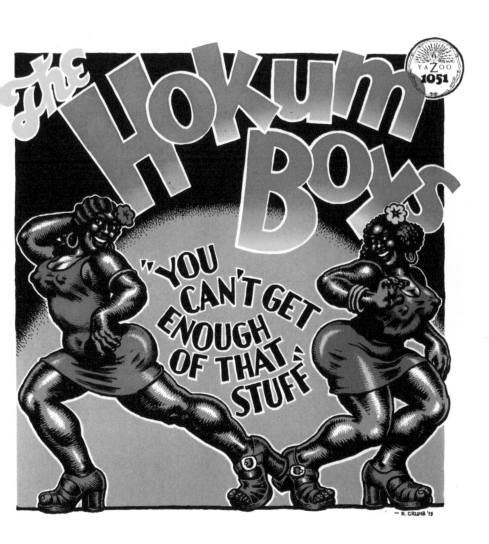

405

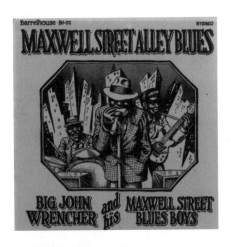

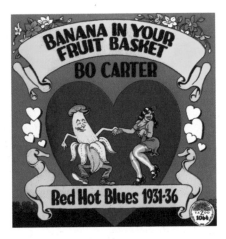

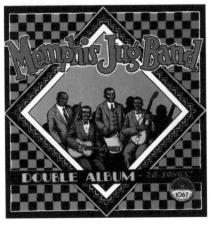

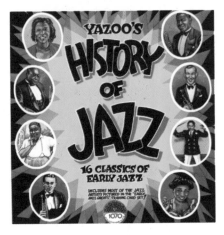

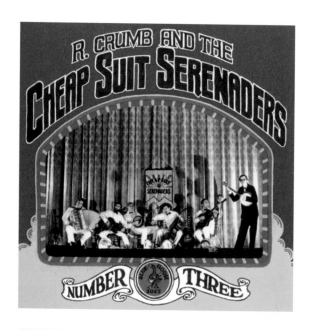

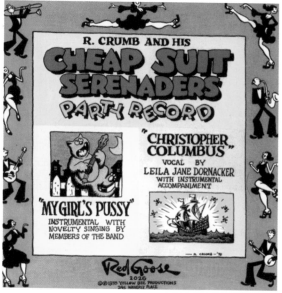

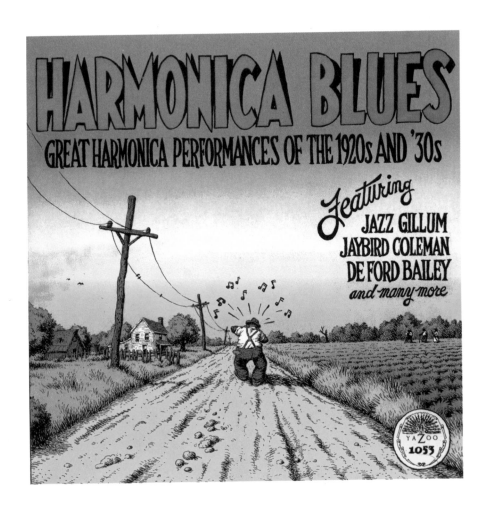

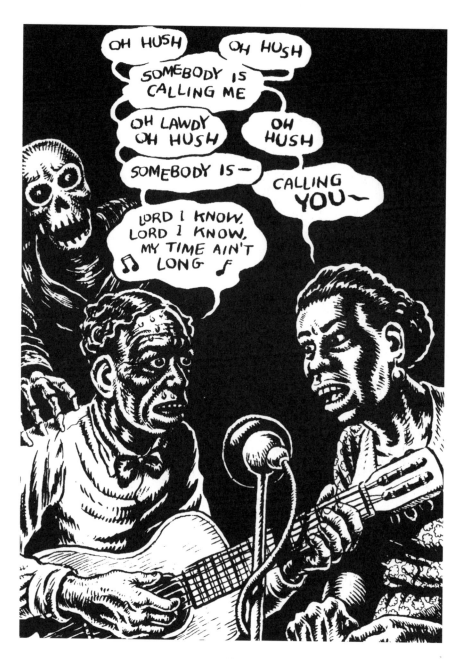

409

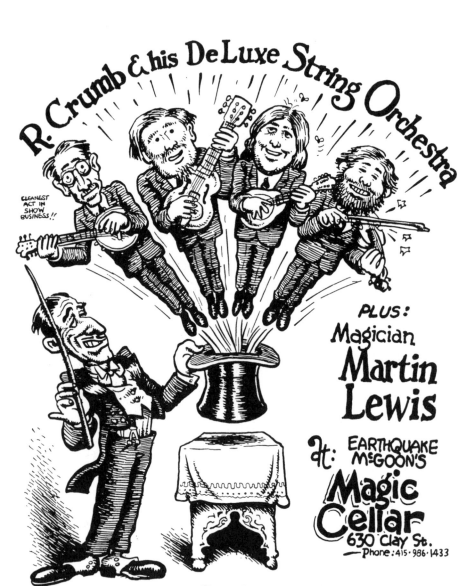

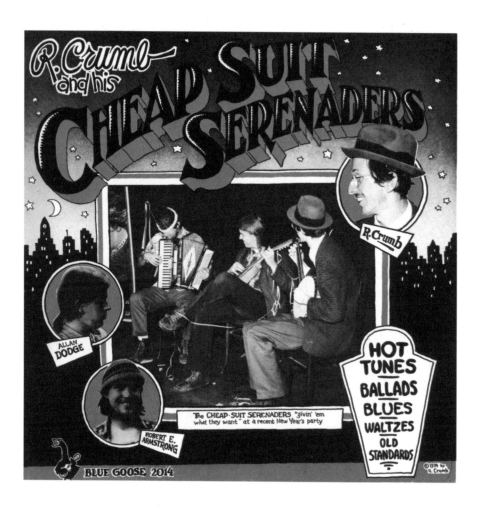

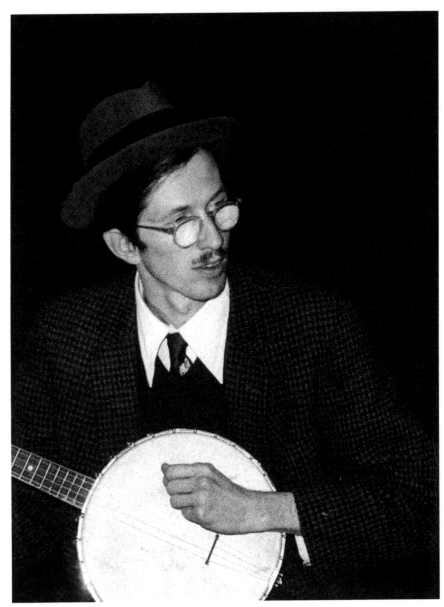

Robert with banjo, San Fancisco, 1975

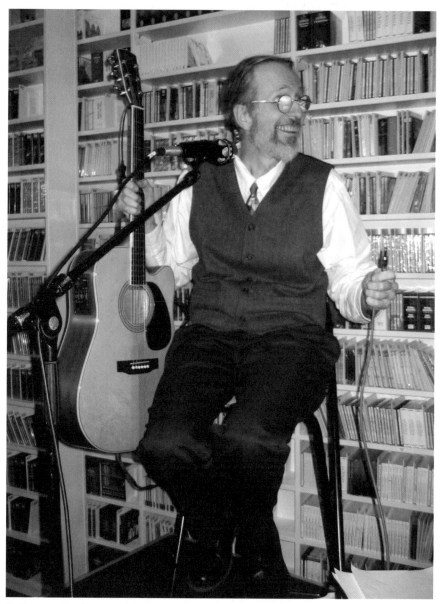

R. Crumb, Zweitauzendiens Bookstore, Hamburg, Germany, April 2003

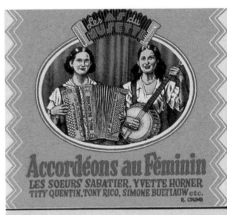

Accordéons au Féminin
LES SŒURS SABATIER, YVETTE HORNER,
TITY QUENTIN, TONY RICO, SIMONE BUTTIAUW etc.
R. CRUMB

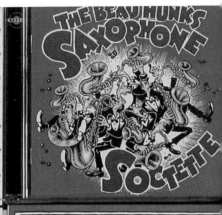

THE BEAU HUNKS
SAXOPHONE
SOCIETTE

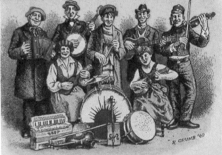

"GAY LIFE IN DIKANKA"
R. CRUMB'S OLD-TIME FAVORITES

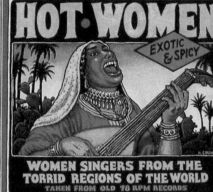

HOT·WOMEN
EXOTIC
& SPICY
WOMEN SINGERS FROM THE
TORRID REGIONS OF THE WORLD
TAKEN FROM OLD 78 RPM RECORDS

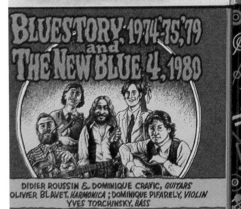

BLUESTORY: 1974,'75,'79
and
THE NEW BLUE 4, 1980
DIDIER ROUSSIN & DOMINIQUE CRAVIC, GUITARS
OLIVIER BLAVET, HARMONICA ; DOMINIQUE PIFARELY, VIOLIN
YVES TORCHINSKY, BASS
"JA VI DE "COCKTAIL D'AMOUR-LES MUSIQUES DU FUTUR, 1986

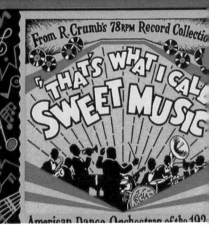

From R. Crumb's 78 RPM Record Collection
"THAT'S WHAT I CALL
SWEET MUSIC"
American Dance Orchestras of the 192...

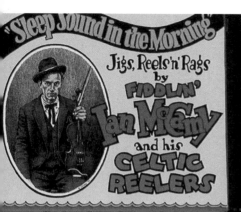

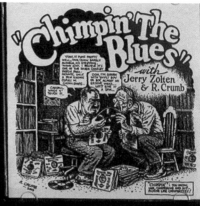

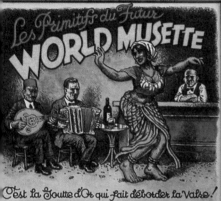

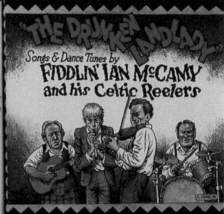

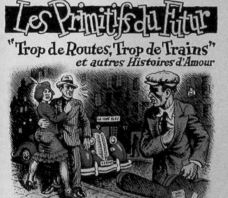

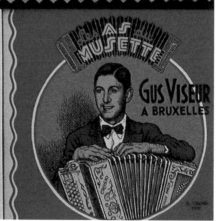

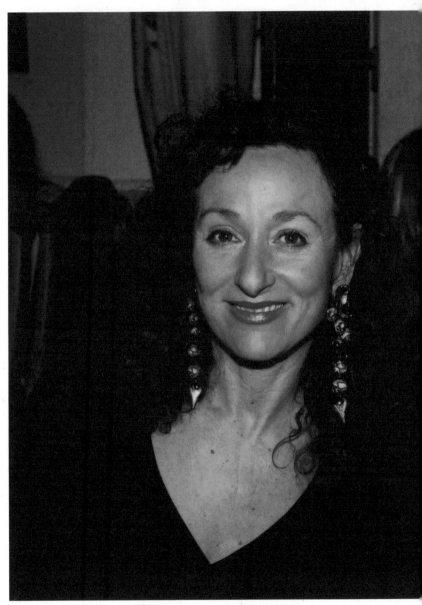

Aline and R. Crumb at Cannes Film Festival, May 2004

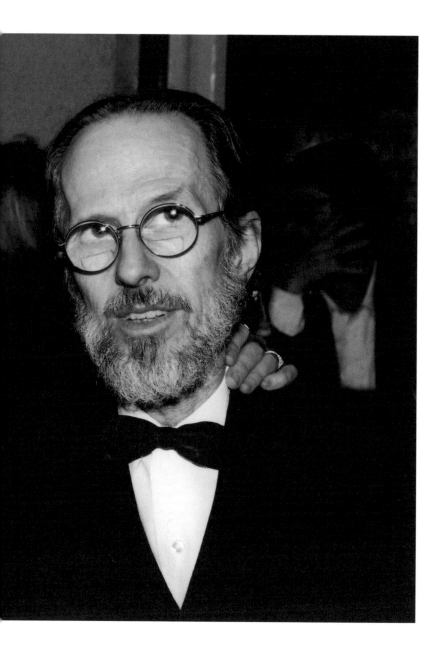

The HEARTBREAK
of the
OLD
CARTOONIST

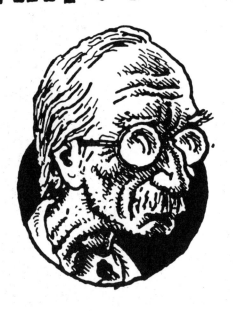

THE OLD CARTOONIST

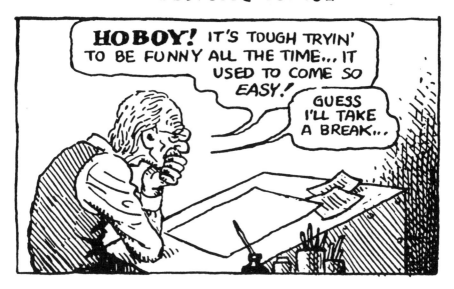

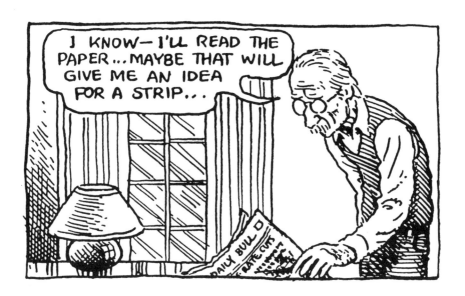

THE OLD CARTOONIST

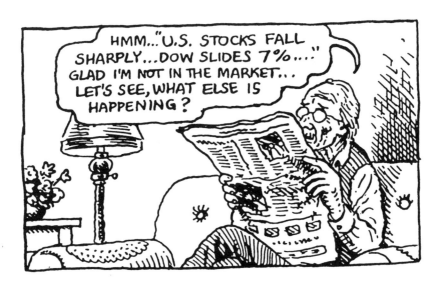

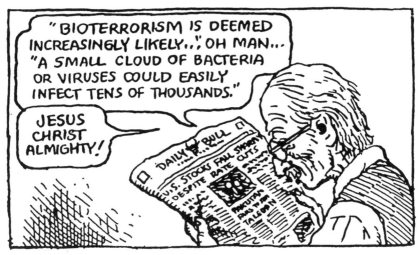

THE OLD CARTOONIST

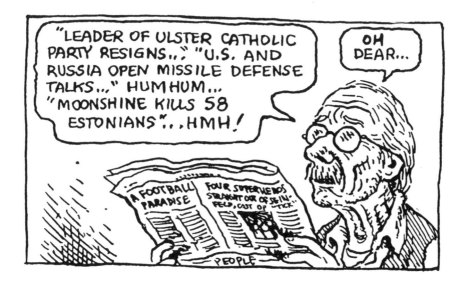

"LEADER OF ULSTER CATHOLIC PARTY RESIGNS..," "U.S. AND RUSSIA OPEN MISSILE DEFENSE TALKS...," HUM HUM... "MOONSHINE KILLS 58 ESTONIANS"...HMH!

OH DEAR...

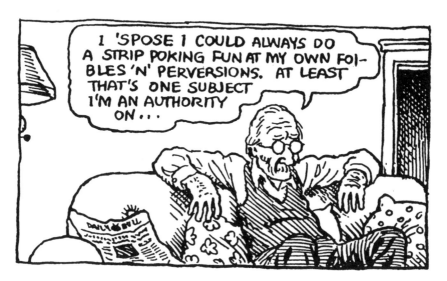

I 'SPOSE I COULD ALWAYS DO A STRIP POKING FUN AT MY OWN FOIBLES 'N' PERVERSIONS. AT LEAST THAT'S ONE SUBJECT I'M AN AUTHORITY ON...

THE OLD CARTOONIST

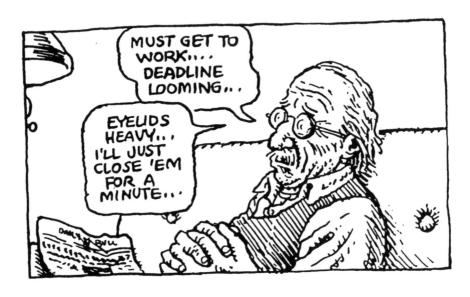

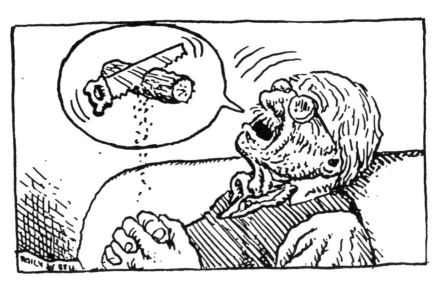

THE OLD CARTOONIST

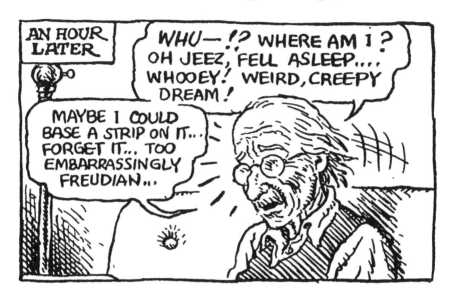

AN HOUR LATER

WHU—!? WHERE AM I? OH JEEZ, FELL ASLEEP.... WHOOEY! WEIRD, CREEPY DREAM!

MAYBE I COULD BASE A STRIP ON IT... FORGET IT... TOO EMBARRASSINGLY FREUDIAN...

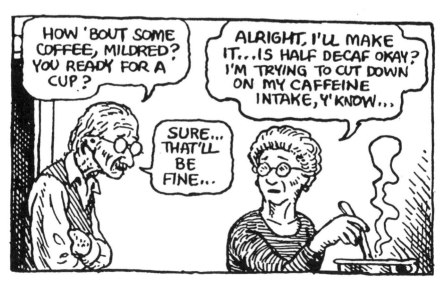

HOW 'BOUT SOME COFFEE, MILDRED? YOU READY FOR A CUP?

ALRIGHT, I'LL MAKE IT...IS HALF DECAF OKAY? I'M TRYING TO CUT DOWN ON MY CAFFEINE INTAKE, Y'KNOW...

SURE... THAT'LL BE FINE...

THE OLD CARTOONIST

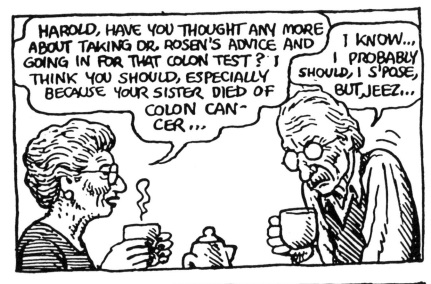

HAROLD, HAVE YOU THOUGHT ANY MORE ABOUT TAKING DR. ROSEN'S ADVICE AND GOING IN FOR THAT COLON TEST? I THINK YOU SHOULD, ESPECIALLY BECAUSE YOUR SISTER DIED OF COLON CAN-CER...

I KNOW... I PROBABLY SHOULD, I S'POSE, BUT JEEZ...

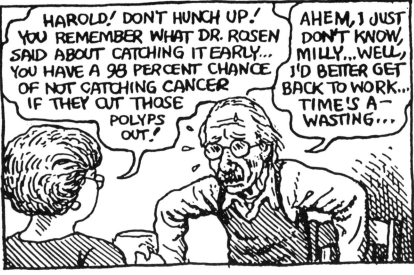

HAROLD! DON'T HUNCH UP! YOU REMEMBER WHAT DR. ROSEN SAID ABOUT CATCHING IT EARLY... YOU HAVE A 98 PER CENT CHANCE OF NOT CATCHING CANCER IF THEY CUT THOSE POLYPS OUT!

AHEM, I JUST DON'T KNOW, MILLY...WELL, I'D BETTER GET BACK TO WORK... TIME'S A-WASTING...

THE OLD CARTOONIST

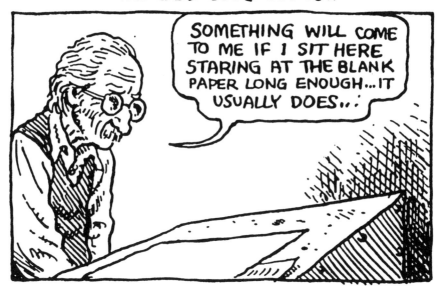

SOMETHING WILL COME TO ME IF I SIT HERE STARING AT THE BLANK PAPER LONG ENOUGH...IT USUALLY DOES...

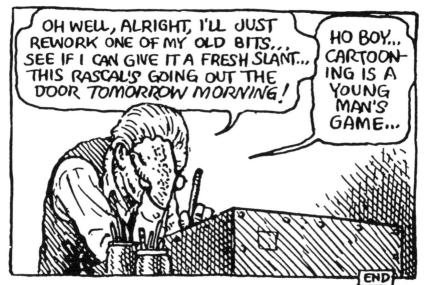

OH WELL, ALRIGHT, I'LL JUST REWORK ONE OF MY OLD BITS... SEE IF I CAN GIVE IT A FRESH SLANT... THIS RASCAL'S GOING OUT THE DOOR *TOMORROW MORNING!*

HO BOY... CARTOON-ING IS A YOUNG MAN'S GAME...

END

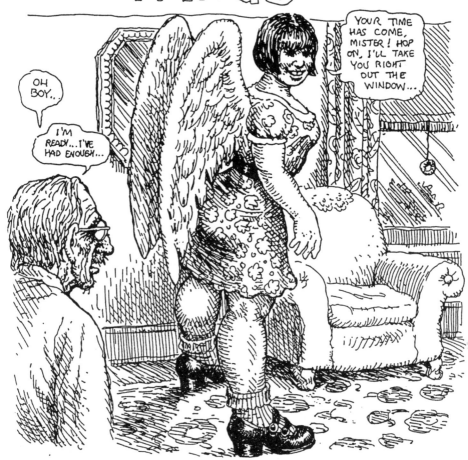

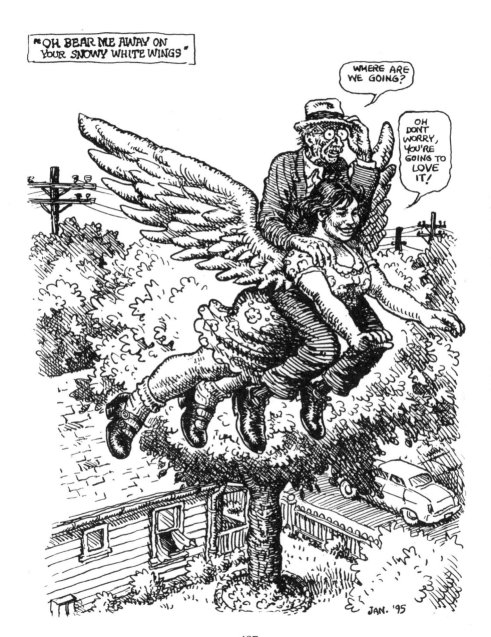

427

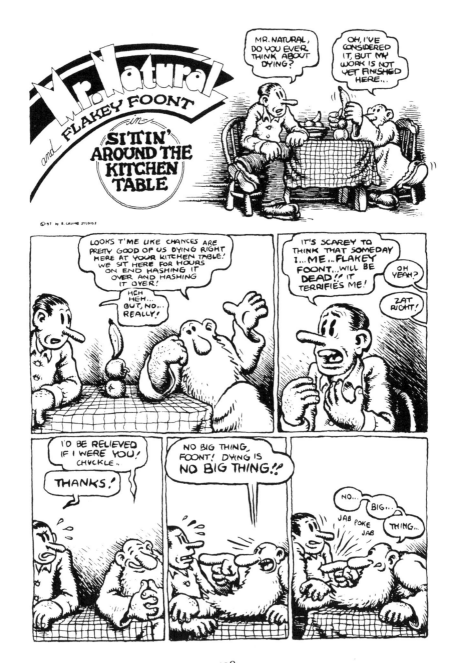

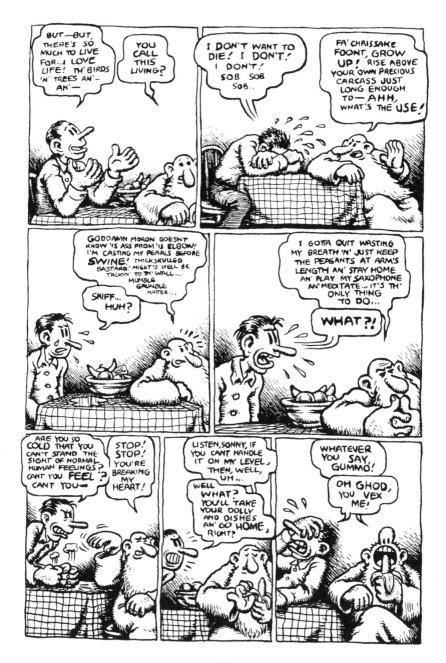

429

POET/WRITER
CHARLES BUKOWSKI

I cracked a beer and turned on the TV. There was a fight on ESPN. They were really slugging it out. The fighters were better conditioned now than in my youth. I marveled at the energy they could expend and still keep going and going. The months of roadwork and gymwork that fighters had to endure seemed almost intolerable. And then, those last two or three intense days before a big fight. Condition was the key. Talent and guts were a must but without condition they were negated. I liked to watch the fights. Somehow it reminded me of writing. You needed the same thing, talent, guts, and condition. Only the condition was mental, spiritual. You were never a writer. You had to become a writer each time you sat down to the machine. What was hard sometimes was finding that chair and sitting in it. Sometimes you couldn't sit in it. Like everybody else in the world, for you, things got in the way: small troubles, big troubles, continuous slammings and bangings. You had to be in condition to endure what was trying to kill you. That's the message I got from watching the fights, or watching the horses run, or the way the jocks kept overcoming bad luck, spills on the track and personal little horrors off the track. I wrote about life, haha. But what really astonished me was the immense courage of some of the people living that life. That kept me going.

from *Hollywood,* by Charles Bukowski 1989

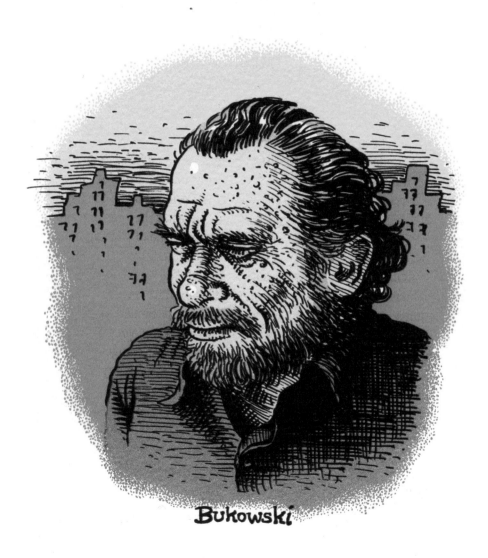

Bukowski

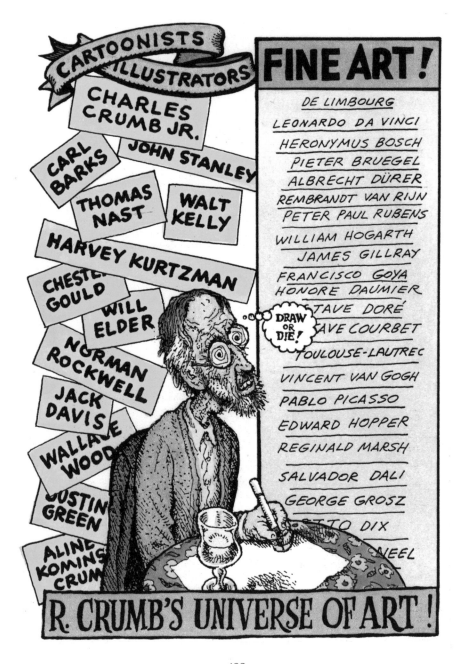

The R. Crumb Handbook Art

Comic Index

434

Picture credits

p55   Everett Collection/Rex Features

p63   Paramount/The Kobal Collection

Illustration credits

The following illustrations are reprinted courtesy of their copyright holders:

Pogo, by Walt Kelly © 1946, Dell; Greetings cards © 1961/62, American Greetings Cards Corp; *Cheap Thrills* © 1968, Columbia Records; *Little Lulu,* © 1946 Western Printing; *Heckle and Jeckle* © 1955, CBS; *Superduck* © 1943, Archie Comics.

All other illustrations are from the private collection of the author

Quotation credits

p18   James Howard Kunstler *The Geography of Nowhere: The Rise and Decline of America's Man-Made Landscape,* Simon & Schuster (1993)

p66   Kenneth Tynan, *The Diaries of Kenneth Tynan,* Bloomsbury, 2001

p174   Steve Martin, *Kindly Lent Their Owner, The Private Collection of Steve Martin, Essays by Steve Martin,* Bellagio Gallery of Fine Art, Las Vegas, G.G. Inc., 2001

p234   Harvey Kurtzman, introduction to *R. Crumb's Carload O' Comics: An Anthology of Choice Strips and Stories: 1968 to 1976,* Kitchen Sink Press, 1996

p290   Carl Barks, *Carl Barks: Conversations,* University Press of Mississippi, 2003

p390   Carl G. Jung, *Man and His Symbols,* Doubleday & Co. Inc., 1964

A big thank you to

The blame for this book firmly rests on the soft but strong shoulders of Zaro Weil and Aline Kominsky-Crumb, two women who periodically upset the applecart of easy living found only in the south of France with an idea that some project is worthy of existence and puts everybody to work making it a reality. This puts us, the authors, in the position of apologizing to ... we mean, we would like to thank the many people who went out of their way to help with the creation of this book by supplying information and images as well as their personal time and talents, specifically: Christian Coudurès, Michel Coste, Rika Deryckere, Caroline Chimenti, for handling the computer, Tony Baldwin, who not only engineered the music CD, but also doubled as a proofreader and copy editor on occasion, Alain Schons, Jean-Pierre Mercier, and Paul Morris for cheerfully submitting to grueling interrogations, Michael Trier, who loaned images and personal photos, Daniela Steinfeld, who sent us her photos of the Ludwig Museum exhibition, Joan Schirle, who dug deep to supply photos, reviews, and promotional material from the Dell'Arte Players Company's theatrical version of "Whiteman Meets Bigfoot", Sergio Ghirardi, who looked for and found in Italy several cinema posters that fit the text, Raoul Philip, who contributed Baubiac wine and objets du Crumb from his personal collection, Tim Van Beek and Sam Kujava, who sent Disney material from America, and finally, Rob Fuke and Millie Dolan, who loaned their computer. This whole can of worms was put on disk by Christian Coudurès, proofread by Aline, and placed in front of our faithful friend, John Casey, to make heads or tails out of! Then, Yvonne Deutch, Gareth Jenkins, Gordon Parker, and Leon Meyer jumped in to tie up all the loose ends, make corrections, add images, and get this to the printer! Additional thanks are given to the many fine musicians who have made music with Robert over the past three decades and who appear on the music CD that is part of this book. Bravo, ladies and gentlemen!

Peter Poplaski

First published by MQ Publications Limited
12 The Ivories, 6–8 Northampton Street
London N1 2HY
email: mqpublications.com
website: www.mqpublications.com

Design: Christian Coudurès
Handbook Series Editor: Gareth Jenkins

ISBN: 1-84072-716-0

10 9 8 7 6 5 4 3 2 1

Printed and bound in France

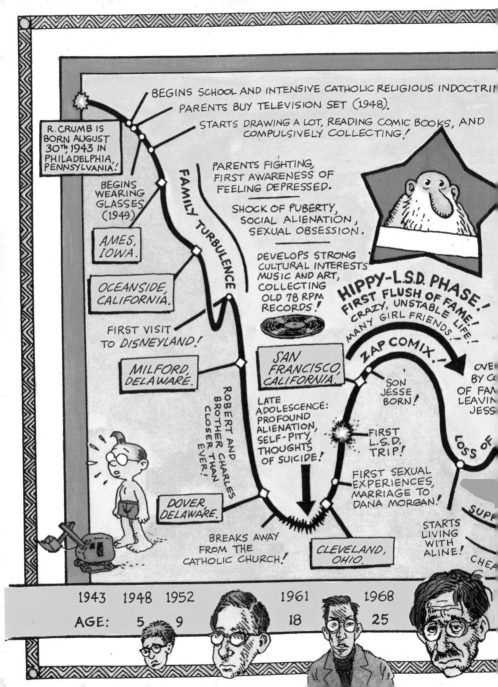